The Missing Stratum

The Missing Stratum

Technical School Education in England 1900–1990s

Michael Sanderson

THE ATHLONE PRESS
London and Atlantic Highlands, NJ

First published 1994 by
THE ATHLONE PRESS
1 Park Drive, London NW11 7SG
and 165 First Avenue,
Atlantic Highlands, NJ 07716

British Library Cataloguing in Publication Data
A catalogue record for this book is available from the British Library

ISBN 0 485 11442 9

Library of Congress Cataloging in Publication Data

Sanderson, Michael, 1939–
The missing stratum : technical school education in England, 1900–1900s / Michael Sanderson.
p. cm.
Includes bibliographical references and index.
ISBN 0-485-11442-9 : $70.00
1. Technical education--England--History--20th century.
2. Technical institutes--England--History--20th century. I. Title.
T107.S26 1994 93-39429
607.1′142--dc20 CIP

Typeset by
Bibloset, Chester

Printed and bound in Great Britain by
Bookcraft Ltd., Bath, England

Contents

List of Tables

Preface

This is a study of England's failure to create a stratum of technical school education in the twentieth century. It is increasingly being recognized that educational defects have contributed to England's relative decline and laggard economic performance compared with her European competitors. This has certainly been so since 1945 and probably for longer. Yet that deficiency has lain not so much in our universities, public and grammar schools. It has been our failure to tackle the problem of what to do with non-academic teenagers of more practical abilities. They have been the victims of an over-selective and over-academic education system. It is a system that has been better geared to produce Nobel prize winners than technology-based entrepreneurs and our economic failure has been a consequence. Our expulsion from the European ERM (exchange rate mechanism) and crises in public sector borrowing and balance of payments are indicative of a society that can no longer afford its aspirations.

These crises also focus the mind on the causes of this decline, and historians and economists have put forward many in recent years. It is the theme of this book that one of these causes has been the unwillingness to develop a stratum of technical schools for early and mid teenagers. We had the junior technical schools from the 1900s and secondary technical schools since 1945. Yet for a complex of reasons they never developed into a large and strong part of our educational system. They were then abandoned in the 1950s and 1960s. This was in contrast to many of our industrial competitors in Europe and elsewhere. The lack of this stratum has left us with shortages of skilled labour even in times of high unemployment. It has also left us with a culture which emphasizes high quality making and doing rather less than some of our rivals. Not least its lack explains something of the present unsatisfactory attempts to reintroduce 'technology' as an ill-defined subject into an educational system which had rejected it. This is an important matter; it lies near the heart of England's malaise about her industrial economy, education and cultural values.

In the course of the research for this book I have incurred obligations which it is a pleasure to acknowledge. Archivists at the Public Record Office and the Manuscript Room of the British Library have been unfailingly helpful. I am also grateful to Trinity College Cambridge for permission to use the papers of R.A. Butler. I have also benefited from conversations with Mr John Neal, Mr Raymond Griffin and Mr Frank Cooper who gave me valuable insights into these schools from the viewpoint of pupils and teachers of the past. Mr Cooper also generously made available various papers of the Association of Heads of Secondary Technical Schools.

While preparing and writing the study I have had the privilege of giving papers based on the ongoing research at conferences at Valencia and Leuven where the comments of Professor Gabriel Tortella, Lars Sandberg and Derek Aldcroft and others have given me stimulating food for thought. So has the opportunity to present papers at seminars at the Universities of Manchester, Lancaster, Belfast and the Institute of Historical Research. I am grateful to them all. I am also especially appreciative of the seminars organized at the Institute of Education University of London by Dr Alison Wolf where as a passive and active participant I have learnt much of present issues in vocational education and training.

The research was greatly facilitated by a grant from the Economic and Social Research Council [ROOO 231860] which I gratefully acknowledge as also initial funding and study leave from the University of East Anglia. Finally various versions of the text were typed by Mrs Sue Rowell whose careful efficiency eased the task.

CHAPTER 1

An Edwardian Problem

Apprenticeship . . . is everywhere decaying and there is nothing except the technical school rising to take its place[1]

R. A. Bray (1911)

The long story of Britain's relative economic decline from being the workshop of the world to a marginal low-ranking economy in Europe is littered with missed opportunities and wrong turnings. Defects in education have often been seen as playing a major part in this decline both by contemporaries and subsequent historians. The public schools, Oxford and Cambridge universities and their former preference for liberal over vocational studies, the lack of involvement or interest in education on the part of the state or the employers have been much criticized.[2] For a century or more, politicians, businessmen and educators have engaged in a 'pass the parcel' of mutual recrimination about the shortcomings of the education system and its culpability for economic decline.

Less discussed has been the failure to develop an efficient system of technical schooling for schoolchildren. This failure is the theme of this book. This stratum of education has been neglected by historians as it was neglected by the shapers of the educational system itself.[3] More attention has been paid to technical colleges, the universities and other forms of technical and scientific education for older people. It is the purpose of this study to examine the evolution of the attempts to create technical schools in England and the limited success of this development. They began with the junior technical schools from 1905 which became the secondary technical schools after the 1944 Education Act. Yet in spite of the high hopes invested in them they declined and were swallowed up into grammar and comprehensive schools. From their Edwardian beginnings the schools were stifled and prevented from becoming a genuine third part of the secondary tripartite system. This failure is one of the major defects in English education for it lies at the heart of our neglect in producing the skilled craftsman, artisan and engineer for manufacturing industry. In this, it may be argued, it was a significant element in Britain's relative economic decline since 1900.

I

The long term decline is painfully clear. The UK share in world trade in manufactures had been as high as 40.7 per cent in 1890 and declined to 29.9 per cent in 1913, to 19.8 per cent by 1955 and to 8.7 per cent by 1976.[4] In 1900, where this book roughly begins, Britain was still the richest country in the world. In 1950 UK living standards were still only behind those of Switzerland and the USA. But by 1985 Britain had become a poor relation of Western Europe with real income per head between a half and two-thirds that of France and West Germany and behind Italy.[5]

To an extent some of this was inevitable and the result of a complex of factors of which education was only one. Yet from the beginning this concern about declining competitiveness was linked with anxieties about educational defects as an underlying cause. This was so from the Paris Exhibition of 1867 where the manifest superiority of French textiles and Prussian steel armaments prompted a generation of propagandizing and new initiatives in technical education. The increasing commercial and military threat of Imperial Germany especially in the 1890s and 1900s heightened the belief that technical education should be part of that revised 'national efficiency' necessary to withstand German imports at home and foreign tariffs abroad.[6]

This broad concern encompassed the development of science at Cambridge, the creation of the civic universities, the polytechnics and municipal technical colleges and youth movements like the Boy Scouts. Within this there was a special late Victorian and Edwardian emphasis upon the boy (and to an extent his sister), the juvenile early teenager, and how best to prepare him for useful work in industry. Around this clustered many problems.

II

Firstly, too many Edwardian youngsters were going into 'dead end' jobs.[7] For the elementary school leaver a range of blind-alley occupations beckoned, easily obtained and fairly lucrative and best done by the young. Such were boy messengers, 'beer and baccy' fetchers for dockers, van boys, newspaper sellers and sweepers-up.[8] Errand boys were ubiquitous, 'to sweep out the shop, clean plate glass windows, walk or bicycle on errands with frequent stoppages for conversation'.[9]

Of 24,145 boys leaving London elementary schools in 1899, 42.5 per cent became errand boys,[10] and two thirds in the 1900s went into unskilled jobs.[11]

The rise of an urban leisured class also provided ample opportunities for the unskilled boy worker. A contemporary commentator observed:

> Boy-workers minister to a heedless public on every hand. They bring our purchases to our doors, sometimes close on midnight. They deliver our telegrams, and carry our private messages. They address our letters, affix our stamps, and shrilly answer our telephone calls. They hoarsely advertise the news of the moment at the street-corners, or they transform themselves into human bookstalls to beguile the tedium of travel, or into refreshment buffets to sustain the inner man. As pages, they stand and wait upon us in hotels, and restaurants, and clubs; they open to us the doors of spacious shops; or round and round in the latest cafe smoke-rooms they bear cigars and cigarettes. They 'caddy' for us on the golf links, bearing stoically with our testy humours, or, judicial and observant, they record our billiard breaks.[12]

Individual towns had their specific needs for armies of such youngsters. Norwich had a vast demand for child packers of mustard, starch and confectionery who were cheaper and more easily replaceable than machinery.[13] In Oxford the University supported 'a good deal of casual labour among caddies, grounds boys and newspaper sellers'.[14]

Yet there was a cruel arithmetic behind many juvenile jobs. A firm of carriers would employ 1,000 drivers and an equal number of van boys. Yet a driver's career would be 40 years and that of his boy only 4. A driver would outlast ten van boys in the service of the firm and 'of every ten boys who dangle their legs over the tailboard of a van only one can stay on and become a driver'.[15] The rest would be unemployed at 17 or 18. Even jobs that seemed to be an entry into serious industrial work could prove to be blind alleys. In a sawmill machine shop, a weaving factory and a cloth finishing mill about the same number of men and boys were employed yet there was no progression for any but a tiny proportion of boys to the adult jobs.[16] In the first, 80 per cent of boys left at manhood, in the second and third 95 per cent. Rather similar to the van lads, many juvenile jobs were not preparation for adult work but distinctive jobs in themselves best done by juveniles.[17]

The danger was imminent unemployment for youth discarded from such jobs. Indeed the Royal Commission on the Poor Law recommended technical education for adolescents as a way of reducing the army of unemployables.[18] While only 1 or 2 per cent of 14- and 15-year-olds (in a survey by Cyril Jackson) were unemployed, this rose sharply to 22 per cent for 17-, 18-, 19-year-olds as they left juvenile work for idleness. In Norwich for example the largest category of 14 year olds were errand boys (30 per cent) but the largest category of 20 year olds were casual and unemployed labours (52 per cent).

Several commentators saw this as not only harmful for the young themselves but for the economy as a whole. The use of juvenile labour retarded mechanization, since employers 'use too little and too antiquated machinery and supplement its deficiency by cheap human labour . . . so long as boys are cheap work will be done by them rather than by machines.'[19] The withdrawal of juveniles from the labour market to undertake more education and training might vacate some jobs for adults, reducing adult unemployment. The consequent increase in demand for adult labour and an increase in their wages would offset the loss to the family income of the foregoing of the contribution of the young worker's wage. It would also encourage the use of labour substituting machinery. This in turn would set up a benign circle by requiring more mechanically sophisticated youth which more technical education would provide.[20]

A particular problem associated with the 'blind alley' situation was the gap between the school leaving age and the starting of apprenticeship. The school leaving age was 10 from 1876, 11 from 1893, 12 from 1899, permissively up to 14 in 1900 but not generally to that age until 1918.[21] Yet most trades did not receive apprentices until the age of 16 with the exception of painting, plumbing and printing which accepted boys at 14. So an elementary schoolboy leaving school at usually 12 or 13 in the 1900s found a chasm before him and time to fill. Accordingly there was a massive change between what boys did at 14 and at 16 when new opportunities became available (see Table 1.1). Casual labour sharply diminished and taking apprenticeships increased, but to a low level. The large gain was simply taking labourers' jobs – where over half ex-elementary boys ended up. A form of education such as the junior technical school supplied between the ages of 13 and 15 would certainly have bridged this gap and decanted a much higher proportion into

Table 1.1 *Changes in occupations of boys aged 14–16 in 1909*

	14 (%)	16 (%)	% change
Apprentices	5.3	13.8	+ 8
Messengers, milk, van boys	47.9	18.8	– 29.1
Labourers	32.6	52.6	+ 20

Sources R.H. Tawney, 'The economics of boy labour', *Economic Journal*, 19 (1909) p.525, a sample of 150 London elementary school leavers. Also R.H. Tawney's memorandum in 1909 XVII Col 4757 *Report of the Consultative Committee . . . Continuation Schools*, p.302.

skilled apprenticed work away from the dull drudgery of labouring. Michael Sadler noted of Liverpool that 'there is a gap between their leaving the elementary school and entering upon their apprenticeship. This gap the work of a manual training school would profitably fill'. Presciently he foresaw that they would be most useful in the engineering trades.[22]

The state made various provisions in these years to ease early teenagers into jobs. From 1899 children were allowed partial exemption from school from the age of 12 – the so called 'half timers'. These were mostly in Lancashire, Yorkshire and Cheshire to enable young children to continue to play their traditional role in the textile industry. In 1908 care committees dealt with various welfare functions of local education authorities (LEAs), including getting a job, and in 1910 the juvenile advisory committees of labour exchanges dealt with juveniles below the age of 17 under the Labour Exchanges Act of 1909. These last two were worthy developments, the first more controversially so. They were all getting children into jobs but without concern for their effective skill-raising training.

The situation was the more unsatisfactory in that there were frequent complaints that employers found the education of elementary schools inadequate; 'employers often complain that the teaching given in elementary schools is not thorough and practical enough.'[23] Elementary schools were accused of having for their aim 'producing a million clerks a year' whereas their children would have benefitted from 'valuable technical training as is afforded by a mechanical laboratory or an engineering shop.'[24] Spencer Gibb summed up,

> that elementary education needs to be reformed in such a way as to bring it into more vital relation with the practical life of the children is the unanimous verdict of all . . . [what is needed is] work of hand as well as head, of which the manual training already very skilfully adopted in many schools is the best.[25]

Others took the view that the defects lay not so much in the lack of practical education in elementary schools but in the failure to create any end-on follow through. Eglantyne Jebb observed in 1906 'we have established at great cost our elementary schools and much of our expense and labour is wasted because we build no superstructure on the foundation we have laid'.[26] In consequence many pupils came to technical college so badly prepared as to be unable to take advantage of the instruction given.[27]

For lack of such a superstructure, ex-elementary pupils wishing to advance themselves had to resort to evening classes. But they had their own limitations. After ten hours work during the day a student would 'find it difficult to concentrate on any subject that has not immediate interest'. Only 'a very small proportion indeed' survived the first six months.[28] In any case only a small minority attended evening classes: in Birmingham 15 per cent, in London 10 per cent of ex-elementary pupils.[29] Ironically the chief study of evening classes in the 1900s came to the view that the system 'is accompanied by an enormous waste of money, time and effort.'[30] Yet this was the distinctive characteristic of technical education in England. Michael Sadler's view was that the reliance on evening classes was the conjunction of two vested interests of teachers and employers. Because of low salaries teachers liked to supplement their income with evening class work and employers were unwilling to release young workers for daytime instruction.[31]

III

The traditional way in which the 'blind-alley' job had been avoided had been through apprenticeship. Yet there were ubiquitous complaints about the decline or decay of apprenticeship. It was observed in 1906

> Apprenticeship has survived in the Provinces, when it has died, or is dying, in London; and in some trades, therefore, such as Letterpress Printing, the more completely trained Provincial ousts

> his Metropolitan rival. Neither among Masons nor bricklayers is real apprenticeship found. The use of machinery in the Carpentry trade has absorbed the work which used to be done by the hand-labour of boys; and, though apprenticeship survives in a more or less complete form in the country, in London it is rare, and among Plasterers and Painters quite the exception.[32]

C.B. Hawkins in Norwich also found that apprenticeship 'belongs to a condition of things which has long since passed away'.[33] In some industries and trades apprenticeship still flourished, in plumbing for example and notably in shipbuilding.[34] But contemporaries were much exercised by 'decay' as a problem.

Various factors lay behind the decline of apprenticeship between 1890 and 1914. There was the introduction of semi-automatic machines, notably the capstan and turret lathes and specialized boring and grinding machines.[35] Mechanization split up processes into a number of different jobs,

> processes forming one skilled craft may be split up into a number of different jobs and the artisan be replaced by the semi-skilled machine minder . . . in large engineering shops there are growing numbers who work each a single machine and most of whom earn wages about midway between those of a mechanic and those of a labourer.[36]

In many trades semi-automatic machines could be worked by boys. The use of interchangeable parts allowed greater tolerances and less need for a precise and lasting fit, while semi-skilled assemblers of engineering parts usurped the role of skilled fitters.

Knox points out that the status of the apprentice also became degraded in various ways. The relation of the employer to him became more exploitative. He was given speedy training on one automatic machine and so received a specialized rather than an all round training. The diminished status was reflected in the narrowing of pay differentials between first and final year apprentices between 1865 and 1915. There was more working of overtime by apprentices and accordingly less attendance at night school. Finally there were complaints that apprentices were less interested in their work and identified more with ordinary workers by participating in proletarian strikes. This was an aspect of the decline of the old personal relationship which had bound master and apprentice, the latter aspiring to the position of the former – 'in these new conditions the old personal feeling between master and man which was so potent a factor in the old apprenticeship system is no longer possible.'[37]

Boys themselves seemed less willing to undertake apprenticeships. They were wary of committing themselves and losing their independence for four, five or six years, 'in an era of such rapid industrial changes he naturally shrinks from engaging himself for a term longer than that which is really necessary for the acquirement of his craft',[38] especially if 'they are tied down to a trade that will soon be as extinct as the dodo'.[39] They may also have been aware that many employers regarded apprentices less as youth undergoing training than as cheap labour and strike breakers.

Behind this contemporary concern about the decline of apprenticeship was the implication that some alternative form of industrial training was necessary. The increased mechanization had not simply led to deskilling but a realignment of where skills were needed. There was more demand for machine minders and less for all round craftsmanship but also more for a higher level of engineer to look after the machines, 'the setting and supervising of these (machines) is work probably demanding a higher level of intelligence than ever before'.[40] N. B. Dearle also pointed to this dichotomy with modern engineering machinery requiring 'a larger number of men whose skill is far less, and a smaller number to set up the machines whose skill is greater than that of the older type of mechanic'.[41] Demand for this level of labour exceeded its supply. If it was to be met then some kind of more formal schooling might fill the gap. R. A. Bray suggested this in the quotation at the head of this chapter. Likewise the Norwich commentator C. B. Hawkins saw a day trade school as the only solution to the decline of apprenticeship in his own city.[42] William Calderwood, Chairman of the Association of Technical Institutions drew the connection explicitly,

> the old practice of apprenticeship has fallen into disuse and everywhere there is a greater demand for more and more specialisation. Employers will not undertake to teach trades and the development of large factories and combinations of interests results in the subdivision of processes with little or no opportunity for the learner to master more than one operation. Thus we find in industrial England an army of unskilled, or at best semi-skilled artisans, . . . This could be done [i.e. rectified] by the institution of Trade Schools with equal opportunities for all. The manual processes of trades might be taught with advantage in the Technical School.[43]

In fact all the main national commentators on apprenticeship and boy labour in the 1900s – Bray, Dearle, Dunlop, Sadler for example – called for a raising of the school leaving age and some form of juvenile technical schooling as the remedy for this problem. And cause and effect linked in this way in practice. C. V. More points out that the precocious development of trade classes in London was probably the consequence of the failure to provide much apprentice training there.[44]

IV

Contemporaries were also concerned about juvenile disorder and delinquency and the possibility of mitigating it through education. There were 30,000 young people in industrial and reformatory schools by the turn of the century. As many as 42 per cent of all convicted larcenists were under 21 (and 21 per cent under 16) and a quarter of pickpockets were under 16. Springhall concludes that 'juvenile crime in short seems to have remained as serious a problem as it ever was'.[45]

Also troubling was not only formal crime but general hooliganism and the fear of street gangs and working class youth as disaffected and aimless. Gillis suggests that while serious indictable offences remained stable at this time yet non-indictable offences by juveniles rose – drunkenness, loitering, vandalism and dangerous play.[46] Elementary schools sought to contain this with an atmosphere of repressive constraint. This in turn prompted its own reactive hooliganism in the form of school strikes – strikes against caning, in favour of shorter hours, just for the hell of it against the restrictive boredom of school life and the stifling hot summer of 1911. There were 50 in 1889, 71 in 1911 and 14 between 1912 and 1914.[47]

If the elementary schools were not containing the spectre of hooligan youth it is plausible that more technical school education might have done so. No junior technical or trade school was involved in these strikes. Work in the junior technical school was more interesting than life on the streets and considerably more so than in elementary schools. There must have been many children whose bad behaviour might have been improved by more practical education. For example, Vic Amey was an intelligent lad of the 1900s, hating his teachers and school and constantly punished for disruption. Yet he yearned for more technical schooling, 'anything mechanical if it worked I wanted to know why or how. I always had an inquisitive turn of mind'.[48] Here hooliganism on the part of the child was linked with the frustration of inclinations and waste of skills. He cannot have been the only one and advocates of the junior technical school could rightly see the JTS as a solution of both behavioural and occupational problems. Indeed it is significant that the Meccano toy construction kits began production around this time, in 1908. These perceptively tapped the interest of boys in building mechanisms that worked and moved. Vic Amey (who would then have been 12) would have loved to have one. The JTSs were to tap identical aptitudes as a basis of education.

V

We may ask whether there was any evidence that getting a training and going into a skilled craft actually paid, compared with going into a dead end boy job and becoming an unskilled labourer. It is clear from a compilation of scattered references to wage rates in social surveys of the time (see Table 1.2) that unskilled boys earned more than apprentices. Yet skilled craftsmen on average earned about twice what could be expected by the unskilled labouring man. The skilled manual worker also earned more than the clerk. It was clear that employers valued skill and had to pay a high differential for it. But it prompts the question of why so many working class boys went into unskilled work. The higher initial wages of unskilled boys compared with apprentices was one element. Another, deplored by contemporaries, was the remarkable ignorance and lack of foresight among working class boys and their fathers who should have been advising them.[49] Even those who thought they were being canny and ambitious by aiming at clerical work were acting with economic irrationality. Alderman Heape of Rochdale regretted that too many working class boys hoped for clerical positions 'instead of applying themselves to mastering a handicraft or fitting themselves for some industrial occupation. Manual work is looked upon as being on a lower plane and hence the outrageous number of applications for a poorly paid clerk's place'.[50]

We may then ask the reciprocal question whether education and the capacity to read actually paid off financially. This can be tested in an unusual survey made by Lady Florence Bell of Middlesborough.[51] She surveyed a large number of working men, noting for many of them their wages and their capacity and inclination to read. Where these pieces of evidence coincide we can compare the two (Table 1.3). It was clear that an ability and inclination to read was a characteristic of the higher earners. Put in another way eight of the nine highest earners (above £2.15) enjoyed reading and the ninth could read but did not care for it. It would have been evident by the 1900s – as it certainly would not in the

Table 1.2 *Weekly wages in certain occupations, 1904–14*

Type of employment	Wages in shillings per week: J	B	T	P	U	H	Pe	Average
Apprentice boy								
cabinet-making						3.5–6.5		4.92
printing, jewellery, engineering							4.5–5	
Unskilled boy	4–5	5	8	7–8	8		7	6.5
Unskilled labourer (man)	17		16–20				30–40	21.7
carter		17–21						
street-sweeper		18						
porter		17–21						
Clerk					25–30 (aged 23)			27.5
Skilled man								43
bricklayer	38–45							
carpenter	38–45							
plumber	40–48							
plasterer	40–48							
stonemason	40–48							
tradesman					35–40			

Sources

J Eglantyne Jebb, *Cambridge, a Brief Study in Social Questions* (Cambridge, 1906) pp. 41, 68–9.
B C. V. Butler, *Social Conditions in Oxford* (London, 1912) p. 51, 53, 54.
T R. H. Tawney, 'The economics of boy labour', *Economic Journal*, 19 (1909) p.529.
P Alexander Paterson, *Across the Bridges, or Life by the South London River-Side* (London, 1911) p.120.
U E. J. Urwick (ed.), *Studies of Boy Life in Our Cities* (London, 1904) pp. 125–7, 130–1.
H C. B. Hawkins, *Norwich, a Social Study* (London, 1910) p.195.
Pe H. S. Pelham, *The Training of a Working Boy* (1914) pp. 68, 72, 77.

Table 1.3 *Literacy levels and wage rates, 1907*

	Median weekly wage (shillings)
6 cannot read	23
18 can read but do not	27
40 can and do read	36

1830s for example – that high working class earnings were underlain by educational literary attainments.

The wages evidence suggests that education, training and skill did receive good differential rewards in wages and that manual skill was considerably more valued than clerical. All this suggested the value to employers of what technical training there was and the need for more of it.

VI

As Britain was beleaguered by foreign trade competition and wary of emergent industrial nations so she kept an eye on foreign educational developments, it became clear that most foreign systems Britain would care about contained some provision for technical schools for school age children.

The rapidly industrializing Japanese Empire placed great importance on engineering and they had junior technical schools from 1885 right through to 1950 covering the age span 12–17, following primary education from the age of 6.[52] The French also had excellent provision for junior technical education.[53] Most important were the *écoles primaires supérieures* under the Ministry of Public Instruction and started in the 1830s. They were for children aged 12–15, sons of artisans and farmers, and combined general education with science and workshop practice. Helped by a financial stimulus in 1906 and 1907 they expanded rapidly from 260 schools with 33,000 pupils in 1895 to 450 schools with 55,000 pupils by 1913. Parallel to these were the *écoles d'industrie* established in 1892 under the Ministry of Industry and Commerce. There were 70 such schools with 14,766 students by 1913. These too included workshop practice and were of particular value for training pupils for Peugeot at Montbeliard and marine mechanics at Brest. C. R. Day regards French technical schools as 'modernised, well equipped . . . (and) closely linked to industry'.

The French influence was especially direct. R. L. Morant of the Board of Education investigated French *écoles primaires supérieures* in the mid-1890s and was deeply impressed by the practical preparation for industrial work they provided for young teenagers. He concluded with some emotion that such schools in France were 'an earnest effort at a social reform which recognises that the backbone of a nation is its class of manual workers'. The significance of Morant's French experience was that shortly after his report in 1897 he became Permanent Secretary of the Board of Education. In this capacity he issued the Regulations in 1904 and 1905 which instigated the junior technical schools – the intended English equivalent of the *écoles primaires supérieures* he so much admired.[54]

Not surprisingly there were similar developments in the United States. In 1884 the Industrial Education Association in New York City was formed to promote manual training in post-kindergarten schools. In the 1900s there was more emphasis on the vocational purposes of such education rather than simply handwork for personal development. The motives were very similar to those arguments used in England: the scarcity of skilled workmen, the decay of apprenticeship and the emergence of industrial competition from Germany. The Massachusetts Commission on Industrial and Technical Education in 1905 was particularly influential in developing the movement for industrial trade school education. Also the National Association of Manufacturers of the USA threw their influence in favour of trade schools for 14–16 year olds to produce the mechanics of the future. Accordingly notable technical school systems arose in the 1900s in Philadelphia, Milwaukee and Columbus and in the States of Massachusetts and New York.[55] A subsequent campaign for Federal aid to industrial schools led to the Smith Hughes Bill which brought this about in 1917.

American experience had a direct influence on English thinking through the Mosely Commission which visited the USA in 1903.[56] The deputation wrote extensively on US technical and trade schools and found much to admire as 'more has been done in America than among ourselves in the matter'. H. B. Gray expressed 'my profound sense of the value of manual training as scientifically carried out in the schools of the United States'. Alderman Heape was pleased at the 'engineering trend' of the schools and the fact that 70–90 per cent of boys went into manufacturing industry. Sir Harry Reichel described schools in ten cities, concluding that 'manual training in all its branches forms one of the most remarkable features of contemporary education in

America, and is exciting special interest in Great Britain'. It all added to the heightened awareness of technical schools in England and the need to match the institutions of our major competitors.

But the chief foreign influence was undoubtedly that from Germany. In the German states of the early nineteenth century compulsory elementary education in the Volksschulen was followed by the trade continuation school, the Fortbildungsschulen. A child could leave the elementary school at 12 and go full-time to a trade school, or at 14 and attend part-time while starting work. The Fortbildungsschule was thus the model root of both the full-time junior technical school and the part-time day continuation school in England. The German trade schools arose from an economy where handicrafts were still important – the toys, clocks, smoking pipes, carving of statues, wrought iron and embroidery which are distinctive parts of the German aesthetic. As the German economy changed, with engineering and metallurgy subjects arising alongside the old crafts, so the schools then became important sources for forming juvenile skill for late nineteenth century technological industry. Important in their own right, they also led students up to more advanced levels, the Fachschulen and Technische Hochschulen. The emphasis on vocational education at all levels, not least the juvenile, was one of the great strengths of the German industrial economy.[57]

A German example that attracted much attention was the work of George Kerschensteiner, the Director of Education in Munich.[58] In that city in the 1900s 92 per cent of boys leaving elementary schools at 14 went into trades requiring training and they combined this induction into work with attending compulsory trade schools. The continuation schools that Kerschensteiner inherited were too academic and he reorganised them from 1900, focusing their work on workshops and practical work in trades. Some 20,000 children were being taught 56 trades free of charge in 7 specially equipped schools ranging from butchers to builders, mechanics to printers and dozens more. Similar developments were also taking place in Berlin, Hamburg, Leipzig and Frankfurt. The Germans had virtually no 'dead end' problem such as troubled England, and they led the way in how to direct the non-academic 13 year old into the acquisition of productive skills. They still do.

Much English attention was directed to trade continuation schools but Edwin Cooley, touring for the Commercial Club of Chicago, reminded observers of the stratum of full time secondary technical schools and that 'these technical secondary schools are very numerous in Germany while they are almost unknown in England and America'.[59]

The lower technical schools took pupils after elementary school and gave them a two year course in building or machine trades. They were highly valued in Germany. There were 561 such schools in the German states, most (297) in Prussia. Cooley also noted 'that England's inferiority in technical education, as compared to Germany is not in the university grade of engineers but in the secondary grade, which is almost unprovided for in England'. Cooley's clear conclusion was that factory production with its minute division of labour had brought about the decay of apprenticeship in England (and America). Accordingly while elementary education should provide a general cultural education yet this should be followed around the age of 14 with vocational workshop-based technical schools. Finally Cooley noted that technical schools in Germany enjoyed strong support from employers – 'the attitude of employers is almost universally favourable to these schools'.

Why then was Britain behind Germany and France in the provision of technical school education? English educationalists saw this backwardness as the result of two factors. Both France and Germany had experienced a slower and later transition from handicraft to large-scale industry in the nineteenth century. The continued relevance of crafts perpetuated and enhanced the importance of schools that served them.[60] Secondly both France and Germany had an earlier and stronger acceptance of publicly aided state education on which its technical schools depended. Britain's rapid factory industrialization and downgrading of handcrafts and its preference for low-level and belated state intervention in education undermined a commitment to the technical school. A third, more modern, argument is that Britain before 1914 was indeed behind the USA and Germany in the reception of the most advanced technology in various industries. Yet this was a rational strategy since Britain's ample supply of skilled labour obviated the need for the labour- and skill-saving machinery appropriate to economies less well-endowed with a skilled labour force. It was these less well endowed nations – USA, Germany, France – which tended to emphasize the importance of technical schools to replenish shortages which they experienced more than Britain.[61] Britain's neglect of technical schools, in this argument, is the counterpart of her being able to rely on generations of ample hereditary, on-the-job trained, skilled labour.

All the factors which we have been considering so far pointed the minds of Edwardian reformers and educationalists in the direction of the need for some form of technical school for the young. The blind-alley jobs, decline of apprenticeship, defects of elementary and evening schools, the problems of juvenile unemployment and delinquency, the manifest high returns to skill and education and the example of foreign systems all provided the background and the impetus for the creation of the junior technical schools to which we now turn.

CHAPTER 2

A Solution: The Junior Technical School, 1905–1918

Let us then sweep our artisan schools clean of the bookish wordly spirit of the pedagogue . . . let us bring in the active spirit of the artisan and craftsman . . . the pride in honest manual labour, the joy in a thing well made[1]

W.P. Welpton (1913)

I

The junior technical schools (JTSs) came into being in the 1900s but they had antecedents in the previous decades. James Kay Shuttleworth, the Secretary of the Privy Council Committee on Education, tried in the 1840s to encourage day schools of industry with grants, as well as ordinary elementary schools. But in 1860 industrial schools were transferred to the Home Office for the treatment of young criminals. So with great misfortune manual and industrial training became 'associated in the public mind with penal discipline and early disgrace'[2] rather than skill training for industry. Ordinary elementary schools, by contrast, were forced to shun practical work by the Revised Code of 1862 which refocused their activities on basic literacy as a condition of earning grants. Both these developments in the early 1860s wrongfooted elementary education on the eve of England's awakening concern about international competition and industrial training.

However, there were other more positive developments. Firstly, after the Great Exhibition of 1851 the Science and Art Department (SAD) was set up in South Kensington in 1853. This encouraged science education by setting science examinations for schools from 1859. Grants were paid to such schools for successful pupils on the basis of payment by results. By 1870 as many as 799 schools with 34,283 pupils were participating.[3] Some schools and institutions were so closely dependent on the SAD that there were 93 of these by 1895.[4] This arrangement fitted in with the aspirations of board schools. The Elementary Education Act of 1870 set up school boards as ad hoc local authorities to build board schools and provide elementary education in their area. These areas were usually small, there were 2,568 of them, and large towns and cities would have their own board. But they soon encountered a problem. The children were arranged in standards I - VII and they moved up these standards as they passed Her Majesty's Inspectors' annual examinations. However, able children could well have passed the Standard VII examination before reaching the statutory school leaving age or before wishing to leave school. For such children an extra classroom called the 'higher top' was often built providing a post elementary pseudo-secondary education. In boards where there were numerous post VII children, especially in large towns, then a separate school would be built, a higher grade school. However these higher grade schools, being post-elementary, were not eligible for grants from the Education Department in Whitehall under the 1870 Act. Accordingly they could apply instead to the SAD at South Kensington. Under these arrangements the schools provided scientific and technical instruction for children.

Other institutions also moved in this direction. In the 1880s Quintin Hogg started setting up polytechnics in London.[5] These were predominantly for youths and adults learning technical trades complementary to work. But from 1886 they also had schools for younger children as part of them - embryo JTSs. In the 1890s these developed: 'a few of the Organized Science Schools connected with the polytechnics began to give instruction more or less definitely preparatory to employment in the engineering industry during the nineties'.[6] By 1898 six of the polytechnics had day schools teaching 1,600 pupils aged 12--15.[7]

From 1889 technical colleges run by local government came into being. These too were growth points for new types of schools for children. For example, Kent had a number of proto-junior technical schools from around 1900 attached to technical colleges: Gravesend (1898), Dover (1900), Beckenham (1901) and Dartford (1904). These provided a curriculum with a heavy emphasis on science and mathematics for pupils aged 12–16, chiefly sons of artisans and clerks.[8] In Bolton a Manual Training School was attached to the Technical College in 1894, providing a pre-apprenticeship engineering course for early teenagers.[9]

Finally, at the elementary school level, drawing, woodwork, metalwork and cookery were increasingly introduced into the curricula of elementary schools in the 1890s.[10] This was partly due to the intervention of the SAD at the elementary level. The SAD made grants for 'manual instruction', and drawing grants were transferred from the SAD to the Education Department in 1898.

The London School Board had actually been doing this in elementary schools since 1887 with funds from the City and Guilds and the Drapers Company before government grants became available. Since 1898 manual instruction 'has been regarded as an ordinary subject of the school course'. There was a strong influence of Swedish Sloyd work – woodworking with knife and sandpaper – and, though not fully followed, the Swedish course 'has made a great impression upon the general lines of manual instruction in London'. Not least it inculcated the view that manual instruction was educationally valuable in its own right as well as being associated with 'the commencement of training of workmen'.[11] In 1909 Acland's Committee noted that 'handwork of all kinds is steadily though slowly forming a larger part of the Elementary Day School course' and that ideally this should be followed by 'a course of further training in day trade schools'.[12] Through these various ways - the work of elementary schools, the SAD, organized science schools and technical colleges - there was increasing acceptance of the idea and practice of providing some form of technical education for children at school. This set the scene for the recognition of the JTS in 1905.

The immediate background was the restructuring of the education system associated with Sir Robert Morant between 1900 and 1911.[13] The Education Department in Whitehall and the Science and Art Department in South Kensington were merged into the Board of Education in 1899. At the local level the school boards were abolished and their work and that of the technical instruction committees subsumed into the local education authorities of county boroughs and county councils. Most importantly the 1902 Education Act created the municipal rate-supported grammar school with access through scholarships from the elementary schools and closely focused on academic subjects.

Morant is often criticized as an academic élitist, projecting his reverence for the classical education of the Winchester of his youth onto the new grammar schools, to the neglect of a more appropriate technical education. Yet, true as Morant's academic élitism was, there were two other aspects of his outlook on education which are more relevant here. First, he was very knowledgeable about foreign educational systems and as part of the Board of Education's Office of Special Inquiries and Reports had written reports himself on Switzerland, France, Germany and the United States. He was aware that most advanced systems had gradations of post-primary schooling that included not only academic but technical and practical schools also, as we have seen in the previous chapter. He approved of this. Secondly, Morant was above all a 'National Efficiency' man. At one level this was expressed in the provision of a 'ladder of opportunity' through scholarships to grammar schools and thence to university. This facilitated the circulation of élites on which the efficiency of the nation depended. Yet at another level he was equally concerned about the efficiency of the artisan class which did not aspire to academic honours. He was as concerned about dead-end jobs and all the attendant problems that exercised the social critics we referred to previously. Hence it was under Morant's administration that the Education Act of 1910 created vocational guidance in schools, not to speak of the school meals of 1906 and medical inspection of 1907. The creation of JTSs in 1905 falls squarely into this area of Morant's concern -not anti-technical academicism but a concern for the physical, occupational and technical efficiency of the skilled working class. Morant envisaged an educational system with *both* grammar schools and technical schools.[14] In this he was surely right, and it may be argued that since the 1950s we have abandoned Morant's vision to our cost.

II

To bring some order to these various early forms of technical school, new Regulations were introduced in 1904 whereby the Board financed technical classes which had formerly received grants as science and art day classes. It defined strictly that

> the course or courses of instruction output to be definitely related - as a preparation, a concomitant or a supplement - to the training available in the actual work of the trades, manufactures or commerce of the district in which it is situated.[15]

This was intended for late teenagers, not for schoolchildren. But the reference to 'preparation' and the close relating of education to future occupations presaged the future JTS. In the following year, 1905, these new Regulations were 'extended so as to include . . . those who may still be devoting a large part of their time to preparation for their work in life'.[16] This new Regulation 42 was the basis for the development of the JTS form.

The 1905 Regulations facilitated the closing of the gap of two or three years between the school leaving age of 12 from 1899 (with the possibility of raising it to 13 or 14 by bye-law from 1900) and starting apprenticeship.[17] These schools of the 1905–13 period were schools for children who no longer had any legal obligation to attend school and who were beyond the school leaving age of 12 or 13. Accordingly they were fee-paying schools, usually £3 a year. They received grants from the Board of £2 a pupil under these new Regulations. The schools were run by the new LEAs of the county borough or county councils and most were conducted in technical colleges 'using the premises and sharing the staff of institutions devoted mainly to evening work in technology'.[18] By appropriate coincidence 1905 also saw the inauguration of the Association of Teachers in Technical Institutions, teachers both in colleges and JTSs.[19]

Most JTSs were intended to 'provide an educational foundation and background for those pupils whose broad intention is to enter industry on leaving school about the age of 16' rather than to train them for one particular grade.[20] They were most appropriate in the two broad industries of engineering and construction. It was nonsense to talk of producing an engineer between the ages of 12 or 13 and 16, and such claims were never made. Yet it was feasible to give a useful grounding in theoretical and workshop aspects that would be applicable later to any of the myriad occupations in the wide spectrum covered by 'engineering'. A pioneer in the movement, J. Paley Yorke who ran the Poplar School, one of the earliest engineering-based JTSs recalled that they had begun too narrowly but, realizing the breadth of engineering occupations, had broadened out the curriculum to what became the normal JTS model.[21]

The HMIs' suggested curriculum for such schools was:[22]

Workshop practice – 6 hours
Mathematics, science (physics and mechanics), English, technical drawing – 5 hours each
Physical training – 1 hour

In practice this seems to have been broadly followed. At Woodhouse and Holbeck Technical Schools in Leeds the balance was:

Practical mathematics – 6 ½ hours
Practical mechanics – 3 hours
Technical drawing – 4 ½ hours
Workshop practice – 6 ½ hours
English – 5 ½ hours
Drill and games – 2 hours

It was emphasized that

> in all the details of the handwork and of the mathematics, mechanics and drawing, the exercises were to be of as practical and workshop-like a character as possible. The pupils were to be faced with practical problems very similar to those existing in the workshop of the city.[23]

A more specialized group within the JTSs was the trade schools 'which are frankly and definitely preparing their pupils for entry into a specific occupation within an industry. They aim at . . . developing a substantial measure of personal skill in the processes of the occupation for which these pupils are being prepared'.[24] They were particularly relevant for specialized London trades where it was appropriate to start acquiring manual skills early. The pioneer was the Shoreditch Technical Institute Trade School which from 1901 taught woodworking and furniture- and cabinet-making to pupils aged 13–16 on a three-year course. This was soon followed by schools of Engineering at Paddington and Engineering and Navigation at Poplar and the Silversmithing School at the Central School of Arts and Crafts in 1906.[25] By 1912 fifteen London institutions were running day trade schools for 13–16-year-old boys in a range of trades - cookery, tailoring, book production, jewellery making, carriage building, as well as engineering and building based activities.[26]

The Board felt able to justify the education of young teenagers for future careers. They pointed out that in those days in many families in many towns sons followed fathers into prestigious trades.

> Certain trades are well known to be taken up by father and son for several generations and for a large number of boys in such towns as Barrow in Furness, Portsmouth, Chatham, Birmingham, Sheffield and many others can be predicted with much certainty. It is for such boys that the Junior Technical School is or should be provided.[27]

These schools were also valuable for girls. The first of these had been that at the Borough Polytechnic in 1904 for teaching waistcoat-making and dressmaking. By 1913 there were 26 girls' trade schools in London and 6 in the provinces specializing in dressmaking (16), millinery (8), domestic service (6), hairdressing (1) and one in photography - a pointer to greater equality with men.[28] Selby-Bigge, Permanent Secretary of the Board of Education thought highly of these schools. He told a London County Council (LCC) councillor 'London Schools were in many ways the pioneers of the Junior Technical School movement, particularly in the case of the Girls Trade Schools and they probably furnish the best examples of well established schools in the country'.[29]

A distinctive feature of these schools both for boys and girls was the provision of workshops. One in such a London school described as 'not elaborate' but 'very serviceable' gives some idea of the provision. The room 20 ft × 29 ft was used in relays throughout the day. It had working tables, sinks, gas burners and benches and most remarkably a lead lined floor. The work had two distinctive features. Since cabinet-making was an important local trade this was taught using cardboard instead of wood for instructional purposes. They also worked in lead (hence the lead floor), making bowls and models which the HMIs found 'interesting work' of 'undoubted value'.[30] It was also a subtle but practical aspect of these schools that the pupils should sit at flat topped tables rather than desks. In this way they already thought of themselves as workmen at a bench rather than as bookish children, or clerks. The Board noted that it created 'quite a different attitude of mind towards their work'.[31]

The curriculum too was heavily biased towards the practical. HMIs proposed the following curriculum for girls trade schools.[32]

English – 5 hours
Mathematics – 2 hours
Art and drawing – 3 hours
Trade work – 18 hours
Singing – 1 hour
Physical training – 1 hour

with trade work making up 60 per cent of their activity. And in practice it was observed that in London girls trade schools 'the pupils give about two-thirds of their time to trade work'.[33]

The success of JTSs and trade schools in London owed much to the support of Robert Blair, the Education Officer of the LCC. A former science teacher, head of Cheltenham School of Science and Inspector of Science in Scotland, he knew the field.[34] He appointed a special organizer for trade schools, H. Cameron Smail, and another for day continuation schools. Although keen on both forms he preferred the industrially related vocationalism of the former to the rather liberal education bias of the latter. Accordingly the LCC provided scholarships to its JTSs and trade schools covering fees and a maintenance grant.[35]

As well as the technical schools there were those with a commercial rather than a technical bias. There was a niche to fill here. The changes in office skills, with shorthand, typewriting and book-keeping, and with the telephone diminishing the role of the messenger, had led to the rise of the skilled female secretary - the 'white blouse revolution'. Many of these young women were trained in higher grade schools or private or correspondence college started by George Skerry from 1880. The number of papers in commercial subjects taken in the Royal Society of Arts examinations rose from 8,900 in 1900 to over 35,000 by 1914. This gives some indication of the strength of the movement.[36]

Accordingly some authorities created junior commercial schools as counterparts to the technical schools. One in North Manchester was described thus:

> The aim of this Junior Day Commercial School is to give a sound preliminary training for commercial life to boys and girls who have passed an entrance examination equivalent to Standard VII and are at the time of the examination between 13 and 14 ½ years of age. The courses of study extended over two years.[37]

The unease felt about early specialization in technical schools extended even more to this commercial work. In 1910 it was decided that no new commercial schools admitting children below the age of 16 should be recognized and that such work should be done in local secondary schools. Existing schools should continue but there were to be no new ones.[38] H.A.L. Fisher, who thoroughly approved of JTSs, did not extend this confidence to the junior commercial schools with their typing, book keeping and commercial French. He thought that 'commercial education for boys and girls has hitherto had little claim to be one valued from the point of view either of education or commerce'.[39] This was rather harsh.

The successful growth of the JTSs, after the Regulations of 1905, prompted the Board to 'clear the decks' in preparation for some ambitious form of JTS which came about in 1913. HMIs were asked to keep an eye on how far secondary schools were doing 'special work of a vocational character . . . [or] having any particular vocational bias, rural, industrial, commercial in the curriculum as a whole'.[40] Reciprocally, HMIs were urged to acquaint themselves with industrial conditions in their areas by visiting factories, workshops and businesses.[41] The Board also suggested that technical and science subjects being taught in arts schools should be transferred to local technical colleges.[42] These were small straws in the wind indicating that the Board was thinking about a closer linking of schools and industrial work. They made this more explicit at the end of 1911:

> it is probable that in the near future [we] will be in a position to press, at any rate in the larger towns, for a development of day work under their Regulations and in particular for the establishment of Junior Full Time Schools.[43]

This presaged the subsequent Regulation of 1913.

In introducing the 1913 Regulations, Selby-Bigge claimed that

> among the educational developments of recent years none have been more interesting and important than the growth of Junior Technical Schools . . . which continue the general education of their pupils while at the same time aiming at preparing them for industrial employment.[44]

The Regulations recognized that 'the Schools have emerged from the experimental stage' and deserved increased grants and detaching from the 'miscellaneous body of work' covered by Article 42 of the Regulations for Technical Schools under which they had operated hitherto.

The courses were not intended to prepare for the professions, universities or full-time higher technical work but for 'artisan or other industrial unemployment'. The curriculum of the JTSs was not specified in detail but 'must be suitable . . . to the circumstances of the locality', must include progressive practical work but should not include a foreign language unless of 'direct vocational value' to occupations for which the child pupils were being prepared. The age of pupils was to be 13–16 undertaking a 2–3 year course. Schools would receive £3 a year for children under 13 at the start of the school year and £5 for older pupils. Pupils could take internal tests but not be entered for external examinations without the permission of the Board, so that the curriculum should not be distorted from local needs by external academic demands. The Board was also concerned that the JTSs should relate closely to occupational needs. Parents were accordingly obliged to certify that their child was intended to enter an employment for which the school provided preparation. Indeed a school could be closed if the future jobs of leavers did not relate to courses offered by the school. Recognizing the importance of practical work in groups, class sizes were limited to 32 or 24 where individual attention was needed. Also to this effect a reasonable proportion of the teaching staff 'must have had practical trade experience'. In the same year residential technical schools preparing boys for the sea became 'schools of nautical training' providing annual grants of £10 per boy. Also in 1913 non-artistic subjects were recognized in arts schools to facilitate the organization of full-time preparatory departments with courses of general education. These were the junior art departments, so called after 1916.[45]

Behind the apparent firmness of regulations and public statements there was a private ambivalence at the highest levels of the Board about the JTSs. Selby-Bigge told Ernest Gray of the LCC that 'the place which these schools will permanently occupy in the educational system is in my opinion rather uncertain. I regard them as largely experimental and we are watching them as experiments very closely'.[46] Selby-Bigge's private personal view was that ideally all children should be in secondary schools between 11 and 16 and that vocational specialism was undesirable. Neither the working classes nor British society at large, he thought, saw much value in education as such. Accordingly both working class parents and middle class employers had to be persuaded of its value by allowing some vocationalisms which would relate to future work. With remarkable frankness he commented,

> the main national interest is to keep children in some good schools at work in which they are interested and which secures a substantial basis of human culture and training for citizenship. If the attainment of this object involves some sacrifice of an ideal curriculum to vocational considerations the sacrifice must be made - in course of time the sacrifice, it is hoped, will become less.[47]

Shortly afterwards he told Spurley Hey, the Director of Education for Manchester, that he had 'quite made up my mind' that the JTS 'is sound policy'.[48] But he did not elaborate on his view that it was a *faut de mieux* sacrifice. In the 1920s Selby-Bigge recalled that 'at one time the anxiety of the Board to establish (secondary schools) led it to look askance on competing types of full time day schools' including the JTSs.[49] The perception of many HMIs - recalled some years later - was that before 1914 JTSs were 'frowned on by the Board as competing with the secondary schools which remained the favourites of the Board down to 1912–14'.[50] They had clearly caught the whiff of the Permanent Secretary's views in Selby-Bigge's corridors of power.

H.A.L. Fisher who became President of the Board in 1915 was favourably disposed towards the JTSs. He admired Michael Sadler and Robert Morant and the system the latter had established including the technical schools.[51] In various public speeches in 1917 and 1918 he also made approving references to the these schools.[52] Perhaps more significantly he expressed these views privately also,

> in certain industries, for example Engineering and Building, . . . there is ample evidence that a course planned with reference to the needs of the future engineer and intelligently pursued, whether it be in Mathematics, Science or Drawing can develop capacity in the pupil . . .[53]

Yet the JTS found no mention in his famous Fisher Act of 1918.[54]

With the issue of the new Regulations of 1913, 41 schools were invited to apply for registration as JTSs.[55] Their geographical disposition was London 20; Lancashire 5 (Bootle, Liverpool, Preston, Salford, Wigan); Yorkshire 4 (Hull, Halifax and 2 in Leeds); Devon 3 (Exeter and 2 in Plymouth) Kent 2 (Gillingham and Rochester); Northumberland 2 (both in Newcastle), 1 each in Leicester, Peterborough, Radbrook, Guildford and Workington. By the end of the school year 1913–14, 27 schools for boys and 10 for girls had been recognized under the new Regulations.[56]

HMIs clarified their policies in the interpretation of the 1913 Regulations. They agreed that courses lasting just one year should be refused, that schools should have not only science laboratories but separate workshops for woodwork and metalwork and that 'a reasonable proportion of the staff of each school has had workshop experience'.[57] JTS students should not be expected to attend evening classes since their course should be complete in itself. The Inspectors were also adamant in those days that JTSs should not prepare for Matriculation which was the task of secondary schools.[58]

In most cases the JTSs were located in larger technical colleges and polytechnics in London. They shared the same buildings and facilities. Indeed this was one of their strengths, since they would use the laboratories and workshops of the senior institutions. The children were there by day and many more adult students were there for evening-class work. Sensible as this arrangement was there was some feeling that it would be better to separate schools, colleges and polytechnics. A Board official noted

> the moment has arrived I think in the metropolitan district for allowing this unnatural growth of a secondary school in a polytechnic to pay the normal penalty due to an unnatural union. A new growth of the same species as the parent stock is waiting to spring up in congenial surroundings.[59]

He made the usual point that there was an urgent need for trade and technical schools to replace apprenticeship.

The polytechnics had their own motives for wanting their JTSs to be hived off. There could be organizational tensions where the principal of a polytechnic was nominally the head of the JTS but had delegated this role to a subordinate with whose independence he may be inclined to interfere. But the presence of a childrens' school in a polytechnic also touched the nerve of another issue. The polytechnics in the 1900s were already trying to take up university work 'for which they were not intended'. They were seeking to drop some of their proper technical work in pursuit of becoming 'sham University colleges instead of places of education for workers either about to be or already engaged in industrial occupations'.[60] Having JTSs and children on the premises ran counter to these higher aspirations and were an unwelcome reminder to the polytechnics of their manual, technical and industrial purposes which they were seeking to abdicate.

The junior technical and trade schools were run by local education authorities. There were some schools operated by firms, for example, British Westinghouse, Cadbury and Boots, for their young employees. But these were part-time day continuation schools for young people in work and allowed some time off during the day.[61] However, there was a rare example of a genuine private enterprise full time JTS which is worth considering here. It was run by William Ford Stanley who owned a distinguished firm in Norwood making scientific instruments and precision tools. He was aware that the young people he employed had been insufficiently prepared by their impractical elementary education. He opened his own Stanley Technical Trade School in Norwood in 1907 when there were very few state JTSs. The school took sons of mechanics for a three year course between the ages of 12 and 15 'to form the ground work of knowledge for a scientific, artistic workman'.[62] The curriculum consisted of mathematics and science, drawing, modelling and English. But central to the school's work were the well-equipped workshops for woodwork up to cabinet making and metalwork up to making lathes (as good as American) which were sold commercially. On leaving school boys were superbly equipped to start apprenticeships with Stanley or elsewhere and they were encouraged to continue their studies at a polytechnic. This was an excellent exemplar of the private JTS. Sir William Crookes wrote to Stanley,

> I am sure your Trade Schools will do much good. They fill a gap left since the discontinuance of the system of apprenticeship, and were capitalists as public spirited as yourself to found similar schools in all the large centres of industry, the general intelligence of the working classes would be increased materially.[63]

With 174 students the Stanley School was the second largest JTS in England in 1916.[64]

The activities of the JTSs were flanked by similar developments both in elementary schools below them and in secondary schools above. Elementary schools were urged to develop handwork including woodwork (sawing and simple turning) and metalwork (drilling, screw cutting and forge and lathe work). This was to be done not as trade training, as in the junior technical school, but for the 'information of character through discipline of the hand and eye'. Indeed Board officials preferred to use the term 'manual instruction' since 'handicraft' 'suggests too much in the nature of preparation for a specific occupation'.[65] In practice this was carried out. Elementary schools taught not only needlework, cookery and laundry but woodwork and even jewellery making in Birmingham.[66] This was not primarily to turn out more craftsmen but to develop the sense of handiness, accuracy and pride in creation, qualities valuable in any worker.[67] It would also be desirable to divert childrens' minds away from clerical work as a preferred employment of elementary children.

Secondary schools also adopted workshop practice and engineering in the curriculum. F.W. Sanderson had pioneered this at Oundle in the 1890s but the 1904–5 Regulations prompted other academic secondary schools to teach woodwork and engineering. The aim was to get boys 'to exercise forethought and intelligence in the use of means towards definite ends in production'.[68] In 1914 the Board investigated engineering at eight secondary grammar and public schools to 'enable an opinion to be formed as to the relation of this engineering work to that done in Technical Institutions and Junior Technical Schools'. They approved their work and the flow of boys they provided into engineering works and evening class studies. They concluded that 'the engineering work in some of these municipal secondary schools follows much the same lines as that in Junior Technical (Engineering) schools, but only half the time is spent on it'.[69] They were content that the work of elementary schools and secondary schools did not obviate the need for a separate stream of JTSs. The elementary work was obviously for younger children and too

Table 2.1 *Occupations of technical school boys in Leeds, 1905–12*

Employment	Boys	Percentage	Percentage of known occupations
Mechanical engineering	134	39.8	49.6
Electrical engineering	23	6.8	8.5
Draughtsmen	23	6.8	8.5
Building trades	14	4.1	5.2
Other skilled occupations	30	8.9	11.1
Commercial occupations	28	8.3	10.4
Unskilled	18	5.3	6.7
Not known	66	19.6	-
	366		

Source W.P. Welpton, *Primary Artisan Education* (London, 1913) pp.243-4.

elementary to compare, while that of the secondary schools was only half as specialized. The JTS had its distinctive niche, though all schools were influenced in common by the perceived need to make education provide more practical skills orientated to industry.

That this new kind of technical schooling was paying off is suggested by the future occupations of the boys produced by the Holbeck and Woodhouse Schools in Leeds between 1905 and 1912 (see Table 2.1). It was clearly gratifying that only 5 or 6 per cent of ex-pupils were going into unskilled work and that 83 per cent were entering worthwhile skilled jobs 'many of them after leaving school have risen to posts of very considerable responsibility in the works in which they have been employed'. Though it was disappointing that the destiny of nearly a fifth should be unknown.

III

The First World War had relatively little effect on the new JTSs. There were so few of them and, unlike in the Second War, there was no need for evacuation. However, the schools had to be defended against officious and indiscriminate attempts to take them over. Voluntary Aid Detachments were trying to commandeer central and technical schools to convert them into hospitals. The War Office made this clear that while this was doubtless done from 'patriotic motives' yet it was 'undesirable at the present juncture'.[70] Generals were told that such schools were not required for this military purpose and still less should they be used for billeting. Indeed any schools which had been used for billeting should be vacated.[71]

The position of staff was also protected. HMIs had the power to advise military advisory committees and local tribunals. They did so on the lines that

> Teachers who have many students under their supervision should generally be regarded as indispensable if it would be impossible to obtain efficient substitutes for them. The Principals and Heads of Departments of important Technical Schools . . . and Junior Technical Schools, would in nearly all cases come into this category.[72]

However, there were ambivalent attitudes about the relative importance of training and actual production in wartime conditions. These were well highlighted by the case of Walter Patterson. Patterson was the holder of a scholarship at Shoreditch Junior Technical School. But in October 1917 he had asked to be released from his scholarship to go to work for Vickers. The LCC asked for a £13 refund since Patterson had stayed for only one and a half years of the three years he had undertaken. This brought to a head a variety of basic attitudes. Sir Auckland Geddes thought that Patterson was right and that JTS courses should all be suspended so that scholars could patriotically work in munitions factories.[73] However this was not the official Ministry of Munitions view since when Sir Robert Blair of the LCC had offered them teachers from the JTSs the Ministry had decided that they were better retained in the schools. The Board of Education of course took the view that it was not worth sacrificing a whole generation of skilled labour by closing JTSs, and the national need for boy labour in munitions was hardly so urgent as to justify strangling the supply of future skilled young adults.[74] H.A.L. Fisher noted that it was now recognized that interrupting medical training at the beginning of the war had been an error. Lord Derby also regretted the stupidity of his unselective recruiting policy at the start of the war which had led to the wasteful slaughter of scientists, industrial technologists and others with civilian skills vital for the war economy.[75] It was important that the views of Auckland Geddes did not prevail. The JTSs continued their work in the recognition that a sensible balance had to be struck between the needs of the fighting forces, productive industry and the training for the latter.

The JTSs continued; they were after all dealing with children not teenagers of military age. Indeed eight more (Plymouth, Darlington,

Turton, Wigan, Kirton, Peterborough, Newcastle (2)) were authorized in the first year of the war.[76] They did relate themselves to the war effort by 'testing materials, and making gauges, aeroplane parts and other engineering details'[77] as did workshops and laboratories in other educational establishments from public schools (like Oundle) to universities. As if to leaven this dour practical work the HMIs were especially keen during the war to encourage JTSs to develop a varied and interesting social life with 'students' clubs, social gatherings, excursions, school magazines [to] encourage a corporate spirit'.[78]

One important side-effect of the war was the destruction of that admiration for German education and culture which had supported claims for the English JTS before 1914. By the end of the war the view was commonly expressed that German technical education had produced a nation totally materialistic in its values and subordinate to the state. Such students were taught to place technological, industrial and hence military efficiency above all other considerations. As J.H. Badley observed, a century of German education had been directed to 'the production of efficiency in the material side of life' creating 'a nation at once the admiration and dread of the rest of the world, in industry as in war'. Admirable as this had been thought before 1914, its proven results thereafter had been a menace and a disaster for Germany itself and the rest of Europe. The implication was that in educational matters 'we have neither to adopt their aims nor copy their method'.[79] On the contrary, the Headmistress of Manchester High School for Girls urged 'we should borrow from our kinsmen and our allies rather than from the Prussians'.[80]

The war and its ending also had the effect of exacerbating trends which before 1914 had drawn attention to the need for more training and education of the young. The mechanization and specialization which critics had seen as undermining apprenticeship before the war intensified during the war. The increased use of machine tools and deskilling was accepted as mechanization enabled war production to be maintained by women, juveniles and the semi-skilled. With the ending of the war 'demobilization returned to civilian life men many of whom, engaged upon casual work as boys four or five years ago, are unequipped for skilled employment, and are therefore brought into direct competition with boys for work'.[81] Both gave greater urgency to the need for the technical education of the young.

IV

The JTSs had to contend against certain forms of opposition. First there was the undoubted preference for liberal education and suspicion of too early vocational training for children. For example, Sir Stanley Leathes, the historian, slightingly noted that schools should adopt an academic approach to practical subjects and that technical schools 'carry with them their own problems. They are supplementary to education, they are not at present a part of general education'[82] - this in the same year that the JTSs received their own Regulations. Another commentator, just after the war, noted the same attitude (which she did not share) that 'in England the practice of the schools for the age group 14–16 is to emphasize the liberal side . . . This is a part of a generally accepted English policy, viz., to defer vocational training till the age of 16–18'.[83] Even educational reformers keen on technical education could be opposed to its premature provision for early teenagers.[84]

For some this was linked with doubts about the material advance of the 1900s. For C.F.G. Masterman, telephones, motor buses and aerial flights were less objects of wonder and delight than apprehension. They represented 'the insistence of things against ideas, the dominance of the material'.[85] Forms of education like the JTSs which emphasized the material to the supposed neglect of the liberal, spiritual, higher values could arouse hostility on these grounds. The long Victorian tradition of respect for 'liberal' non-vocational education enshrined in the public schools, the ancient universities and the Morant view of the 1902 grammar schools made it difficult to accept the notion of the technical vocational secondary school. It was a prescient pre-echo of Martin Wiener's current view of the English 'industrial spirit' being stifled by gentlemanly liberal arts values in education and the neglect of hard edged technical vocational training.[86] The JTSs had to establish themselves in this sceptical climate of attitudes.

Even the headmasters of JTSs, while deeply convinced of their value, appreciated the unease of their opponents, a small element of which they shared. They were defensive about the accusation that their schools provided a narrow premature trade training and wanted to stress their educational value. They even tried to get the 1913 Regulations changed. They wanted the deletion of words about 'preparation for artisan or other industrial employment' and their substitution by claims 'to provide a liberal education based upon instruction in science . . . which may or may not prepare for industrial employment'.[87] They were not successful but their initiative suggested a sensitivity, a desire to prove that they really were providing education, even 'liberal' education, and were not merely anterooms to forge and factory as their critics suggested.

Part of this scepticism and hostility came from the Left. They saw that the middle and upper classes enjoyed a liberal education which rounded their minds and characters before they embarked upon professional training. Consequently the working classes resented that their own education, by contrast, should pre-empt their future occupations and prematurely stunt their broader intellectual development in the interest of the narrow acquisition of skills. The Workers' Educational Association which since 1903 had been providing specifically non-vocational liberal education for adult working men 'had headed a reaction against the prevailing conception of vocational education' for boys and girls since by fitting them to be breadwinners it led 'to the neglect of their real capacities and above all of their spiritual gifts and needs'.[88] J.M. Mactavish, the Secretary of the Workers' Educational Association (WEA) was bluntly dismissive of JTSs, 'specialisation under the age of 14, or even 16, stereotypes the mind and checks natural development'.[89]

The trade unions also had more mundane motives for being suspicious of JTSs. They feared that the training of large numbers of young people in technical subjects would increase the availability of skilled labour. This would lead to competition which would drive down the wages of workmen, undermine the strength of the unions and advantage none but the employer and his profits. N.B. Dearle was aware of hostile attitudes in the trade unions - 'we feel bound to discourage attendance at the Technical Schools. Lads of all sorts go to them and naturally turn to the Woodworking Trades which get overstocked. We object to manual training before they leave school for the same reason'.[90] Dearle thought these 'overstocking' fears were diminishing, but they were certainly around. Major Ernest Gray of the LCC found that many people regarded the 1913 Junior Technical School Regulations 'and all similar movements as attempts to side track children from secondary schools, furnishing as they think an abundant supply of cheap labour for the benefit of parsimonious employers'.[91]

Moreover this benefit to the employer and disadvantage to the worker would be paid for by the taxpayer. A.H.D. Acland's Committee on Continuation Schools observed in 1909 that the trade unions suspected technical education 'of being a device of the employers to increase, largely at the cost of public funds, the supply of young workmen sufficiently skilful to take their place in a skilled industry and so numerous as to reduce the wages of labour'.[92] Of the 98 witnesses to the Acland Committee only six people spoke positively in favour of the JTSs or trade school. Three of them represented working-class interests but two of them (George Lansbury, J. Sexton) noted that their positive views were unusual in the Labour movement. In short, socialists and trade unionists feared that school technical education would produce young people to oust adults from jobs, it was a capitalist ruse to increase profits at the expense of the taxpayer and trade unionist, it denied the young worker that spiritual dimension derived from general education.

Such views exasperated H.A.L. Fisher, President of the Board of Education, who wished to press forward with more vocational education. Fisher at the end of the First World War deplored that 'school of working class opinion which is very suspicious of technical education . . . which is likely to make the workman more useful to his employer'.[93] Yet he thought that official Labour attitudes were at variance with grass roots working class opinion which 'would really have preferred a more definite bias to bread-and-butter studies'.[94]

The number of schools was small. Between 1905 and 1913 they rose to 37 schools with 2,900 pupils and by 1918 they had expanded to 61 schools.[95] In 1916 the Board analysed 30 JTSs which revealed something of their internal arrangements. A half of them took children from the age of 12 and the other half from 13 with the most common age of entry 13–14. Nineteen of them provided a two-year course and eleven a three-year course. They were also rather small, with the average size being 81 pupils.[96]

In spite of these negative views and the small size of the sector, by the end of the First World War there was much public enthusiasm for the JTS. On behalf of the Lewis Committee, 120 education committees were asked by a circular whether they considered that there was a need for an increase in junior day technical instruction. They found

> there was practical unanimity on this question, only eight Committees being of the opinion that no increase of junior technical instruction is required . . . There seems no doubt that a system of junior technical training for children from 12 to 15 is felt to be an urgent need, with possibly a parallel scheme of junior commercial schools.[97]

Of the 97 individual witnesses the majority who expressed a view approved of JTSs and their purposes and of 24 chambers of commerce only two expressed opposition to them. The Board too found much to approve: 'there appears to be little doubt that the schools are producing useful citizens and successfully fulfilling the object for which they were established'.[98] With their formative years over and this blessing the schools entered the interwar years.

CHAPTER 3

The Problems of the Junior Technical Schools, 1918–1939

Education has neglected the boy whose skill lies in making things rather than in writing about them.[1]

Boots Pure Drug Co. (1925)

There is probably no type of school in the whole system of English education whose reputation . . . stands higher than that of the Junior Technical School.[2]

British Association of Commercial and Industrial Education (1934)

I

For the first 25 years of their existence the junior technical schools were borne along by frequently stated public approbation. By 1918 they were praised for producing useful citizens and successfully fulfilling the object for which they were established. After ten years experience 'the Board can say with confidence that these schools have justified themselves, in that they are of practical benefit to the students and are appreciated by employers in the industries concerned'.[3] The JTSs also impressed Sir Joseph Thomson's Committee which was looking at science education in 1918. They regretted that there were not more of them and recommended that they be 'strengthened and developed'.[4] By the late 1920s it was noted that JTS boys had no difficulty in getting jobs in industry, 'indeed in some cases, the demand on the part of the employers far exceeds the supply of such students'.[5] If the 1920s had praised the JTSs for fulfilling their purpose and being useful to industry, comment in the 1930s moved to a more euphoric plane finding a high moral tone in the schools. The Board of Education put it strongly in 1930,

> The pupils attack their work with a seriousness and satisfaction not always found in schools for pupils of their age. They concentrate because they are interested, they are interested because they have no

Table 3.1 *Numbers of junior technical schools and pupils in England and Wales, 1913–38*

	England		Wales		England and Wales	
	Schools	Pupils	Schools	Pupils	Schools	Pupils
1913/14					37	
1918/19					69	
1919/20					78	9 811
1920/21					84	11 235
1921/22					89	12 256
1922/23					89	12 206
1923/24					87	11 988
1924/45					89	11 954
1925/26					92	12 704
1926/27	101	18 704	3	629	104	19 333
1927/28	104	19 541	3	659	107	20 200
1928/29	108	18 243	4	634	112	18 877
1929/30	115	19 537	5	680	120	20 217
1930/31	177	21 066	12	932	189	21 998
1931/32	182	21 033	12	942	194	21 945
1932/33	191	21 445	12	1 025	203	22 470
1933/34	200	23 090	13	1 040	213	24 130
1934/35	208	24 532	15	1 077	223	25 609
1935/36	216	26 071	16	1 283	232	27 354
1936/37	226	27 395	17	1 352	243	28 747
1937/38	230	29 036	18	1 421	248	30 457

Sources: Bill Bailey, 'Technical Education and Secondary Schooling 1905–1945' in Penny Summerfield and Eric Evans, *Technical Education and the State since 1850* (Manchester, 1990) pp.100–101 provides the best figures derived from the *Annual Reports of the Board of Education*.

> difficulty in realising the direct bearing of their work on their future lives. They have the air of knowing exactly what they are doing, and exactly why it is worth doing.[6]

The Board returned to extol the 'zest and purposefulness' and 'spirit of industry' of the schools in 1934 and the Spens Report enthused over the 'atmosphere of vitality, keenness and happiness' of the JTSs they visited four years later.[7] Yet this consistent and increasing praise for the JTSs in the interwar years contrasts with the modesty of their development in this time. The growth of the JTSs was as shown in Table 3.1. This growth might at first sight appear creditable but there are problems within the figures. The figures up to 1925 are clear enough and reflect the slow growth of the depressed years of the early 1920s. The decline in student numbers in 1929 was the result of changing the mode of calculation from all students who had attended at any time during the year to those attending on 31 March 1929. The increase in numbers from 1931 was partly due to the inclusion of housewifery schools and the reclassification of a school as a group under a head teacher rather than an institution in which a school was run. Finally from 1935 nautical schools were added to the list. So to compare the Board figures for 1920 with those of 1938 is to exaggerate the expansion by not comparing like with like. However, these considerations are quite marginal when we see in context just how small this sector and its growth were.

We can see the limited role of the JTSs in other ways. For example, the Hadow Report in 1926 estimated that only 0.3 per cent of children aged 11–16 were in JTSs.[8] The Board in 1930 admitted that their growth had been slow, 'steady but not spectacular', with only 100 schools and less than 20,000 scholars after 20 years. The Board concluded realistically if gloomily that 'measured by numbers the Junior Technical School is not a major element in our educational system'.[9]

Two other indicators confirmed this. In the 1930s the percentage of elementary school children going to JTSs was a consistently tiny 2.6 per cent of boys and 1.4 of girls. Looked at another way it was possible to tell how geographically limited JTSs provision was in 1937.[10] (See Table 3.2.)

That JTSs were to be found in fewer than half of units of local government of populations less than 200,000 was an indication of the limited development of the junior technical sector. There was growth but it was from the minuscule to the very small. Let us then turn to consider some factors which account for this constrained growth.

II

A major obstacle to the establishment of JTSs was the question of cost. The Chief Inspector of Technical Education, A. Abbott, observed that the 'cost of this type of school is relatively high. This is due mainly to the fact that so much of the work is done in laboratories, work rooms and drawing offices and consequently the classes are small'.[11] The Principal of Derby Technical College a few years later agreed and was more explicit:

Table 3.2 *Junior technical schools and local education authority size, 1937*

	Population (in thousands)				
	Over 300	200–300	100–200	60–100	50–60
No. of county boroughs	7	10	23	29	7
No. with JTSs	7 (all)	8 (80%)	7 (30%)	12 (41%)	4 (57%)
No. of municipal boroughs and urban districts	-	-	9	22	14
No. with JTSs	-	-	4 (44%)	4 (18%)	4 (28%)

Source: *Review of Junior Technical Schools in England*, Board of Education pamphlet no. 111 (1937) p.8.

> The cost of the [Junior Technical] Schools is relatively high . . . the cost could hardly be low, a highly trained staff is necessary . . . Again expensive equipment is necessary, the use of which requires much material. Classes cannot be large (with a staff student ratio of 1:18, lower than for secondary schools). Did not most of these schools form part of a Senior College, sharing with it both staff and equipment, the cost would be greater.[12]

The HMIs summed up clearly:

> vocational education with equipment is expensive, staffing is difficult . . . the point of cost is important. If there is to be more vocational education teaching will become more expensive . . . this is one of the reasons for the slow development of Junior Technical Schools in the provinces.[13]

Firstly the schools were costly to build. This was not always possible to discern since JTSs were usually part of larger technical college buildings with which they shared premises. In the 1920s the capital costs of building a secondary school were reckoned to be about £100 a place.[14] In the mid 1930s the cost per student was still £100+. This is confirmed by some rare data about the building costs of some JTSs structurally independent of technical colleges (see Table 3.3).

However, the building costs were only the start. The JTSs also entailed considerable equipment costs. It was assumed that JTSs would have extensive facilities. The Board itself proposed typewriting rooms for 30 places each with a modern typewriter and individual lighting,

Table 3.3 *Building costs of junior technical schools in the 1930s*

		Cost (£)	Pupils	Cost per pupil (£)
1931	Stoke JTS	24 000	212	113[1]
1936	Birmingham Bordesley JTS	22 908	202	113[2]
1937	Bexley Day Technical School	22 342	231	96[3]
1935	South Essex Technical College Barking	131 273	900	145[4]
1939	Sunderland	56 202[5]	?	?

1 ED 22/155 Survey of technical school accommodation, 29 Apr. 1935. HMI: J.L.Manson's calculation for N.W. Division.
2 ED 98/129 Stoke Junior Technical School.
3 ED 22/219 Provision of new premises. Building costs, 12 Apr. 1939.
4 *Technical College Buildings, their Planning and Equipment* (ATI and APTI, 1935) p.118.
5 ED 98/189 Sunderland Villiers Street Junior Technical School.

workshops for metal and woodwork, foundry and forges with benches, vices, lathes, drilling, planing and milling machines and so forth.[15] The Board's specifications of 1937 made the setting up of a JTS sound a very difficult and expensive business, which it was. One may readily imagine many a financially hard pressed Chief Education Officer reading this and deciding to have nothing to do with such schools. Cost was a deterrent. This equipment element raised costs further.

It was the workshops in JTSs which caused the high costs in addition

Table 3.4 *Building and equipment costs in junior technical schools*

	Building £	Equipment £	Total £	Equipment as % of total	Building and equipment costs per pupil £
Barking	131 273	44 500	176 273	25.5%	145
Bordesley Green	22 908	4 667	27 575	17%	136
Bexley	22 342	1 368	23 710	5%	102
Stoke	24 000	3 231	27 231	11.9%	128

Sources: *Technical College Buildings, their Planning and Equipment*, Association of Technical Institutions and Association of Principals of Technical Institutions (London, 1935), p.118; ED 22/219 Provision of new premises, 12 Apr. 1939; ED 98/129 Stoke Junior Technical School.

Table 3.5 *Running costs of junior technical schools, 1937*

	£
Net costs to rates and taxes	131,275
Income from fees	12,444
Income from other sources	947
Gross expenditure per annum	144,666
Number of pupils	5636
Average cost per pupil per annum	£25.66

Source: *Review of Junior Technical Schools in England*, Board of Education pamphlet no.111 (1937) p.33. This pamphlet misleadingly calculated cost per pupil at £23.2s by dividing only the net costs to rates and taxes by the number of pupils. This recalculation is a truer figure.

to the laboratories. At Stoke the fitting up of laboratories cost £1,347 but the workshops and drawing offices cost another £1,250. Indeed the metal workshop was quite the most expensively equipped part of the whole school with motor and shafting, benches and vices and milling machines. When the Principal of Borough Polytechnic was asked whether it would be feasible to equip secondary schools with the kind of equipment apparatus found in technical schools he replied, 'No, it would be too expensive'.[16]

However, the third element was the annual running costs. These caused particular concern to administrators. A series of jottings about Manchester schools by Board officials caught this anxiety

> I expect the school is very costly per pupil . . . we have found the other Manchester Junior Technical Schools amazingly costly . . . the cost of the Manchester Junior Technical Schools at Newton Heath and at Openshaw prove to be very high . . . the figures are very difficult to defend.[17]

This concern prompted the Board to find out more exactly just what the schools did cost from the returns of 42 inspected schools in 1937 (see Table 3.5).

Perhaps on the basis of these figures, when Accrington proposed a JTS in 1938 for 50 students at an annual cost of £30 a head they were told that this was too expensive.[18] Yet some running costs were remarkably high. A girls' trade school in Bloomsbury was cited as £48 a head in the 1920s[19] and a London needlework school as £60 in 1939.[20]

Table 3.6 *Relative running costs of junior technical schools and grammar schools in the 1930s*

	Annual per capita cost (£) Junior technical school	Grammar school
Barrow (1935)[1]	30	25
Workington (1933)[2]	28	22
Bootle (1933)[3]	£1 higher than Grammar School	
Leicester (1933)[4]	26	24

Notes

1 ED 98/53 Barrow in Furness Junior Technical School.

2 ED 98/4 Workington Junior Technical School.

3 ED 98/59 Bootle. Ald T.A. Patrick 29 Mar. 1933.

4 ED 10/153 Memorandum by E.C. White, n.d. 1934.

The Board did not publish the relative running costs of JTSs and grammar schools. Yet it was evident that in a number of places the JTS was more expensive to run than any other kind of school. The National Association of Inspectors noted that 'A trade school in London (13–16) costs rather more than a Secondary School per head'.[21] Here was a curious paradox that a sector of schooling largely for working class children who had failed to get into grammar schools was costing more than the prestige secondary education from which they had been excluded.[22]

An element in the high costs of JTSs was that their staffing ratios had to be kept low. This was due to the practicalities of workshop practice. Demonstrating machinery and working with tools at benches could only be undertaken with smaller groups than the large classes possible with academic subjects. Staff student ratios in JTSs ranged from 1:13.6 at Wolverton to 1:29.2 at Preston. Most were in the range 1:19 to 1:25.[23] W.A. Richardson considered 'the average ratio of staff (considered on the basis of full-time service) to students is 1 to 18 - smaller than the ratio for secondary schools'.[24] The NUT urged the Board to keep practical classes in technical schools low on safety grounds and were reassured that although no serious danger had been experienced the HMIs were keeping an eye on the situation.[25] As staff student ratios were low, so almost all JTSs were small. Only about 16 per cent had more than 200 pupils and 54 per cent had fewer than 100 by the late 1930s.[26]

III

Teachers were to be a particular problem for the JTSs. Sadler saw this at once - 'the chief difficulty would be to find the right teachers'.[27] They would have to have the academic qualities of orthodox schoolteachers and the skills of the workshop craftsman. The paragon junior technical school teachers

> must be as well qualified academically as teachers in secondary schools; others must, in addition, have had industrial or commercial experience; yet others, engaged in teaching practical subjects, must be skilled craftsmen, having not less than five years adult experience in the industry or occupation for which they are preparing students.[28]

Yet such supermen were to be attracted by salaries so modest (£120–200 but most under £160 in 1913) that educationists agreed they were unable to attract men of quality and 'secondary teaching does not offer a career worth training for'.[29]

Low salaries might satisfy teachers of ordinary arts school subjects with low market value or no alternative market. But JTSs were caught in a double bind. 'There are workmen enough, but they cannot teach, and there are teachers enough but naturally they know nothing about the industrial processes which it would be their business to teach'.[30] In practice dual staffs evolved: academic teachers for the academic subjects and those with industrial experience for the practical work. One might wonder about the motives of the latter. So did the Board. They thought that the technical teacher 'will be induced to leave his trade for teaching on account of the shorter hours, the more regular work and the longer holidays' but unless they were decently paid the JTSs risked 'being staffed with derelicts'.[31]

The Board was aware of the need for attractive salaries for technical staff. In 1919 the Burnham Committee was set up to determine national salary scales for teachers and schools. It set out the scales shown in Table 3.7. Yet no decision was taken on salaries for principals, head of departments or instructors, i.e. those with five years industrial experience (after the age of 21), the very men undertaking the craft workshop instruction. Lord Burnham told Fisher that they were not able to make recommendations on scales for instructors 'owing to the many and various types of schools and the wide divergence of local conditions'.[32] Accordingly LEAs were left to decide on appropriate

Table 3.7 *Salaries of junior technical school teachers, 1921*

	Graduate assistant					
	Masters			Mistresses		
	Min.	Annual increment	Max.	Min.	Annual increment	Max.
England and Wales	240	15	500	225	15	400
London	290	15	550	275	15	440
	Non-graduate assistant					
	Masters			Mistresses		
	Min.	Annual increment	Max.	Min.	Annual increment	Max.
England and Wales	190	12.10	400	177.10	12.10	320
London	210	12.10	450	197.10	12.10	360

Sources: ED 108/17 Report of the Sub Committee on Scales of Salaries for Teachers in Junior Technical Schools 1921. *Report of the Standing Joint Committee . . . on Scales of Salaries for Teachers in Junior Technical Schools* (Lord Burnham) 1921.

salaries at their discretion. There was a good deal of sense in this since the employment of technicians was much more subject to local labour markets than, say, graduates in English or History. At that time, 1921, the balance of teachers in technical schools was as shown in Table 3.8. Accordingly a large element of JTS staff were not covered by Burnham. Tantalizingly the LEAs and teachers proposed some figures for the missing grades. (See Table 3.9.)

These are interesting as indicative of the kind of salaries that actually were paid but they had no Burnham authority behind them. The lack of scales for many JTS staff had an ironically protective effect. Since there were no scales for instructors it was very difficult to assess the overall

Table 3.8 *Types of teachers in junior technical schools, 1921*

Graduate	Men	Women
Graduate	780	145
Non-graduate assistants	562	99
Non-graduate instructors	1189	508

Source: ED 108/17 Teachers in technical schools in England and Wales, 1921.

Table 3.9 *Proposed salaries for junior technical school teachers not on Burnham Scale, 1921*

Instructors	LEA proposals	Teachers proposals
England & Wales	Min. 190 – 240 Max. 300 – 350	Min. 220 – 250 Max. 300 – 350
London	Min. 300 Max. 400	Min. 300 Max. 425
Head of depts	490 – 600	500 – 1000

Source: ED 108/17 Report of the Joint Sub Committee on the Financial Considerations n.d. (1921?).

cost of these salaries and there was no uniform scale which could be neatly cut by a decided percentage. This created difficulties for the Treasury putting pressure on the Board as part of the public expenditure cuts in the early 1920s.[33]

In the late 1920s, while still not filling in the missing scales, Burnham made suggestions of increasing generosity. He suggested that headmasters be paid a minimum of £600, that years spent in industry, professional or research work be taken into account when deciding on LEA discretion salaries, then service in HM Dockyards or as instructors in the Forces.[34] The new scales of 1927 were as shown in Table 3.10. This suggests that in the more buoyant industrial conditions of the late 1920s the LEAs were having to compete by being more generous to

Table 3.10 *Salaries of junior technical school teachers, 1927*

Graduate assistants	Masters			Mistresses		
	Min.	Annual increment	Max.	Min.	Annual increment	Max.
England and Wales	234	15	480	216	12	384
London	276	15	528	264	12	420
Non-graduate assistants						
England and Wales	186	12	384	174	9	306
London	204	12	432	192	9	342

Source: *Second Report of the Standing Joint Committee . . . on Salaries of Teachers* (Viscount Burnham) 1927.

their Junior Technical School staff to retain 'the services of teachers who would be of great value owing to their industrial experience'.[35]

As a result of the slump and financial crisis, teachers' salaries were cut by 10 per cent in 1931. Paley Yorke, the headmaster of a notable JTS in Poplar and a member of the Burnham Committee, vehemently protesting against the teachers' 10 per cent salary cuts in 1931 said

> he knew the difficulty of getting the right kind of men and women. The salaries offered did not attract them . . . it was necessary to recruit people who had some industrial experience . . . it was perfectly well known that the salaries now offered were not good enough to attract the teachers required.[36]

Paley Yorke was still persisting in this vein four years later, meeting the bland denial of Alderman W.B. Kenrick for the employers who denied that the remuneration of technical teachers had failed to recruit 'a steady flow of satisfactory teachers'.[37]

In 1934 Burnham's scales of 1925, which had been subject to the 10 per cent cut in 1931, were partly restored by 5 per cent. They were fully restored to their former level in 1935 and were then set to continue to 1939. Accordingly in 1938 a Committee was set up by the Chief Inspector E.G. Savage to see if the qualifications of non graduate technical staff in JTSs could be related to graduate qualifications in secondary schools. This might facilitate the belated drawing up of Burnham scales for such teachers. But yet again they decided that it was not practicable to suggest any combination of qualifications suitable for relating technical school craft teachers to graduates in secondary schools. Mr Marris noted

> the technical school teacher . . . is in most cases a man employed in giving instruction in workshop practice for whom the art training required to obtain the qualifications suggested for the secondary school teacher would not be appropriate . . . there are at present no organised courses of training for technical school teachers and consequently such a qualification is not obtainable.[38]

Accordingly the key technical teachers in JTSs still remained without a scale, taking or leaving what the LEA thought fit to offer.

So what did JTS teachers actually earn? The salaries of JTS teachers seem to have been quite attractive especially in the unemployment of the 1930s. Some typical ranges were

Chipping Wycombe, Bucks[39] (1933)

£173, 211, 218, 251, 258, 262, 270, 281, 319, 345, 345, 345, 369

Average £280

Barrow-in-Furness[40]

£283, 291, 293, 307, 344, 345, 345, 345, 345, 361, 396

Average £332

Dorothy Pannett found that in London JTSs graduate women started at £264 and rose to £420, non-graduates from £192 to £342, instructors from £230 to £330.[41] This seems to have been typical and adequate. It was noted in 1940 that Junior Technical School salaries 'on average rise from a minimum of about £250 to a maximum of about £400. These scales would be more than adequate for the handicraft instructors . . . they have hitherto been sufficient to attract suitable staff from industry.'[42]

Headmasters, of course, were better provided for. When Norwich proposed £600 for the salary of a JTS head in 1935 the Board sent a typical range of headmasters' salaries: £520, 550, 600, 620, 700, 750, 800, 850, 960.[43] The Barrow head received £700 a year. So Norwich was on target, though low.

Table 3.11 *Salaries of junior technical school headmasters, 1935–6*

	£	JTS salaries above this point	
Higher professionals	634	7	headmasters
Managers	440	4	
Lower professionals	308	12	other JTS teachers
Foremen	273	5	
Skilled workers	195	6	
Clerks	192		
Semi-skilled	134	1	
Unskilled	129		

Source: Guy Routh, *Occupation and Pay in Great Britain 1906–1960* (London, 1965) p.104.

We can compare JTS headmasters' and teachers' salaries with the spectrum of average earnings 1935–6 (see Table 3.11). So JTS teachers' salaries were in the range of skilled workers, foremen and lower professionals with the best reaching up to managerial and professional levels. It would suggest that they were quite realistically pitched. In addition were the psychological satisfactions - important in the 1930s - of regular work, guaranteed employment, pensions and holidays and perhaps the awareness among some technically skilled men and women that they lacked the personality or capital to make the transition from being good employees to being successful employers in business in those risky decades.[44]

These salary scales and conditions seem to have attracted a generally satisfactory teaching body. JTSs needed a distinctive mixture of graduates for academic subjects and others with industrial experience who need not be university graduates. Overall, Spens found that about 55 per cent of JTS staff were graduates, and 'a salient feature is the employment of teachers who have had experience in industry and commerce'.[45] For example at Chipping Wycombe 60 per cent, at Barrow 66 per cent and at Bootle 50 per cent of the staff had industrial experience. At Bolton Junior Technical School it was claimed that the whole of the staff had been in industry[46] and at Hull that 'the full time teachers were largely drawn from men with experience in industry . . . the curriculum had a vivid touch of realism about it'.[47] This was the great value of these schools and the benefit to their pupils.

> There are on the staffs graduate teachers of engineering who have in real industrial competition designed steel frame structures or electrical transformers or possibly diesel engines . . . There are excellent craftsmen who have made tools and master gauges for famous pieces of engineering production. All this is a great thrill to the schoolboy . . . the boy feels he is already under the foreman, a first class craftsman who has made good on real jobs himself.[48]

Although teachers in JTSs 'will in all probability have received full time training in teaching prior to entry into such schools' yet there was no special provision for specifically technical school teaching.[49] There were a number of part time courses in the 1920s for teachers in work - in engineering at Birmingham University, dressmaking at Regent Street Polytechnic. By 1925 there were 4 weekend and 9 part-time courses of one or two days a week for a month or more.[50] These were usually refresher courses for existing teachers. In the 1930s the Board began to think whether something better could not be provided. It was not regarded as feasible to set up a training college specifically for technical teachers nor did university departments have a sufficiently industrial outlook.[51] At the part-time level HMI Savage told inspectors that teachers in Technical Schools could have 30 working days leave to bring their knowledge up to date.[52] But further thinking about training had to wait until the war.

IV

The JTSs were not free, like elementary schools, but charged fees like secondary grammar schools. In the early 1920s these were usually 30s to £3 a year.[53] However, many pupils had scholarships. In London JTSs in the late 1920s about 52 per cent of pupils were fee payers but 40 per cent had LCC scholarships and 8 per cent other local scholarships since they came from outside the LCC.[54]

Table 3.12 *Fees in junior technical schools, 1937*

Charges	Schools
free	6
up to £3	18
£3	13
up to £6	15
£6	19
£6.6s	8
£6.15s	2
£9	1

Source: *Review of Junior Technical Schools*, Board of Education pamphlet no.111 (1937) pp. 31–2.

In response to the 1929–31 slump, public expenditure including education was cut. Part of this package was a change in the scholarship system such that from 1932 the free places were replaced by special places. The special place scholarships were means tested to save money. The Board's view was that ideally all places in JTSs should be special places with all students eligible for total or partial remission of fees subject to a means test. Thus admission to school should be entirely on merit. However if LEAs wanted some full fee payers then they should not be discouraged. They also recognized 'that a considerable variation of fees as between Junior Technical Schools in different areas is justifiable'.[55] In prosperous areas £5 or £6 a year would be chargeable but so high a fee would not be appropriate in certain areas e.g. Lancashire and Yorkshire. They considered that junior commercial schools (JTCs) could charge 50 per cent higher fees than JTSs. Their reasoning was that students at commercial schools 'may be expected on the whole to obtain better paid posts'. Also they were 'drawn on the average from families with better means' and JCSs were in competition with private enterprise schools which charged substantially higher fees in any case. In practice this was so. Annual fees in JTSs in 1933 ranged from £6.6.0. to 30s. Those for JCSs ranged from £9 to £2.5.0. Table 3.12 shows the range of fees charged by a sample of 82 schools charged the following range of fees in 1937. About a half of pupils paid full fees, a proportion not very different from that in secondary schools. The burden of fees was mitigated by two considerations. First, 'Junior Technical School fees are on average only about one-third of secondary school fees'.[56] Second, there were complex schemes of sliding scales relating the income of the parent, the number or his dependent children, his eligibility for a scholarship grant and level of fees and fee remission. For example in the London JTSs scholarship scales a father earning over £500 a year would receive no assistance of any kind for one child aged 13. A parent earning less than £150 would receive free tuition plus a £17 grant for a child over 14, and there was a spectrum of concessions in between.[57]

Nevertheless parents of children going to Junior Technical Schools were liable not only for fees but for uniforms, sports kit and books (like grammar school pupils) and also for 'protective covering for practical work'. If parents could not afford to send a child to grammar school then they could hardly do so to a Junior Technical School. The Board claimed that the raising of fees in September 1932 had not adversely affected enrolment to the JTSs.[58] Yet D.W. Thoms finds this optimistic, 'even when a junior technical scholarship was obtained the value was often insufficient to compensate adequately for lost earnings and other costs so children from low income families were automatically disadvantaged, particularly during periods of unemployment'.[59] If JTSs had been a free or much cheaper alternative to the grammar school for intelligent working class children then they might have boomed. That they were not limited their attractiveness.

There were also problems with the entrance examination into the JTS. The children would already have had the opportunity to take the 11+ examination and had either failed or passed it and declined a grammar school place. But since entry to JTS was two years later, at 13, a separate test was held with a Transfer Board to investigate requests for transfers at 13.[60] However these tests rarely took account of the special aptitudes needed for JTS work. The LEAs 'were able to make no more than a gesture in the direction of picking out the children with aptitude for practical technical work'.[61] There were tests in English, mathematics and drawing, rather on the lines of the secondary school entrance examination, and reports from headmasters. London tried to be more practical with two-part entrance tests first in English and mathematics then secondly in handicraft, for example needlework, and drawing with geometry for building. Those selected for aptitude were then interviewed.[62] Perhaps the most innovative school was the Gateway School, Leicester, under H.C. Dent.[63] As well as the academic component he used 10 tests of practical ability, 5 artistic and 5 in handling materials. But it was regrettable that in most cases the non-practical bias of the test tended to perpetuate the view that entrance to a JTS was merely a second academic creaming rather than a fresh test of genuinely different aptitudes.

V

A major recurrent problem which the JTSs regarded as their chief handicap was the obligatory age of entry at 13. It was set at that age on the grounds that 10 or 11 was too young to decide on a child's future career and that it needed two more years of general education before receiving the vocational bias that the JTS would provide. Psychologists also did not believe that it was possible to detect technical aptitudes before the age of 13. It was also argued that staff in technical colleges, who also taught in the JTSs, were not used to dealing with very young children. Yet the obvious disadvantage was that whereas children started in secondary grammar schools at 11 yet the potential entrant to the JTS had to mark time for two years. This 11–13 purgatory, so to speak, was spent in the elementary school or a central school before proceeding to the JTS. This dog-leg double change disruption of school life after 11 was clearly undesirable. Though less so, in the belief of the time, than a premature pre-emptive channelling of a child into vocational training.

After the 1914–18 war there was pressure especially from LEAs in the North to be allowed to reduce the age of entry and give the JTS parity with secondary grammar schools. But the Board considered that there were no grounds for altering the existing arrangements.[64] This by no means settled the matter. The pressure intensified as the age of entry restrictions were accused of strangling the expansion of the JTS. It was regarded as perverse that the war had brought a heightened awareness of the importance of technology and a great expansion of secondary schools but not commensurately of JTSs. It was suggested bitterly that the regulations of the JTSs were designed 'to burn a ring patch round the secondary school to keep it safe from the fire of competition'.[65]

Developments elsewhere in the educational system also began to overtake the situation. Firstly there were recurrent moves to raise the school leaving age to 15. H.A.L. Fisher had assumed this could happen sometime after his 1918 Act which had raised it to 14. When Labour was in power in 1926 and 1929–31 Sir Charles Trevelyan tried without success to bring it about. Oliver Stanley's 1936 Act did raise it to 15 at last but the outbreak of war in 1939 intervened before it could be implemented. However the totally reasonable assumption of educational administrators in the interwar years was that the leaving age would be raised in the near future. The implication of this expectation was that with a school leaving age of 15 it would be less acceptable for children to spend all their school lives in an elementary school. It would increase the need for different types of secondary school, of which the JTS would be one, all given parity of age of entry.

The position of the JTS was paradoxically weakened by improvements in other levels of schooling. In their early years in the 1910s and 1920s the JTSs had attracted a considerable portion of children prepared to stay at school a little longer and it was claimed that 'the average intellectual level of the pupil was high'.[66] However, following the Hadow Report in 1926 the structure of schooling was changed. Ideally children were to attend primary schools until taking the 11+ exam whereafter they were to be decanted into grammar schools, modern schools and the JTSs. But as the grammar schools expanded far more than the JTSs so working class chances of attending grammar schools rose sharply from 1 per cent to 7–9 per cent between the 1900s and the end of Second World War.[67] This siphoned off many able children who might, pre-Hadow, have attended JTSs. This was appreciated at the time,

> it is probable that some of the talent which would previously have entered the Junior Technical School, is now diverted elsewhere . . . it is perhaps possible that the stream of children into secondary schools is carrying with it a considerable number who would have been more suitably provided for in Junior Technical Schools.[68]

It was argued that the starting age of 13 was a particular handicap to the JTSs, especially after Hadow. The 13-year-old entry age was justified by two inevitable boundaries. The occupations ex JTS pupils were likely to take up usually began at 16. Also courses had to be 2 or 3 years in length to be of value to the student and employer and they had to start late enough to enable children to decide on a career without encroaching too far on their general education. This left little option other than 13. But after the 11+ many able children had already entered some other form of secondary school from which they would have to make a conscious (and unlikely) decision to transfer at 13. In practice it was improbable that a youngster who had secured a scholarship place at a secondary grammar school would move to a JTS after a couple of years. Accordingly entrants to the JTSs tended to be ex-elementary or modern school pupils who had failed to pass into the grammar schools. Consequently 'today the complaint is general that the quality obtained is lower than it used to be owing to the fact that these other schools of the secondary type have had a first skimming'.[69] It also meant that pupils were selected for JTSs not on the basis of special technical aptitudes but because they had just failed to qualify for an academic school.[70] Thus non-academic was assumed to equate with potential technical capability. The Board put it bluntly,

> the field of recruitment for Junior Technical Schools at 13 years of age was, therefore, reduced to those who were unable, or did not desire, to pass on to a secondary school . . . the Junior Technical School is almost inevitably at a disadvantage.[71]

The solution would be to lower the age of entry to JTSs to 11 (as was done after 1944) but the Board remained adamant against too early vocational studies which were the distinctive characteristic of the JTSs. Others advanced the idea of the composite school, a modern school for ages 11–13 end-on to a JTS for ages 13–16. The Board rejected this view also on the grounds that the same staff could not teach in both parts of the school, especially in the more general 'modern' section and yet retain their credibility as practical experts with industry and employers. The Board remained clear that JTSs should retain their quite distinctive character and age of entry and length of course and not be absorbed into the rest of the secondary education system.[72] It retained the purity of the concept and lessened criticisms of premature (at 11) specialization but made the position of the JTSs more difficult especially in the post Hadow reorganization.

Several LEAs wanted to lower the age of entry of JTSs. Indeed there was scarcely an issue over which the LEAs more troubled the Board. Smethwick was perhaps the first *cause célèbre*.[73] They applied and were refused every year from 1928 to 1930. The Board's position was that if they wanted to have an entry at 11 they should turn the JTS into a secondary grammar school. The LEAs' position was that they wished to retain the distinctive characteristics of the JTS but starting earlier. Norwich applied in 1930 but on the precedent of Smethwick was refused.[74] Norwich's problem was that a large central school in Duke Street provided ample non-academic secondary education which kept the JTS weak and small. Denied the possibility of expanding the JTS by taking 11-year-olds, a new Director of Education in 1935 wisely decided to restrict entry to the central school to enhance the JTS. Here the Board's policy of holding firm had a salutary effect on the policies of an LEA. Bolton too tried to reduce the age of entry on the grounds that in the depression local employers preferred younger boys of 14–15 who paid no National Insurance, and the school wished to adjust the entry age down accordingly.[75] The Board was not impressed by that argument either.

The example of Sunderland raised a major consideration rarely made explicit. In 1931 they made the familiar request for age 11 entry with the classic argument 'If the Junior Technical School age of entry were reduced to 11 many of those who now go to secondary and central schools would choose the Junior Technical School which would thus secure the best material'.[76] It met the usual block. Yet behind the block lay some financial motives rarely disclosed. E.G. Savage explained that 'admission [to a Junior Technical School] of children from an elementary school at the age of 11+ involved a higher cost to the public since they would be taught by teachers who were on a higher grade of salary'. JTS teachers earned about a third more than elementary teachers.[77] Moreover since the Board paid 50 per cent of administrative costs of JTSs but only 20 per cent of those of central schools so more children in JTSs and fewer in central schools would shift more cost to the Board. Elementary schools and central schools were the typical 'holding tanks' for children waiting to enter JTSs at 13. Earlier entry at 11 would entail higher costs or a changed disposition of cost. This was clearly recognized by an HMI James Strachan who wrote in angry and personal terms to Savage, 'the long controversy on the age of entry seems to be boiling down to a question of cost'. In his view Board Regulations were too restrictive, applications to lower the age of entry were justified: 'I feel sure this type of Junior Technical School is worth saving'.[78]

Behind the scenes opinions about entry at 11 or 13 were rifting and shifting. As the 1930s began, Albert Abbott understood clearly the arguments for reducing the age of entry to JTSs in the light of changes elsewhere in the system. He noted

> the raising of the school age and the reorganisation of provision for children of 11+ up to the leaving age, will make central and senior schools ultimately more attractive than they are now . . . unless something is done to enhance the advantages of the Junior Technical School it may not fill so easily at present.[79]

He was aware that Directors of Education were divided; Thomas Walling of Newcastle wanted 11 but Sir Percy Meardon of Lancashire and Sir George Gater of LCC still favoured 13.[80] Opinion was shifting. When G.E. Savage began his inspections in 1933 he said he was keeping an open mind on 'the controversy regarding the age of admissions to Junior Technical Schools'.[81] Likewise Percy Meardon, whom Abbott had considered an orthodox conservative in 1930, by 1935 said that he would be prepared to accept entrants to JTSs at 11 with a general curriculum for the ages of 11–13. In the evidence presented to Spens, Abbott (now retired) and the Inspectorate still held to 13 but the ATI, APTI (Association of Principals of Technical Institutions), the Association of Education Committees and Association of Directors of Education had moved to prefer 11.[82] This was Spens's view too and subsequently recommended by him in his Report.

The Board did allow some notable exceptions to its policy against lower age of entry. The most famous was the Leicester Gateway School which opened in 1911 and organized as a JTS in 1913. In 1928 they proposed to merge the JTS and a JCS and move to a separate building with admission at 11. Abbott and the Inspectors thought that this might be an acceptable experiment. Leicester was keenly interested in technical education and 'here if anywhere such an experiment is likely to be successful'.[83] Indeed it was and in 1934 the Gateway School moved from its Tudor houses in the Newark (now a local history museum) to a central site in Leicester. The other notable experiment was Workington. In 1929 their request to reduce the entry age to 11 was denied. But Workington was most unusual, as a JTS, a secondary school and a technical college were all housed in the same building under the same headmaster. In these peculiar circumstances the JTS and secondary school were allowed to have a common 11 age of entry. This proved an undoubted success, the whole making 'a singularly complete system of education'.[84]

In the late 1930s one or two other institutions followed this path.

In 1936 the South East Essex Technical College in Dagenham opened as a JTS with an age 11 entry with a general course 11–13 and an engineering or commerce bias thereafter.[85] These schools were forerunners of later developments, the technical secondary school with entry at 11 recommended by Spens. Workington looks like a kind of grammar technical school which became popular in the 1960s, or even the multilateral. Between the Spens Report in 1938 and the outbreak of war, Walthamstow and the new Villiers Street JTS in Sunderland were sanctioned as age 11 entry schools. *Education* enthused

> it is hoped that a new era for Junior Technical Schools of this type will be established through the wider facilities available in the new school with eleven plus entry and that the experiment in Sunderland - the first of its kind in the country - will prove the effectiveness in the system of a Junior Technical School which is really part of the system.[86]

They set the pattern for the Secondary Technical School which followed the 1944 Act, freed of the differential entry conditions which had hampered their development in the interwar years.

VI

The most serious missed opportunity to give the JTSs a boost in the interwar years was the Hadow Report of 1926.[87] Sir Henry Hadow, musician and Vice-Chancellor of Sheffield University, was asked to consider the education of the adolescent. The importance of his report was the principle that all children had the right to secondary education subsequent to primary education and scholarship selection by the 11+ examination. 'Secondary education for all' was to replace 'the ladder of opportunity' as the watchword of policy. The types of post primary education envisaged by Hadow were the secondary grammar school, the modern (former central) school and the existing JTSs. Hadow accepted that the JTSs did admirable work and hoped that they would continue. He had no intention of changing the 13 age of entry, agreed with the assumption that JTSs should lead immediately to work and not to further study. In short he was happy to accept the situation as it was without change or striking expansion. Indeed he was clear that the major expansion should be that of the modern schools giving a 'practical bias' without the narrower vocational aims of the JTS. He saw the JTSs and the modern schools as having quite different purposes and considered that the specificity of the former made them unsuitable for expansion into that mass general non-academic role to be fulfilled by the modern sector. The tone of Hadow towards the JTSs was appreciative and accepting but cool, and certainly not seeing them as an area of major advance beyond the specialized niche they already occupied. It may be noted that two of the most influential left-wing (and WEA) liberal educationalists, R.H. Tawney and Albert Mansbridge, were leading figures on Hadow's committee and their views may also be reflected in the Report. The official Board of Education pamphlet explaining Hadow contains a mere seven unenthusiastic factual lines about the JTS.[88] Lord Percy saw through this and was politely disappointed - 'my mind did not move on quite the same lines as the Hadow report'.[89] Percy would have wanted much greater emphasis on two parallel ladders - secondary school to university and JTS to college of technology. Hadow's achievement and legacy was the reorganization of the 1930s which greatly increased the chances of all to attend grammar schools. But the JTS was not a shining peak in the Hadow vision.

VII

The JTSs were not well provided with social corporate life in the interwar years. The shortness of the course and transience of the pupils, compared with secondary grammar schools, militated against the running of societies. One area where JTSs did notable work was dramatic societies which gave full scope for practical technical skills backstage. Another was holiday camping - 'some developed high standards in this, taking pride in the ingenious pieces of apparatus they often invented and made. Before the war (1939) some regularly extended their camping to continental countries'.[90] More modest but practical schools emphasized trips to factories, locomotive works and so forth to widen the pupils' industrial culture and focus their minds on imminent careers.[91]

Many of the JTSs were hampered in that they did not usually have their own buildings. Of 82 schools inspected by HMI only 16 were in buildings apart from the main technical college. Parents were often not aware of JTSs as distinct institutions, still less as distinct places. What accommodation they had was often unprepossessing - 'it is generally true to say that the premises of JTSs are not calculated to make a good impression on either parents or the business community'. Common rooms were 'rarely provided', facilities for meals 'often non-existent', 16 per cent had no libraries.[92] One gas-lit JTS opened in 1919 was described with relish as horribly dark. There are dark dungeon-like passages. One of the rooms used as a laboratory has to serve as an assembly hall and as a dining room. The dust and grime that collect in the rooms seem to dishearten the cleaners, who tend to give up the unequal struggle.[93]

VIII

The JTSs were not supposed to take external public examinations. The reason for this was the belief that schools should relate themselves to the varied needs of their local communities and that this purpose would be warped by the uniformity of preparing for national syllabus examinations. There were a few exceptions. Following a request from Exeter the Board agreed that students should be allowed to take RAF entrance examinations.[94] Also the rather specialized Westminster School of Retail Distribution took the examinations of the Incorporated Association of Retail Distributors and the National Association of Outfitters.[95] By the late 1930s JTS pupils took the entrance examinations for the Royal Navy, RAF and Admiralty Dockyards but since they did not prepare for the School Certificate, parents and employers regarded the JTS as 'something vaguely inferior'. Accordingly an influential Joint Committee of bodies in technical education proposed a JTS leaving certificate to be endorsed by the Board and issued by LEAs.[96] But nothing was done before the war and the 1944 Act changed the whole position.

IX

Finally the JTSs had problems of 'living with the neighbours', the central schools. Central schools, which operated still as elementary schools, took early teenage boys and girls. The girls very largely learnt clerical work and the boys engineering, 10 per cent of them going into engineering or skilled trades.[97] Here, as two Board officials noted, they 'were thus moving in the direction of the Junior Technical Schools'.[98] This set up tensions since many LEAs that were keen on central schools, with their engineering element, saw no need to establish JTSs. Rutland for example had excellent central schools and four-fifths of their children at 11+ went to five central schools to the satisfaction of their parents. The only people in Rutland who disliked the centrals were the local gentry who feared that their raising the aspirations of girls would lead to a shortage of serving maids.[99] Warwickshire had 21 central schools and felt no need of JTSs beyond those in Birmingham and Coventry. Gloucestershire too had an excellent JTS in Gloucester but little demand elsewhere in the county, where they relied on centrals. Spurley Hey, the Director of Education for Manchester, was also keen on central schools.[100] Some authorities took a contrary view. James Graham, Spurley Hey's counterpart at Leeds, did not like central schools which he regarded as 'a makeshift, a *pis aller*' and preferred secondary grammar and JTSs, as did Benjamin Gott of Middlesex.[101]

The borderland relations of the JTS and central schools were important on various grounds. In a sense they were competitors though the latter were nothing like so specialized as the former. In areas like Gloucestershire, Warwickshire and Rutland the widespread use of central schools obviated the need for JTSs, whereas in Middlesex and Leeds it was vice versa. D.W. Thoms found that

> the development of the central school system was a particularly serious threat to the Junior Technical Schools since not only were they commonly regarded as second-best grammar schools, but also their mildly vocational bias contributed to the belief that there was little difference between them and the Junior Technical Schools.[102]

Secondly, a question of administrative jurisdictions also added tensions to the relations of the JTS and the central school. The issue was that Part III Authorities which could run elementary schools favoured central schools because they too operated under the Elementary Education Regulations. These Part III Authorities did not like JTSs since they could not be administered by them but by the LEA of the borough or county council. This would entail an overlapping of jurisdictions, a JTS in the territory of one authority but administered by another. These Part III Authorities were abolished by the 1944 Education Act but in the mean time 'this question of control appears to stand in the way of Junior Technical Schools in some places.[103]

Thirdly, centrals could stifle the growth of JTSs. Because of the 13 age of entry to the latter, pupils transferred to JTSs from central schools which they entered at 11. It was strongly suspected by Abbott that some central headmasters were impeding or discouraging this transfer. So did Percy Meardon, the Director of Education of Lancashire who 'spoke in no uncertain way of his intentions if he found that Central School headmasters were impeding reasonable transfer from their Schools to the Junior Technical Schools'.[104] Finally, as the central school was the forerunner of the secondary modern so the conflict of interest, central versus JTS, in the interwar years foreshadowed the choice facing LEAs

Table 3.13 *Proportions of children in types of schools in the 1930s*

Children over 11	(%)
828,000 in senior schools	42.1
672,000 in all age elementary schools	32.2
440,000 in grant aided secondary (grammar schools)	22.4
27,000 in Junior Technical Schools	1.4

Source: ED 136/214 *Education after the War* (The Green Book) June 1941.

in the 1940s and 1950s of whether to adopt secondary technical or secondary modern schools. In the later period even more than in the 1920s and 1930s the latter won, until both were swallowed up in the comprehensive schools of the 1960s.

X

As a result of all these inhibiting factors by the end of the 1930s the JTSs occupied a disproportionately lowly position in the structure of education for post 11-year-olds. They had not developed into a genuine third part alongside the grammar and senior schools and this was to transmit a problem into the years following the 1944 Butler Act. Yet however small, the JTS sector justified itself through its close connections with service to industry. How important was this?

CHAPTER 4

The Junior Technical Schools and Industry, 1918–1939

The JTS was peculiar amongst full-time schools for boys and girls in that it normally had very close relationships with industry.[1]

Albert Abbott, (1924)

I

The chief purpose of the JTS was to provide an education of service to industry in a variety of ways. Many of the reasons that had prompted the initiation of JTSs in the 1900s continued in the interwar years and some further ones heightened the urgent need of industry for the JTS. Firstly apprenticeship continued to decline in some areas and remained generally low. In 16 industries studied by the Apprenticeship Inquiry in the mid-1920s indentured apprentices as a proportion of boy trainees declined from 36.2 per cent in 1909 to 30.1 per cent in 1925. Less formal verbal agreements were taking the place of the old apprenticeship. Looked at another way, proportions of journeymen to apprentices or learners varied considerably between industries and trades. In building there were more apprentices per journeyman in 1925 than in 1909. But in engineering there was a decrease in apprenticeship among engineering fitters, machine tool workers and mechanics over the same period. So it was also with cabinet makers and upholsterers. These were all trades for which the JTS was relevant and the decrease of apprenticeship in them placed a greater importance on the schools. In any case apprentices were only a seventh (14 per cent) of all male workers under 21.[2] There was a lot of leeway to make up and the JTS could contribute to this. An HMI noted, 'the increased use of semi-skilled labour in industry and the relatively few opportunities for boys and girls to enter skilled trades makes it imperative that the school should increasingly supply a type of education that industry itself once supplied'.[3]

Table 4.1 *Age of starting apprenticeships, 1909 and 1925*

Age of starting apprenticeship	Percentage of apprentices starting at a particular age 1909	1925
14	40	34
15	30	20
16	26	43
	the rest would have started later	

Source: *Report of an Inquiry into Apprenticeship and Training*, Ministry of Labour, 1925–6, vol. 7, p. 77.

Secondly, even of those who started apprenticeship, 9.2 per cent of those in engineering failed to complete their qualification.[4] The implication was that more JTS pre-apprenticeship schooling would have prepared young people better and reduced this failure rate. Thirdly 23 per cent of engineering firms claimed to have difficulty in getting recruits for apprenticeship 'difficulties in obtaining apprentices are however, complained of by a substantial number of employers'.[5] Again, more JTSs would have increased this flow. Moreover this problem was likely to be aggravated by the steady decline in the birth rate from 25.5 per thousand in 1920 down to 14–15 from 1933 to 1939. Fourthly there was a marked rise in the age of starting apprenticeship in the 1920s. Employers were demanding higher educational qualifications from their apprentices than merely attending elementary school. They accordingly pitched their starting age higher than the new (post-1918) school leaving age of 14. In 16 major industries the apprenticeship starting age rose (see Table 4.1). This was especially evident in the engineering and building industries. The increasing gap between the school leaving age assumed and required some form of schooling, and the Apprenticeship Inquiry drew the explicit conclusion, 'the Junior Day Technical schools act as pre-apprenticeship schools . . . and where they exist, fulfil admirably the function of bridging the gap between the school leaving age and the age of entry into industry'.[6]

Fifthly, the continued development of large scale production in industry made training on the job increasingly difficult. Conveyor belts could not be stopped, it was costly and wasteful for experienced workers to direct their time to training the young. This gave more urgency to hiving off part of the training into various types of classes and

Table 4.2 *Specimen curricula for junior technical schools in the 1920s and 1930s*

	Hours		
	a[1]	*b*[2]	*c*[3]
English subjects including history and geography	5	6	6 or 7
Maths and geometry	5	} 8	5 or 6
Science and technology	5		6
Technical drawing	5	3	4
Workshop practice	6	4 ½	6
Physical exercise	1	3	2
Pool including foreign language	-	3	
Total	27	27 ½	30

Notes:
1 ED 24/1849 Recognition of New Junior Technical Schools 23 Nov. 1920.
2 *Report of the Consultative Committee on Secondary Education* (Spens Report) p.277.
3 Butler Archive RAB H 70/198 Frank Bray to James Pitman 28 May 1945.

schools including the pre-work JTS.[7] Finally there was some concern that nepotism, preferentially giving jobs to sons of existing workmen and foremen, was stunting the quality of the labour force. Again the JTS was seen as a solution to this problem: 'it is obviously necessary that nepotism in this connection should be eradicated. The selection of apprentices should be made by a competent member of the works . . . with the Headmasters of the Junior Day Technical Schools'.[8] So the JTS was seen as relevant to meeting these various problems of the interwar years - the decline of apprenticeship, failure rates in completion, difficulty of recruiting, the age gap of starting skilled work, the need to hive off training and to combat stultifying nepotism.

II

A leading way in which the JTSs related to industry was through what they taught. Three specimen model curricula for JTSs are shown in Table 4.2. The first (*a*) was the guidelines laid down in 1920 for recognition of new JTSs, the second (*b*) was a specimen printed in the Spens Report. The third (*c*) was an explanation of what was normal, given to someone writing a report for R.A. Butler, 'there are of course variations of all kinds but in general this is the curriculum we advise

Table 4.3 *Timetable of Newton-in-Makerfield Junior Technical School, 1924–5*

	1st year		2nd year	
	hrs	mins	hrs	mins
English subjects	6	0	5	0
Mathematics	4	0	5	0
Science	6	0	6	0
Drawing	6	0	6	0
Manual instruction	6	0	6	0
PT	1	30	0	30
Weekly record	0	30	0	30
Total	30	0	30	0

Source: ED 10/147.

in engineering JTSs'. This heavy emphasis on mathematics, science, technology and workshop practice (usually about three-quarters of the total), while not neglecting English, was of great value in preparing for industry.

How this was carried into practice can be seen in one or two working curricula. That of Newton-in-Makerfield, a small Lancashire JTS, in the mid-1920s is very similar to what was recommended (see Table 4.3). What was taught in a London JTS at the same time may be seen from the curriculum of the Borough Polytechnic JTS of 1925 in weekly hours (see table 4.4) with a fairly constant 77 or 78 per cent of the curriculum devoted to science, technology and practical subjects. In the 1930s in what was depicted as a typical London JTS, pupils devoted 77 per cent of their time to science, technology and practical subjects in the second and third years, but received more general education in the first year (see Table 4.5). It was evident that under the vigilance of the HMIs such schools kept to rather similar guidelines with slight discretionary variations. These were sensible and very strongly oriented towards industry.

The particular strength of the JTS was preparing boys for engineering in industry rather than higher education. It particularly annoyed the HMIs when grammar schools tried to intrude inappropriately in this area. These were through so-called Alternative Courses in which grammar schools allowed boys to drop Latin and take woodwork, metalwork and engineering instead. This feature had begun in Tynemouth in 1910

Table 4.4 *Timetable of Borough Road Polytechnic Junior Technical School, 1925*

	1st year		2nd year		3rd year	
	hrs	mins	hrs	mins	hrs	mins
English, geography, history	5	0	5	0	5	0
Mathematics	6	40	5	50	6	40
Mechanical drawing	4	10	4	10	4	10
Applied mechanics	-	-	2	30	2	30
Physics	-	-	3	20	3	20
Chemistry	3	20	-	-	-	-
Art	1	40	0	50	-	-
Metalwork	5	10	5	0	5	0
Woodwork	1	40	1	40	-	-
P.T.	1	40	1	40	1	40
Workshop materials	-	-	-	-	0	50
	29	20	30	0	28	10

Source: ED 10/147.

and grew apace in the early 1930s, especially in Yorkshire where 17 schools were doing this. It clearly was a nonsense in the view of HMIs who thought that such boys should have been in JTSs. Grammar schools, conversely, should not have been compromising their academic curricula. More important (unlike JTSs) they did not have the facilities to do this ambitious work properly, 'in very few did it appear to approach the scope and standard expected in Junior Technical Schools'.[9]

Another specialized curricular form was the Junior Commercial School (JCS) preparing children for office and business life. There were 50 of these schools in 1935–6 and 'many more' were established in the years before the war though the Board had no complete statistical return.[10] A typical JCS curriculum was that at Wandsworth (see table 4.6) with 39 per cent of the whole curriculum being devoted to very practical subjects - book keeping, commerce, shorthand and typewriting - let alone the obviously relevant but more generally educative arithmetic, and English.

These schools had their supporters. Sir Robert Blair, the influential Chief Education Officer of the LCC thought them especially valuable in London and wanted more of them.[11] The Goodenough Committee of

Table 4.5 *Timetable of a typical London junior technical school (unspecified), 1934*

	1st year		2nd year		3rd year	
	hrs	mins	hrs	mins	hrs	mins
English, geography, history	5	10	3	30	3	30
Mathematics	6	40	5	50	6	50
Geometric and mechanical drawing	3	20	5	0	3	20
Applied mechanics	-	-	2	30	2	30
Physics	3	20	1	40	2	30
Chemistry	-	-	1	40	2	30
Art	1	40	0	50	-	-
Metalwork	1	40	3	20	5	0
Woodwork	3	20	1	40	-	-
P.T.	3	20	2	30	2	30
Materials	-	-	-	-	0	50
Assembly and prayers	0	50	0	50	0	50
	30	0	30	0	30	0

Source: ED 10/151 J.W. Bispham, Memorandum on Junior Technical Schools, 23 Mar. 1934.

1931 found that few of their witnesses knew of the schools but that those who did referred to them 'in very favourable terms'. They came to the view that JCSs 'would be a definite asset to the educational provision in all business centres' especially for retailing[12] and the Board noted that 'they are popular with parents and pupils . . . and their product is readily absorbed into suitable occupations'.[13] However there were reservations. Selby-Bigge and H.A.L. Fisher had doubts about this form. So even had Chief Inspector Albert Abbott who thought that 'it was unlikely that any Junior Commercial School would enlist much interest on the part of the commercial firms' since what they needed 'was a supply of youths of good general education'.[14] Spens was appreciative, 'we are entirely convinced of the importance of the work done by these schools and of the real educational value in themselves of the special subjects, as these are often taught'.[15] Yet while he wanted the engineering-based JTSs to become technical high schools of grammar school status he could not see such a future for the commercial equivalent. His view was that secondary schools had to be built around 'a range of systematised knowledge and theory'. Engineering and technology met this requirement but in his view the

Table 4.6 *Timetable of Wandsworth Junior Commercial School, 1934*

	1st year hrs	1st year mins	2nd year hrs	2nd year mins	3rd year hrs	3rd year mins
Arithmetic	4	30	3	0	2	15
Book-keeping	1	30	3	0	3	0
Commerce	1	30	1	30	2	15
English	3	0	2	15	2	15
French	3	45	3	45	4	30
Geography	1	30	1	30	1	30
History	1	30	0	45	-	-
Science	2	15	2	15	-	-
Shorthand	3	0	3	45	5	15
Typewriting	2	15	3	0	3	45
P.T.	1	15	1	30	1	30
Assembly	2	30	2	15	2	30
	28	45	28	45	28	45

Source: ED 10/151 Curriculum of Wandsworth Junior Commercial School, 22 Nov. 1934.

practical skills of book keeping, shorthand and typing did not. For him the commercial equivalent of engineering was economics but since this was 'beyond the capacities' of pupils under 16 it could not be the basis of a secondary school. However in their day, notably the 1930s, they served a very useful purpose especially for girls.

Just how useful may be seen by considering the alternative. If girls were not going to university or teacher training then going to a grammar school could actually be a disadvantage. Grammar schools did not usually teach secretarial skills which were thought inappropriate in an academic curriculum. The absurd result was that girls leaving grammar schools at 16 often went into relatively unskilled jobs - library and shop assistants, post office clerks and hotel receptionists - overeducated but undertrained.[16] Or they could take privately paid courses to acquire the secretarial skills denied them at school.[17] A girl going to a JCS was better placed to start a career.

The JTS trade schools, which dated from 1904, continued to flourish. They were even more closely related to specific industries than the more general JTSs for engineering and construction, though in London the term 'trade school' was dropped in 1938 and they were all referred to as JTS. Boys were allowed to follow quite specialized curricula in trade schools devoted to furniture making and coach-building; indeed trade schools were regarded as preparing for a specific trade rather than a broad industry. They were also especially valuable for girls entering the needle trades and their numbers had risen from 6 in 1912 to 32 by 1929.[18] These were mostly in dressmaking and millinery while one or two specialized in photography and hairdressing and a few in cookery and domestic service training. These were all areas which were 'to a very great extent carried on by women'.[19]

Some of this trade school training was especially appropriate for girls. There was a very good School of Hairdressing in Barrett Street (near Bond Street) which especially impressed the education officers of the LCC who thought that many of the pupils were of the calibre soon to run their own businesses.[20] There were also 10 JTS trade schools in London in the 1930s, teaching dressmaking, tailoring, millinery and embroidery in some combination. Dorothy Pannett found that they 'form a valuable, possibly essential, bridge between the slightly unreal world of school and that of industry'. Although not so professional as the equivalent Parisian *écoles professionelles* for couture their keen staff produced totally satisfactory ex-pupils in great demand with the West End fashion and tailoring firms.[21] Finally there was a JTS trade school for photography in Bloomsbury, the lady portrait photographer having emerged as a distinct profession during the First World War.

Some trade school JTSs especially in London could have a curriculum heavily biased towards a particular trade.[22] An HMI regarded 18 hours out of a total of 30 hours a week (60 per cent) devoted to trade instruction as being normal for a trade school junior technical school.[23] For example at the Regent Street Polytechnic Junior Motor Body Building School 55.8 per cent of the curriculum was devoted to panel beating, woodwork, chassis work and drawing for body design. The rest was the normal science and arts curriculum. At Shoreditch Junior Furniture Trade School 66.6 per cent of the time was spent on furniture making, craft lectures, drawing design and costing and estimating. A typical girls dressmaking junior technical school curriculum allowed for 70 per cent of the time being spent on trade needlework and technical drawing for it.[24] This was both a strength and a weakness of the system. These high proportions of practical work were of direct relevance to industry and must have given satisfaction to young people with such aptitudes. Opponents of the schools might deplore that all this panel beating, cabinet-making and embroidery was inevitably at the expense of more general education. Yet parents had no such qualms. The trade school

Table 4.7 *Occupations of girls from four housewifery junior technical schools, mid-1930s*

Occupation	School a	b	c	d	Percentage of pupils (average)
Needlework trades	18	28	34	12	23
Domestic service	10	34	32	13	22.25
Saleswomen and shop assistants	18	12	9	22	15.25
Clerical	12	13	15	20	15
Factory work	1	4	3	7	3.75
Hairdressing	3	5	2	4	3.5
Further education	11	-	1	-	3
At home	25	2	4	10	10.25
Not known	2	2	-	2	1.5

Source: ED 10/151 Data on careers of pupils from four junior housewifery schools by Miss H. Johnston HMI, 26 Jan. 1934.

'was a very popular type of school . . . so great was the demand on the part of parents anxious to secure further education as well as practical training'.[25]

A further specialized form of girls junior technical school was the junior housewifery school. There were 14 of these in the mid-1930s with an annual output of 600.[26] These were difficult to classify since they had various other names, home training schools or schools of domestic economy. As their name implied they prepared girls for cooking, children's nursing or domestic service. Quite frankly housewifery training was reported as being for the dullest girls. The best went into the needle trades; those who could not gain entry to needlework schools were offered housewifery as a fallback[27] but at least it was more stimulating than the elementary school.

What happened to girls from junior housewifery schools may be seen from data gathered by an HMI from four schools over two years in the mid-1930s (see Table 4.7).

This data covered two years, but in another school for the period 1913–31 the longer passage of time had polarized the occupations of the ex-pupils more sharply. Over half (54 per cent) had gone into domestic service, and another quarter (24 per cent) had got married and left their needle, shop or clerical work.[28]

Another particular industry which junior technical schools supplied was shipping. When the 1913 Regulations were promulgated five

Table 4.8 *Courses in junior technical schools, 1924*

	Provinces	London
Engineering	24	5
Construction	7	2
Needle trades	7	8
Commercial	22	2
Domestic science	9	4
Nautical	3	-

Source: ED 10/147 List of junior technical schools, showing particulars of the courses provided, March 1924.

nautical training schools were recognized as JTSs.[29] One of these was the Elmham Watts Naval School in north Norfolk which was a Barnardo's Home opened in 1906.[30] This prepared destitute waif lads for naval and seafaring careers with shore-based training and summer cruising in the North Sea on their substantial yacht. As in the 1930s, fewer boys went to sea and more to civilian trades, so the Board rightly obliged the school to move away from flamboyant gun and anchor drill (intended to impress subscribers) to more solid general education of more use to the boys. The shift in activities was a response to the decline in shipping activity in the 1930s compared with the 1920s. Accordingly the six nautical Junior Technical Schools of the 1920s had shrunk to three, in Hull and Cardiff as well as Elmham, by 1931 producing 160 or 170 boys a year who actually went to sea in the 1930s. This paradoxically was by no means enough: only 40 per cent of boys went to sea with any training in the 1930s.[31] Inquisitive as to what actually went on at sea the HMI most closely concerned, F. Bray, made a trawler voyage from Hull to the Faroes. What struck him most forcibly was that because of lack of education the available advances in technology and nautical astronomy were not being used, a 'simple faith in the infallibility of the compass'[32] sufficed.

A snapshot view of the specific industrial orientations of Junior Technical Schools may be gained from the list presented to the Hadow Committee in 1924 (see Table 4.8). In addition in London there were more specialized trade courses in photo-engraving at the City School, photography, printing, bookbinding and silversmithing at Holborn, cabinet-making at Shoreditch and hairdressing at St Marylebone. Many JTSs were simply listed as 'trade preparatory' or 'technical'.

III

A recurrent curricular issue of the interwar years relevant to industry was whether the JTS should be allowed to teach foreign languages. The Regulations of 1913 had specifically forbidden the inclusion of languages other than English or Welsh, 'unless such instruction can be shown to be of direct vocational value in connection with the occupations for which a preparation is provided'.[33] This was in keeping with the policy that such schools were not to be preparatory to university or the professions. Yet there was eloquent testimony of the value of languages for the technician. W.F. Stanley, the tool and instrument maker who established one of the largest early JTSs found 'I needed a knowledge of French, so I determined to learn it'.[34] So this loophole of 'vocational value' had been left causing scope for argument.

The First World War greatly heightened the awareness of the importance of foreign language teaching by increasing contacts with foreign allies and enemies. In 1917 the ATTI recommended that the opportunity for studying foreign languages should be provided in JTSs[35] and at the end of the war Sir Stanley Leathes' committee stressed the importance of languages for the economy.[36] These influences set up pressures in the early 1920s for permitting language teaching in JTSs. In August 1922 Mr Myers, MP for Spen Valley Yorkshire, asked H.A.L. Fisher if JTS Regulations could be relaxed to allow language teaching for 'educational value irrespective of any vocational value'. Fisher demurred, as he did two days later when Walter Smith, MP for Portsmouth, complained that Portsmouth Junior Technical School had been refused permission to include languages.[37] In practice in the 1920s JTSs wanting to teach a foreign language for good reason were often allowed to do so. For example in Preston the JCS taught French for three hours a week. The Board approved and praised the Principal for his ability to 'modify his product to suit his customers . . . knowing the requirements of local trade or commerce'.[38] German was taught at Hull JTS.[39] Workington JTS in 1929 asked permission to teach German[40] and in the mid-1930s shared this teaching with the secondary school, 'owing to the bearing of German science on the local industries'.[41] All JTSs in Kent taught a modern language by the late 1920s.[42] Colchester, Sunderland and Doncaster Junior Technical Schools also taught French in the 1930s, though not without some controversy.

These cases should not suggest that the Board had dropped its resistance to language teaching in JTSs. As well as the lasting influence of the 1913 Regulations they had good reason. In the first place there were obvious limits to any curriculum. Adding a few hours of languages must have entailed cutting back some other subject, probably a technical one. Moreover it was suspected that introducing languages was a means of preparing boys for matriculation and university entrance 'so turning the Junior Technical Schools into an imitation secondary school'.[43] At Colchester French was embroiled in this particular issue. The Junior Technical School, driven by the headmaster and supported by the Old Boys was trying to move the school away from technical and more towards academic purposes.[44] The Board thought that this was merely becoming 'a cheap and inferior type of secondary school education' including French for School Certificate preparation and for the sake of this 'the work by the whole school was prejudiced'. This was the suspicion: that French in a JTS without good industrial reason could be an indicator of a JTS trying inappropriately to turn itself into a grammar school, paring away its technical function.

Sunderland JTS's naive application to teach French so that its pupils could go to Durham University (!) promoted the Chief Inspector E.G. Savage to strong language. He told the Governors that 'he was very sceptical as to the value of attempting much in the way of foreign language teaching in a Junior Technical School. In many schools no foreign language should be admitted'. For him university admission was totally irrelevant.[45] Finally at Doncaster the HMIs disapproved of language teaching but the Junior Technical School local councillors prevailed on them to keep it.[46] This little incident had a significant sequel which added a fresh dimension to the debate. Within a few years John Neal joined Doncaster Junior Technical School as a boy. He rose to be head of production engineering for International Harvester for Europe, working in Europe and using French.[47] This was the kind of career which the Board had never conceived possible for a junior technical boy. The truth was, though it could not have been foreseen at the time, that many JTS pupils were going to rise to managerial and professional positions well beyond what was expected by the shapers of JTSs. For them a foreign language could certainly be relevant to their careers. We shall see more of these ex-JTS high-flyers shortly. In perspective, of a sample of JTS files, 25 schools did not teach languages and had no wish to do so. Six JTSs did, three with the full approval of the Board and three with some reservations. So language teaching was a minority activity, the Board would be flexible but retained its reservations.

IV

Were employers actually keen on technical education and these schools? There was a good deal of conflicting impressionistic evidence about this. There was a consistent thread of knowledgeable complaint about employers' apathy. Sir Michael Sadler, acting as a consultant to Liverpool LEA, was dismayed to find 'the indifference with which . . . the majority of businessmen still regard the needs of the secondary schools'. He was surprised that employers did not expect much educational attainment from young people nor insist on it as a qualification for employment. He attributed this to Britain's long start in industrial and commercial progress, the momentum of past success, and the suspicion of state education on the part of believers in individual enterprise.[48] So it was in Kent where in 1906 'employers of labour in the County appear to have little confidence in the value of technical instruction'.[49] The Acland Committee in 1909 found the same for the country at large 'the majority of employers are quite indifferent to the education of their work-people'.[50]

In spite of the stimulus given to an interest in technology by the First World War, attitudes remained remarkably the same in the 1920s. The Malcolm Committee in 1928 was still deploring the 'disquieting indifference on the part of many employers to the desirability of securing the best possible training for young workers'.[51] By the 1930s it was clear that the enthusiasm for technical education came much more from the providers of education than their potential end-users. Lord Eustace Percy was disappointed that concern for technical education 'has not been a demand made by industry itself for a high standard of training for its workers'.[52] The Board put it succinctly in 1937 'provision has been developed in response to a demand from the employee rather than any direct demand from the employer'.[53] Even among firms noted for their keen interest in education and training generally, few had much specific interest in the JTS. A survey of 13 such firms in the early 1930s revealed only one - Metropolitan Vickers - which referred to the JTS as part of the desirable education it expected from its pre-apprenticeship entrants.[54] The struggling shoots of technical education had to make their way in the cold air of employer indifference.

This often observed apathy was attributed to the fact that technical schools were concerned to teach the principles underlying a particular trade rather than the practice of the trade itself. This 'tended to repel some employers who have over hastily concluded that the schools are aiming at academic study divorced from the practical content of any particular branch of industry'.[55] The Malcolm Committee found that 'it had been urged upon us by a number of bodies that the methods and aims of the schools are academic in the bad sense, that is to say, unpractical and abstract'.[56]

This suspicion of the 'academic' nature of the JTS prompted some firms to establish their own works schools - Metropolitan Vickers, Cadbury, Tootal Broadhurst, Boots for example. Yet the Board had reservations about relying on privatization as a way of providing the country with technical schools. H.B. Wallis said

> I do not believe that any large number of firms would voluntarily establish schools of their own . . . our experience is that whereas a works school can provide admirable workshop training it is apt to be weak on the more theoretical side.[57]

Abbott also well appreciated that the kind of firms that were enthusiastic about education through organizations like the Association for Education in Industry and Commerce (AEIC) were 'mainly the rather philanthropic firms'.[58] In any case the kind of schools established by firms tended to be continuation schools providing part-time education for young people who had left school and were in work. They were not full-time schools for pupils of school age - nor could one reasonably expect firms to supply this form of schooling.

Where employers had direct experience of particular schools in their city they were often very enthusiastic about the local JTSs. In Sunderland the local engineering employers were 'heart and soul' behind the JTSs.[59] In Hull 'the school was immensely popular with local industrialists'[60] and at Newark 'the leading engineering employers in the District approve wholeheartedly of the course'.[61] Chief Inspector Abbott summed up his finding 'the employers who receive boys from Junior Technical Schools are everywhere very satisfied with them'.[62] The realistic situation was that employers could value a school on their doorstep from which they could recruit apprentices. Indeed by definition a JTS could not have survived without such local support since its existence depended on an output to local industry which was closely monitored by HMI.

In some cases firms actually took the initiative in pushing LEAs to set up technical schools. Vauxhall for example found no technical provision in Luton and voiced their needs to Bedfordshire LEA, 'it needed recruits from schools where boys had a sound training with tools. They asked at once for a Junior Technical School to be established and this was done.' Stewarts and Lloyds at Corby also saw a similar need, pressed the LEA for a school, 'set aside part of their own land and put up the first instalment of the buildings on their own initiative'.[63]

Different firms of course had different educational requirements of their young people. Boots did not need any specific preparation for any trade but wanted schools to give a 'better conception of the object and conditions of our business houses and industrial concerns' and wanted more handwork. They ran their own continuation school for their young employees. So did Cadburys who wanted more craftsmanship and awareness of industry in schools. R. W. Ferguson, the Director of Education for the firm, had himself been headmaster of a higher elementary school in a technical college before the First World War and strongly believed in this sort of school as providing 'a very sound type of education for children who proposed to enter industry'.[64] Although neither Boots nor Cadburys mentioned JTSs specifically, what they approved of in education was ideally provided by the JTSs. ICI had considerable reservations about JTS type education. They claimed that

> boys and girls who have received the best general education and who have the widest interests are given preference over those who have started specialising at an early age to the detriment of their general education . . . the less the specialised aspect of education is stressed the better.[65]

By total contrast A.P.M. Fleming of Metro Vickers thought that 'there can be no doubt that the introduction of the Junior Technical type of School has been advantageous to the engineering industry'.[66] Variations in attitude between firms and between industries were inevitable.

The Board and other government bodies were interested in this matter of differences in enthusiasm for technical education between industries and regions and sought to classify it in various ways. In 1934 the HMIs ranked some major industries in terms of the relevance of JTSs to them. Most concerned were building and engineering, then specialized skills such as furniture, photography and the needle trades. Agriculture they mentioned as an activity where the JTS should have been more relevant than it was in the 1930s. Bottom of the list were textiles where the JTS had little to contribute since the work was 'so largely routine in character' and mining and the chemical industries.[67] In the latter there was a demand for large numbers of ordinary labourers and more highly educated graduates but relatively small demand for technicians and minor supervisors. This was a commonsense assessment based on observations by men with long experience in the field.

The HMIs' view was amply confirmed from other quarters. The engineering industries especially valued the JTS. Sir Dugald Clerk's Committee in 1931 received 'almost uniformly favourable opinions as to the work of schools of this kind [junior technical] which prepare for the engineering industry' and concluded that 'Junior Technical Schools provide a most valuable type of recruit'.[68] Employers in the industry welcomed the JTS though they did not want more specialized training in secondary schools. The JTSs accordingly played their part in Midlands engineering with two in Birmingham (Handsworth and Smethwick) and one in Coventry, 90 per cent of whose boys went into engineering.[69] In mechanical engineering it was considered that a youth who had been to a JTS followed by part-time study could reach a level of knowledge scarcely inferior to a degree.[70] In electrical engineering likewise the JTS was commended for pre-apprenticeship training[71] and for marine engineering Balfour noted that 'there are Junior Technical Schools in all the English shipbuilding areas'.[72] The building industry also liked JTSs. It praised the 'splendid training at the Technical Schools' and noted that 'builders throughout the country realise that the Technical Schools are turning out the right type of lad for apprenticeship'.[73]

That the engineering and construction industries were active recipients of JTS pupils fitted in with the basic dilemma of this form of education. How specialized and usefully vocational should it be? In 1909 it was observed that 'it is no use so to specialise the powers of a boy of 14, 15 and even 16, as to unfit him for any occupation but the one he has learnt'.[74] Any later change of trade conditions, domicile or simple inclination could sharply change the relevance of too specialized a JTS education. Yet too general a curriculum would be of limited use to employers, while too narrow would limit the range of occupations to pupils. Moreover there was increasing specialization of such that 'what was formerly a trade in itself has now become subdivided into dozens or even hundreds of small trades'. Accordingly trade schools should begin

> with a training in those processes which are common to all, giving a certain amount of general instruction in the trade as a whole, and finally leading up to that point at which the final specialisation may safely be left to the trade itself.[75]

Engineering and construction were industries large enough, each with a substantial core of basic expertise, educationally valuable in itself, which could lead to widely diversified specialisms later on. A JTS education was especially appropriate and acceptable in such fields.

By contrast certain important industries were quite aloof from the JTS. Of coal H.B. Wallis noted

> there is no full time preparation for boys who intend to enter the industry comparable to what is provided in Junior Technical Schools for the Engineering and Building Industries. There has been no demand from the Mining Industry for such schools.[76]

The needs of this industry were for graduates and large armies of labourers rather than those intermediate craftsman skills most evident in engineering and building. So it was in the chemical industry where 'little if anything is done to train workers and foremen . . . no demand for such instruction seems to have arisen'.[77] It was an interesting contrast that electrical engineering had a quarter of its labour force in skilled, technical, foremen and managerial posts whereas the chemical industry had only 13 per cent at most.[78] The cotton textile industry had no use for JTSs, 'no special pre-employment school training of those who will enter the industry in the ordinary way has ever been attempted'.[79] This was attributable to the nature of the industry 'based on production by automatic or semi-automatic machines' and the virtual elimination of any surviving handicraft tradition which was often a feature of industries using JTSs, however mechanized.[80]

Agriculture was an area where the JTS did not take root. Some schools in the countryside had a rural or agricultural bias in the curriculum. In Oxfordshire in the early 1920s many senior elementary schools included nature study, gardening and woodwork relevant for farm work. But it did not go beyond that. In this grim area of poor isolated villages, stultified horizons and apathy and hostility to all forms of education, 'there is little realisation of the value of technical instruction in agricultural subjects and consequently little real demand for such instruction'.[81] Northumberland had two senior schools for agriculture at Haydon Bridge and Alnwick[82] and in Lancashire Kirkham

Grammar School ran an Agricultural Sixth. Leicestershire had elaborate schemes of applied biology for farming in rural central schools.[83] Yet while biased elementary, senior central, or even grammar schools seemed acceptable nobody seemed interested in JTSs for agriculture.[84]

Yet well-meaning bodies kept recommending the creation of agricultural JTSs. The County Councils Association in the 1930s thought that such schools would be especially appropriate for Wales.[85] The Spens Report recommended them[86] and so did the National Union of Agricultural Workers.[87] H.B. Wallis wondered why the JTS had not been received in agricultural areas. Basically it was because farmers felt no need for such schools because agriculture, unlike engineering, lacked intermediate technician gradings between farmer and labourer.[88] This is rather surprising in the light of the expansion of tractor and other mechanization in the interwar years. Yet the major problem was the rural lack of density of population. JTSs were best grounded in London and industrial cities which could absorb their output. An agricultural JTS producing farm technicians would either have had to be rather small or have an extremely wide catchment area. It is significant that only one agricultural JTS survives, Brymoor in Wiltshire, and that 'Tommy Archer' son of the fictional 'Tony and Pat Archer' is depicted as attending this school as a boarder.[89]

More precision on differences between industries was sought from figures compiled in the mid 1920s by the HMIs for the Board and used subsequently by the Malcolm Committee.[90] From these we can calculate what proportion of firms in 44 industries used sandwich courses, allowed time off work for training, provided work school classes or apprentice supervisors. From this we can get some idea of the inclination to be interested in or provide technical education across a range of industries. The top nine, highly involved with technical education, were (in order) shipbuilding; structural engineering; pharmaceuticals; cabinet making; vehicle building; watches, clocks and jewels; electrical engineering; printing; and mechanical engineering. Of these, shipbuilding, structural engineering, cabinet-making, vehicle building, electrical engineering and mechanical engineering, i.e. six of these nine, were industries for which the JTS was notably prepared. If we take the bottom nine, those where technical education was little pursued, they are cotton spinning; glass, pottery and porcelain; carpentry and joinery; painting and decorating; gas manufacture, brickwork; leatherwork; textile engineering; dressmaking. Here only three of the nine – carpentry and joinery, brickwork and dressmaking – were

Table 4.9 *Percentage of firms recruiting apprentices from junior technical schools and secondary schools in the 1920s*

Industry	Percentage of firms recruiting apprentices from JTSs and secondary schools
Electrical supply[1]	20.0
Gas[2]	19.6
Mercantile marine[3]	14.7
Shipbuilding[4]	11.8
Foundry[5]	11.2
Electrical engineering[6]	8.8
Mechanical engineering[7]	'a fair number'
Building[8]	2.0
Motor building[9]	'a few firms'
Scientific instruments[10]	'a few firms'
Silversmithing[11]	'some firms'
Glass[12]	'occasionally'
Furniture[13]	'only rarely'
Hosiery[14]	'serious apathy'

Source: *Report of an Inquiry into Apprenticeship and Training*, 1925–6: [1] vol. 5, p.36; [2] vol. 5, p.44; [3] vol. 5, p.71; [4] vol. 6, p.58; [5] vol. 3, p.17; [6] vol. 2, p.98; [7] vol. 6, p.14; [8] vol. 2, pp. 8,17; [9] vol. 6, p.97; [10] vol. 6, p.101; [11] vol. 6, p.134; [12] vol. 3, p.43; [13] vol. 2, p.74; [14] vol. 4, p.51.

traditional JTS industries. It may seem paradoxical that these three industries, closely associated with the JTS, should otherwise be little concerned with technical education. It suggests that in these cases early training at school followed by the increasing acquisition of skill at work was sufficient. This was in contrast to the great engineering industries which are found in the top nine.

We can put this in perspective by considering what proportion of firms in various industries recruited their apprentices from JTSs. The Apprenticeship and Training Inquiry 1925–6 tried to glean statistical or verbal evidence on this but grouped technical and secondary schools together. The spectrum of available data was as shown in Table 4.9.

It was evident that although JTSs were prominent in training for the building industry and particular trades such as silversmithing and furniture-making, yet their pupils made up only a very small proportion of apprentices in these industries. The gas industry is an intriguing anomaly. In the Malcolm Report figures it was an industry

Table 4.10 *Gifts to technical schools and colleges*

	%	
East Midlands	22.7	High 65.9%
North and North-East	21.7	
London	21.5	
Lancashire and Cheshire	13.6	Medium 32%
West Midlands	12.3	
Yorkshire	6.1	
East Anglia	1.4	Low 1.9%
South-East, Surrey, Hants, Kent	0.5	
South-West	nil	

Source: ED 22/146 List of gifts, money and equipment to technical colleges and junior technical schools to 29 Jan. 1926.

with an overall low involvement with technical education but in the Apprenticeship Inquiry data it was disproportionately receptive of JTS and secondary school pupils as apprentices.

A third way of considering the issue is to compare the relative enthusiasm of businessmen in various regions for supporting their local technical colleges and JTSs with gifts of money and equipment.[91] Up to 1926 the total was £120,137. The proportions of that total by region are shown in Table 4.10. Most of the gifts were engineering machinery, Rolls Royce engines, turbines, oil-fired boilers, baking ovens, dynamos and so forth. This reflected the engineering bias of the schools and was in turn reflected in the geographical spread depicted in Table 4.10.

V

The great virtue of the JTSs was that their former pupils went into productive industrial careers. We can see this from the occupations entered by JTS leavers in 1930 (see Table 4.11). Over three quarters of boys went into building and engineering. Over half the girls went into office work and about a third into the needle trades.

In particular places the output of JTSs related closely to local needs. Indeed had it not been so, steps would have been taken to correct or close schools. For example, in spite of a severe trade depression in the early 1920s, of the 240 boys who had passed through the Bristol Junior Technical School, 176 had obtained engineering jobs, in Gloucester 65 out of 73 and in Worcester 23 out of 32. The regional HMI regarded this as 'highly satisfactory' and firms came back for more boys.[92] In

Table 4.11 *Occupations entered by junior technical school leavers in 1930*

Boys	%	Girls	%
Construction	46.7	Commercial	56.5
Engineering	29.9	Dressmaking	17.8
Commercial	12.3	Tailoring	7.1
Building	5.6	Domestic Service	4.5
Nautical	1.2	Millinery	3.2
		Upholstery	2.5
		Cookery	1.7
Less than 1 per cent		*Less than 1 per cent*	
Cookery		Hairdressing	
Book production		Miscellaneous	
Photography		Photography	
Rubber trades		Constructive trades	
Music trades		Laundry work	
Tailoring			
Hairdressing			
Silversmith			
Painting and decorating			
Farming			
Boot and shoe			
Miscellaneous			

Source: 1930–1 XII Board of Education *Annual Report 1930.*

Sunderland 70 per cent of boys every term went into the shipbuilding and engineering industries.[93] Similarly in Barrow 60 per cent of the 509 boys who left the JTS in 1926–32 went into shipbuilding.[94] In a quite different industrial structure, 53 per cent of boys who passed through Chipping Wycombe Junior Technical School went into the furniture industry and 31 per cent into engineering and building.[95] In a quite widely diversified economy like Leicester 20 per cent went into engineering, 18 per cent into clerical work, 12 and 13 per cent each into printing and sales and 7 per cent each into textiles and carpentry.[96]

The JTSs directed their pupils into industry and commerce and especially into industry in the case of boys. It is interesting to compare what would have happened if these boys had gone to public and grammar schools instead. In the late 1930s the output of 21 boys' public and grammar schools was studied (see Table 4.12).

Two or three points are evident. The higher the social status of the

Table 4.12 *Occupations of pupils from independent and grammar schools, 1936–8*

	Commerce (%)	Industry (%)
8 Independent schools	18.6	8.7
4 Direct grant schools	26.7	17.7
3 Aided schools	31.5	28.4
6 Maintained schools	45.5	13.1
Norwich secondary schools	32.8	14.7

Sources: ED 12/479 Returns on Occupations of pupils at independent and grammar schools 1936–8. Data for the Fleming Committee passed to the Norwood Committee; C. Rackham ed. *Education in Norwich, an Independent Survey 1920-1940* (Norwich, n.d.) p.28.

school the less likelihood there was of their boys going into business and industry. Second, these schools tended to bias their leavers more towards white collar commerce rather than manufacturing industry. Thirdly, these modest figures are far lower than those for the JTSs. A boy going to a JTS would be directed to an industrial career. If he had gone to a grammar school or public school a minority might go into commerce but only a very small minority (14% out of this total sample of 2,540 boys) would have ended up in industry.

There was corroborating evidence from 4 London grammar schools collected by Balham Rotary Club in 1937.[97] They found that of 435 boys 151 had failed to get the kind of work they wanted and 117 were positively dissatisfied, 257 (59%) were merely low grade clerks and only 70 (16%) were in technical jobs. Most tellingly, only 36 (8%) were in professional careers to which they might have expected a grammar school to lead. The grammar school served badly those who were not going on to higher education and many of these boys would have been far better off in a Junior Technical School. This was a view shared by many in government circles. Sir Philip Dawson MP deplored that 'many such boys get only into banks and insurance offices doing clerical work' whereas there were better opportunities in industry. But headmasters and parents had a negative attitude towards industrial employment and 'tend to think too exclusively in terms of black coated jobs'.[98] Herbert Schofield, the Principal of Loughborough College, observed and deplored this in the East Midlands. He found 'that the better type of boy in a secondary school . . . was diverted away from industry', such that Rolls Royce preferred to recruit keen elementary boys rather than disappointed second-rate grammar school products. He drew the conclusion that what was needed was secondary schools 'with an industrial atmosphere' - the enhanced JTSs.[99]

VI

There are various questions we may ask about the JTSs in the interwar years to see further how far they related to the industrial needs of the period. First, could ex-JTS pupils expect to be paid more? There are no known figures for the wages of ex-JTS pupils but there is circumstantial evidence to suggest that this was so. The Board noted of girls' junior technical schools in the 1920s that 'their pupils on entering the trades obtain wages above the trade union rates for workers of the same ages'.[100] One expert thought that ex-JTS trade school pupils entered industry at wage levels at least three years ahead of their contemporaries.[101]

Also the types and levels of occupations for which the JTS prepared enjoyed a greater increase in earnings than most others. C.F.G. Masterman thought that in the 1920s skilled workers and engineers had moved from fourth out of six to second in the earnings hierarchy, overtaking the clerical and lower professional classes. It suggested a greater importance for the JTS as the producer of this rising group.[102] More systematically Guy Routh has shown that between 1913–14 and 1935–6 foremen's earnings rose from 141 per cent of the average of all occupational groups to 160 per cent. Whereas professionals, clerks and the semi-skilled had fallen relatively, foremen were the big gainers of these years.[103] It reflects the over-production of the grammar school product and the short supply of the JTS product whose earnings rose accordingly and disproportionately.

Moreover in spite of deskilling in various industries, the requirement for skilled labour was still considerable. For example, at the Austin Motor Works foremen, overlookers, designers, draughtsmen (precisely the kind of people whom JTSs would produce) made up 31.4 per cent of the labour force compared with 65.3 per cent who were semi-skilled or labourers. The equivalent balance in four locomotive engineering works was 48.2 per cent in the skilled grades compared with 30.6 per cent semi-skilled or labourers.[104] There was a large swathe of labour for whom a JTS education was the most appropriate.

Secondly, various factors were making it less likely that training in industry would be an effective alternative for producing a skilled labour force. The very rise in wages of the foreman class made it much more expensive to have skilled men spending their time training apprentices. The substitution of piece rates for time rates also meant that experienced workers were less willing to give time and attention to young workers. Also the speed up of production and sub-division of labour all militated against wider training.[105] One major source of engineering training was disappearing due paradoxically to the replacing of the horse by the motor vehicle. This was the blacksmith's smithy. A government report deplored

> the almost complete extinction of apprenticeship in the country smithy, which was once regarded as one of the best trade training schools for boys on account of the varied nature of the work usually performed under the direct supervision of the master smith.[106]

Third, JTSs were becoming so highly valued in industry that many of them were rising to levels of employment considerably higher than those for which the schools were originally intended. As early as 1928 the HMIs noted of the London JTSs that

> cases may be quoted of boys from these schools who have risen to posts as managers, chief engineers, heads of departments, designers, research workers etc., others have subsequently set up in practice for themselves as consulting engineers, architects etc . . . the record of the past students of some of the London Schools is really remarkable.[107]

As the schools remained only limited in number so the relatively few students they produced did not always remain in rank and file jobs. As many pupils were promoted to positions of greater responsibility so the JTSs became more like seed beds for managers who could rise from a technical base. In one firm in the mid-1930s only nine per cent of its JTS apprentices remained craftsmen whereas 82 per cent of its elementary schools boys did so.[108] In another firm the designations of the workforce from different educational backgrounds was as shown in Table 4.13.

It was indeed paradoxical that the JTSs, established to produce craftsmen for industry, should have a smaller part of their output doing this than any other form of school by the 1930s. Evidence of this upward drift of JTS students also came from individual schools. At Accrington, 'many old Junior Technical School boys now occupy positions of

Table 4.13 *Educational background of workers in an engineering firm in the 1930s*

	Overall numbers	Elementary	Secondary	Central	Junior technical
Craft work	37	74.5	23	40	10
Test hands	15	7	18	7	28
Production processing	9	5	9	7	14
Drawing office	36	13	46	43	45
Commercial	3	0.5	4	3	3

Source: W.A. Richardson, *The Technical College* (Oxford, 1939), p.471.

responsibility in industry and commerce'[109] and in Stoke-on-Trent 'the great majority' of ex-pupils 'are now holding important positions in industry'.[110]

In 1946 Antony Part, suspecting that JTSs had a more impressive record than people supposed, sought to give a boost to the new secondary technical schools and interest his Minister Ellen Wilkinson. He asked schools to send him lists of notable old boys.[111] The result was quite remarkable. Loughborough Junior Technical School reported majors, engineer commanders RN, a group captain RAF, while 'in industry some have reached positions of Directors of Companies, works managers, staff superintendents and a good many are making a success of their own business'. Sunderland Junior Technical School had produced

> 4 chief designers and research directors (including one with Rolls Royce and one with a Yale DSc)
> 4 managers of shipping and shipyards
> 3 architects
> 2 chief chemists, pharmaceutical chemists, dentists, clergymen
> 1 chief engineer, optician, accountant, civil engineer, technical college principal

and 'in addition there are numerous Chief Marine Engineers, Master Mariners and designers'. From Hull 25 ex-JTS boys had gained chemistry and 16 engineering degrees between 1936 and 1946. The Heaton Junior Technical School, Newcastle upon Tyne, produced

> 6 engineering managers, 4 architects, 3 managers of plantations or

> docks, 2 master mariners, 1 naval architect, doctor, professor of naval architecture, engineer designer, engineer commander RN, clergyman

Similar lists were received from other schools. Such careers were not remotely what Morant and Selby-Bigge had envisaged for JTS boys at the beginning of the century. But it was clear that the schools were already taking on the role of the technical grammar schools in the decades before the 1944 Act. Antony Part was very concerned to raise the image of the JTS and the STS in line with its reality, 'the business of putting over the Secondary Technical School is very important . . . it does seem very important to make people realise that there are other possibilities in secondary education beside the grammar school'.[112]

If the JTSs were so successful did their pupils suffer or largely escape unemployment? The peculiar position of JTSs made it highly unlikely that unemployment among their ex-pupils would be tolerated for long. The Board made it clear that JTSs would not be sanctioned

> unless the demand of a particular industry or trade is sufficiently great to absorb the output of the school, and the number of pupils annually admitted to the school is restricted to the absorptive power of the industry or trade for which it prepares.[113]

In areas lacking industry or with industries, like textiles and mining, for which JTS education was not traditional or appropriate, then the creation of JTSs would not be permitted. In areas where economic recession created unemployment this could remove the reasonable expectation that JTS pupils could be absorbed into industry. Schools had to keep records of the employment of their pupils. If this varied significantly from the stated intention of scholars when they entered the school then the Board could encourage such mismatched JTSs to convert into being ordinary secondary schools.[114] However, I know of no such case. Herwald Ramsbotham, opening the Sheffield Junior Technical School in 1933 reiterated the Board's policy:

> It has always been our policy . . . to assure ourselves as far as possible by enquiries amongst local employers, that there will be adequate vacancies for the young people that have been trained in these schools and unless we are so assured we have refrained from promoting their increase.[115]

The very policies that restrained the growth of the Junior Technical Schools also saved their pupils from high levels of unemployment.

If the Board had to be satisfied that the products of JTSs could be absorbed, this raised nice questions of catchment areas. It was argued in the 1930s that an area of 30,000 population was the smallest in which a JTS could be established with any prospect of success,

> it is unlikely that a smaller area could absorb into the trades for which the school prepared the twenty five pupils or so who are turned out annually by the smallest school of this type which can be carried out with proper regard to economy.[116]

Problems of catchment area were even more acute with trade schools, specialized forms of JTS dealing with, for example, silversmithing, photography, printing and the like. Of the 31 schools of this type 27 were in London in the mid 1930s. This was inevitable: the more specialized the trade, the fewer potential recipient employers, the larger the catchment area in terms of population and space. Indeed trade schools outside London were rarely if ever viable in a single LEA. Accordingly 'the provision of trade schools in the provinces appears to depend to a considerable extent upon the development of schemes of regional co-ordination'.[117] There were one or two, the Yorkshire Council for Further Education (1928) and the West Midlands Regional Advisory Council (1935) and a co-ordinating committee for the Manchester area in the latter years.[118] But the unavoidable limitations of catchment area outside London in turn restricted the development of the JTS and kept unemployment levels mercifully low for their pupils.

No figures were compiled on JTS unemployment but in a rare example Middlesborough Junior Technical School provided this supererogatory evidence. At Middlesborough 45.6 per cent of 'unknowns' were unemployed. Using this proportion we might make estimates of unemployment levels at some other institutions from their 'unknown' figures (see Table 4.14).

These figures may be compared with the national rates of unemployment (see Table 4.15). It is evident that JTS levels of unemployment were considerably lower than overall national averages in these years. They were also much lower than findings for juvenile unemployment. One study found 15 per cent unemployment among Bermondsey boys in 1923 and 27.7 per cent in 'Z street'.[119] Another in 1933 found 22 per cent of boys and 18 per cent of girls unemployed three months after leaving school.[120] For the area of Lancashire County Council of boys leaving school in the summer of 1932, 21.2 per cent of elementary school leavers were still unemployed three months later,

Table 4.14 *Unemployment levels of junior technical school pupils in the 1920s and 1930s*

Calculated unemployment								
Middlesborough	1926–32							
	4.8							
Bootle	1926	1927	1928	1929	1930	1931	1932	1933
	12.6	17.8	9.1	18.8	20.7	15.7	21.0	13.0
Gloucester	1926–9				1929–32			
	4.2				5.6			
Doncaster	1926–9				1929–32			
	4.9				5.2			
Manchester Dressmaking	1926–9				1929–32			
	7.9				7.4			

Source: ED 98/147, 59, 29, 152, 72

20.4 per cent of secondary school leavers, but only 15.1 per cent of JTS leavers.[121] This is what contemporaries would expect. In the 1920s the Malcolm Report found of JTSs that 'the demand for their pupils is far in excess of the supply'.[122] A perceptive observer of JTSs in the late 1930s deplored the high unemployment among grammar, public school and university men yet 'at the same time, leaders of industry find it hard to obtain either skilled craftsmen or intelligent recruits for manual work'.[123] Likewise a leading authority on London trade schools and girls employment observed that 'even in years when employment is scarce, ex-trade school workers are seldom unemployed'.[124]

Table 4.15 *National unemployment levels, 1926–32*

Year	Unemployment rate (%)
1926	12.5
1927	9.7
1928	10.8
1929	10.4
1930	16.0
1931	21.3
1932	22.12

Source: A.H. Halsey, *Trends in British Society since 1900* (London, 1972) p.118.

Table 4.16 *Output of junior technical school pupils in relation to total employment in certain trades*

	Employment	Trade school annual output
Dressmaking	755,964	115
Laundry	179,000	30–40
Millinery	2,864	30

Source: 1917–18 XI Cd 8512 *Final Report of the Departmental Committee on Juvenile Education in Relation to Employment* (J.J. Lewis).

The problem was not that JTS pupils did not go into industry or that they were unemployed but that there were so few of them. This was evident at various points. In 1909 the 13 girls day trade schools produced 600 girls a year to 11 different trades. Yet this was tiny in relation to the total numbers employed (see Table 4.16).

In 1937 the Board estimated that 'the number of better class industrial jobs for boys may be estimated at something approaching 400,000', i.e. apprentices and learners. Accordingly the annual intake needed to replace this stock would be 60–70,000. Yet the annual output of JTSs who might be expected to enter industry was only about 7–8,000 boys.[125] H.B. Wallis thought that the JTS annual output to industry was 10,000 boys and 1,000 girls but even this raised estimate was only a fifth to a sixth of what was desirable.[126] Finally R.A. Butler in his campaign before the 1944 Act pointed out that in 1938 there were 45,000 elementary school leavers and 47,000 secondary school leavers but of the latter only 7,000 went into industry. Yet only 8,000 pupils left JTSs and most of those did go into industry.[127]

VII

The assumptions of this chapter so far have been that JTSs could provide an education closely related to industry and that this was self evidently desirable. Yet in the interwar years there were two influential bodies who dissented from or were sceptical of this view. These were broadly the Left and the psychologists. The attitude of the Left remained cool. R.H. Tawney was educational adviser to the Labour Party and a member of the Hadow Committee and his views were accordingly significant. He was hostile to the JTS and wanted them and central schools to be merged into schools of indeterminate but certainly less vocational and more general purposes. With a revealing touch of venom against the JTS he maintained that Labour can make no truce 'with the vulgar commercialism which conceives of the manufacture of typists and mechanics as the primary object of adolescent education' and he stigmatized JTSs as 'inferior substitutes' irrelevant to the 'development of a really adequate system of secondary education'.[128] The WEA remained well known for its liberal rather than vocational preferences. Their secretary saw schools as primarily concerned not with equipping workers to make a living but to 'evolve their own culture and express their own emotional, intellectual and volitional life'.[129] Their president, the future Archbishop William Temple and a close friend of R.H. Tawney's, put it bluntly, 'the WEA has no affection whatsoever for manual training'.[130]

The Trades Union Congress (TUC) in the 1920s took a cautious view, welcoming curricula which would raise the status of handwork in comparison with bookwork but ruling out trade schools and opposing 'any attempt to impose instruction of a narrowly vocational type, or to confine the training of young people to preparation for employment in local factories'.[131] By the 1930s they had moved to a preference for the multilateral school and welcomed an extension of technical school work within that context. Where this was not possible

> the General Council (of the TUC) had no objection to Junior Technical Schools for the purpose of training certain children, provided that these children were not earmarked for a particular occupation and that the work done in the school was envisaged primarily from the educational point of view.[132]

The National Union of Teachers (NUT) similarly hedged their approval for JTSs with reservations that they should not be sharply geared to specific occupations.[133] In the 1930s they welcomed the fact that JTSs had moved from being artisan training schools and now provided 'an education of a more truly liberal character'.[134] So the attitudes of the Left remained unsupportive, ranging from the outright hostility of Tawney and the WEA to the more flexible views of the TUC and NUT which were prepared to modulate in so far as Junior Technical Schools became less narrowly industrial and more 'liberal' like other schools. But the suspicion was still there. D.W. Thoms notes that when Labour gained control of the LCC in 1934 enthusiasm for JTSs diminished 'since they were seen in some quarters as providing an inferior education designed specifically for working class children'.[135]

Attitudes to the JTS could also be negative among other educationalists not at all left-wing. When Norwood asked 'is it desirable or practicable to introduce any preparation for industrial careers by bias in the curriculum or otherwise?' only nine of 38 respondents (a minority of 23.6 per cent) thought so. Most thought that any industrial career bias should not start until well after the minimum school leaving age or not at all.[136] Rather academically minded grammar school headmasters saw little role for JTSs and thought their work could be done equally well in secondary schools, while their assistants wanted technical schools merely as bilateral wings of secondary schools.[137] The HMC Headmasters Conference (of public schools) loftily admitted that they knew nothing of JTSs but, with artless irrelevance, thought that the inclusion of Scripture in the JTS curriculum might be a good idea.[138] There was little sense of industrial urgency here. It was not only the Left and proponents of liberal education who had doubts about the JTS and its links with industry. The psychologists of the 1930s too had problems.

Since the JTSs claimed to prepare young children for future skilled jobs in industry they found themselves in the middle of a psychological debate in the interwar years about aptitudes. The activities of the JTSs assumed that specific technical and mechanical aptitudes were capable of detection and selection at an early age (11 or 13) and of education thereafter. Especially since the First World War there had been an increasing interest in industrial psychology and the identification and testing of skills. But many psychologists, while accepting the relevance of these matters for adults, had difficulty in relating them to children. This had the effect of casting doubt on the legitimacy of the work of the JTS.

The anatomists were sceptical. Professor H.A. Harris of Cambridge pointed out that physiologically there were no definite nerve centres relating to one aptitude or another.

> One boy at 14 learns the rules of the subjunctive mood, another learns to cut a square or circle in wood. The former has no 'nerve centres' which mark him off from the latter. In fact the latter may have been spending his time to better effect.[139]

Dr Cyril Burt was the doyen of educational psychologists and he had decided and unchanging views. Indeed he sent the same evidence to both the Hadow Committee in the 1920s and the Spens Committee in the 1930s saying that he had no reason to change his opinions.[140] His view of psychological, educational and occupational levels neatly corresponded to five groupings.

1. Secondary school scholarship children	
Mental ratio 130+	Professional, administrative and executive
10% of population	
2. Higher grade or central school	
Just fail to win scholarship	
Mental ratio 115–130	Clerical and technical
10% of population	
3. Ordinary children	
Stay at elementary school and leave at 14	
Mental ratio 85–115	Skilled labour, commoner industrial and commercial
68.5% of population	
4. Dull and backward	
Below mental ratio 84	Unskilled labour
10% of population	
5. Feeble minded	
Below mental ratio 70	Institutional life or casual labour
1.5% of population	

Accordingly in his view 'the degree of a child's intelligence roughly marks him out as fit for callings of a certain grade'. He thought that general intelligence was fairly constant from early years and confidently testable at 11. Yet he was equally clear that up to the age of 14 'it is extremely difficult to demonstrate the existence of special aptitudes or abilities on any large scale . . . manual and mechanical (abilities) seldom seem definitely established in any high degree until puberty or even later'. This was no support for the JTS and indeed he made no mention of the JTS in his five level scheme. He appeared before Spens Committee and reiterated his view of technical selection.

> Professor Burt said that it was exceedingly difficult to isolate special aptitudes at the age of 11+. In point of fact, it was unlikely that any special aptitudes would have emerged at the age of 11+ since they do

not begin to become apparent till the period of puberty.[141]

Professor C.W. Valentine of Manchester also held that although experiments were being made to devise tests of linguistic, mechanical and other aptitudes, 'there was little accurate knowledge in these branches of testing'.[142]

The scepticism of psychologists about selection for the JTS effectively prevented the lowering the age of entry from 13 to 11. Yet many of their beliefs supported by implication the activities of the schools. Burt was strongly of the view that the curriculum of secondary grammar schools was too academic and needed more practical subjects. H.A. Harris and Professor F.A. Cavanagh of London agreed with this. Burt and Cavanagh also agreed that it was a myth that studying useless academic subjects could be justified as providing an all round 'training of the mind'. In particular Burt, Cavanagh and Valentine agreed that the study of Latin had no special value whatever, there was no 'transfer' of mental qualities developed in one area to another. Their emphasis on the practical, their scepticism of the academic and their call for a greater variety of secondary schooling worked in favour of junior technical work. But their disbelief in the possibilities of selection for it limited their support for the JTS as a specific form. The implication was that more JTS-type work should be carried on in grammar schools. This was the view Burt came to after the war, with decisive results.

Industrial psychologists held a more enthusiastic view of the JTS than their educational colleagues. The National Institute of Industrial Psychology was clear that 11 was too early to detect mechanical aptitudes: 'mechanical aptitudes appear to be of late development'. However they were quite confident that tests of mechanical aptitude had been constructed and 'these abilities are reliably estimated by the tests in children as young as thirteen years of age'. They were 'strongly in favour' of their introduction into JTSs.[143] They had no such confidence in predicting mathematical and linguistic aptitudes. However on the crucial issues the National Institute backed the JTS - it did cater for discernable special aptitudes, these were detectable at 13 and they were useful for industry. It was perhaps appropriate that the JTS gained more support from psychologists orientated towards industry than from those in the world of education.

In the meantime the JTSs flourished providing a useful education for industry and without doubt benefiting their pupils. But their enemies, the Left and some psychologists, had already flagged their hostility and were to play their part in undermining the technical school system in the postwar years.

CHAPTER 5

The Junior Technical Schools and the Second World War, 1939–1945

> *the technical institutions of this country have, in spite of the gravest handicaps . . . played an invaluable part in safely bringing Britain through her time of greatest peril and placing her on the high road to victory.*
>
> H. C. Dent, 1944.[1]

The outbreak of war in September 1939 presented the JTSs with severe problems but unpredictable opportunities. Just before its onset the Board contemplated its implications. 'Junior Technical Schools and still more Trade schools will be the hardest hit, for they are the more highly specialised in their aims than any other type of school.' They would have to be billeted, though it was recognized that it was unlikely that they would be able to carry on all their technical work. It was hoped that they would retain subjects like engineering drawing along with general education and otherwise 'make best use of the time in the discovery of new interests in physical education and broadening the general outlook of pupils.'[2] It was a pessimistic view but things proved better than they hoped when the realities of war overtook them within a few weeks.

I

On the declaration of war a broadcast announcement required the closure of all schools as a precaution against aerial onslaught. The immediate problem was evacuation to avoid the unexpected bombing. Three types of areas were designated: evacuation areas where children and schools were to be removed from danger, reception areas which were to receive them and neutral areas which should neither evacuate nor receive. Four days after the outbreak of war it was further announced that schools in evacuation areas should remain closed, those in reception areas should re-open and those in neutral areas could re-open after 11 September at their discretion.

The consequence for JTSs was initially rather chaotic. The Board noted:

> in view of the complexity of the transport arrangements for the Greater London evacuation areas it was impossible to allocate any school from this area to any particular district in the reception area and the final arrangements were based on the assumption that the children would have to be transported on the first available train at the London terminal station. In consequence some schools of this type found themselves billeted in remote rural districts where none of the special accommodation required for their work was available.[3]

During the autumn of 1939 the expected German bombing did not come about and, lulled into false security, there was a steady flow of children back to their parents in the evacuation areas. LEAs wanted to re-open secondary schools and JTSs in these evacuation areas. The Board was initially cautious, fearing that the wholesale re-opening of schools and flow back of children to evacuated areas would increase the risk of some disaster. HMIs were told that they must not suggest any re-openings themselves.[4] However on 1 November 1939 it was announced that all schools in evacuation areas that could be made available might be re-opened. It was recognized that JTSs were especially disadvantaged by evacuation and so 'it has been decided that if an Authority proposes on its own initiative to bring back a school as a whole, the proposal can be entertained if a satisfactory case is made out.'[5] Mistakenly they thought 'it is now possible to be a good deal more optimistic about the future of Junior Technical School work than it was a month or two ago.'

After the 'phoney war' evacuation once again became urgent between the Battle of Britain in September 1940 and the ending of the Blitz in May 1941. By the end of 1940 there were 19,809 pupils in JTSs and 6,999 in JCSs, representing a creditable 83 per cent of prewar enrolment.[6]

Before the war about a half of JTS courses were in future evacuation areas and a quarter each in neutral and reception areas. Of these courses in evacuation areas a third stayed put or were allowed to return, a third were carried on partly where they were and partly in a reception area, and a third were wholly evacuated to a reception area. It was therefore misleading to think that even in this second evacuation phase there had been a wholesale transfer of JTSs from endangered evacuation area cities to safer reception area towns. In London this was so with only five courses remaining. But in Manchester, Liverpool, Leeds and Sheffield JTSs were more likely to stay put. A balance of disadvantages had to be taken into account. Schools and courses that evacuated were less likely to be interrupted by war dangers, but suffered other setbacks. Enrolment on evacuated JTS courses was only a half (52 per cent) of what they had been prewar. Also there was no doubt that some of the accommodation receiving JTSs in 'village and other halls and private houses' made it difficult to carry on genuinely practical technical education with proper equipment. By staying put, JTSs sustained much higher enrolment rates (79 per cent) with the familiar pupils attending their familiar school.

Of the prewar junior commercial courses a third each had been in the future evacuation, neutral and reception areas. Of the 20 courses in evacuation areas a half stayed put, 30 per cent were carried on partly where they were and partly in a reception area and a fifth were wholly evacuated to a reception area. The JCSs were less affected by the war. Their demand for premises and equipment was less specialized than for JTSs and in turn they were less vulnerable to poaching for industrial or army training. They had no difficulty in placing their school leavers and found that 'war conditions have created an increased demand'.

London was the most important evacuation centre from which JTSs were dispersed. Prior to the war there were 6,000 boys and girls at these schools but on the outbreak every one of the schools was evacuated with the exception of the School for Retail Distribution. Many of these schools joined other JTSs in the provinces but several courses found more makeshift homes in reception areas:[7]

> Hairdressing is taught to boys in the upstairs room of a cottage in a remote Somerset village, and engineering and tailoring are taught in nearby halls and garages. Expert dressmaking and fine embroidery are taught on platforms of church halls or in disused school buildings in Devon, Hertfordshire and other counties. Lithography and book production are taught in an Oxfordshire village.

All the art schools were merged into two units, one in Northampton and one in Trowbridge. Perhaps the most unusual evacuation was the training ship *Exmouth* which used to be moored at Grays and run by the Metropolitan Asylums Board. This ship was transferred to the West Country and converted into a JTS. It was a poignant aspect of the evacuation of London JTS pupils that many of them were already refugees. It was noted that

> there is one interesting feature of Junior Technical Schools which is worthy of mention; the refugee elements in this country often appreciate them more than do the native born. Before the war, many of the children who were refugees from Nazi oppression found their way to these schools.

Devon, reciprocally, provides a good example of a reception area for JTSs. There had been a JTS at Plymouth but with the destruction of the town it moved to Torquay. Torquay became not only host to this school but to Croydon Trade School and Woolwich Polytechnic JTS. Exeter JTS which had 80 engineering students received an evacuated London JTS and elsewhere in the city a girls needle trade school, also from London, was accommodated. Another JTS was transferred to Budleigh Salterton. All this was probably a valuable cultural import into Devon, otherwise notable for its 'virulently conservative' attitudes to education and its neglect of the technical side.[8]

II

If evacuation was one problem then another was the need to defend the JTSs against potential predation in the early stages of the war. The status of their valuable equipment and staff had to be defined. The Board was dismayed to find at the outbreak of war that 'occasionally it happens that local officers, sometimes quite junior officers, attempt to walk into a building and commandeer it.'[9] The local ARP, the Army and the Office of Works were cited as guilty intruders. It was recognized that specialist laboratories and workshops 'may be of the highest importance to the fighting services' but they must not be taken over 'as billets or offices nor must machinery be taken away'. The LEAs and HMIs were enjoined to resist any attempt at 'invasion' and to co-ordinate demands with chief constables and the War Office. By 1940 industrial training courses and training for army tradesmen were using some JTS facilities. There was less concern about the latter which was 'mainly work with hand tools' and made 'comparatively small demands on machine tool workshops'. But if industrial training courses put pressure on the Army or JTS work then more classrooms could be converted to workshops to ensure 'that the interests of the Junior Technical School pupils are safeguarded'.[10]

Staff too were a problem in wartime, especially those of such specifically technical engineering skills as the JTSs employed. The shortage of teachers was causing concern early in the war,

> instructors have either been called up or volunteered for munitions. It is only recently that the training of young technicians has come to be regarded as having sufficient importance to justify exemption . . . teachers with specialist knowledge such as metal work and engineering subjects have taken up posts in munitions, training centres etc.[11]

The JTSs could not withdraw production workers from industry and they had hoped to recruit handicraft teachers from elementary schools but found them insufficient in quantity and quality.[12] HMIs discussed this with directors of education but this could not conjure up the teachers with the industrial experience they needed.

A clear order of priorities was established. All schools had to cede to the claims of A priority which was providing teachers for courses for training radio personnel. Thereafter the situation was as follows,

> having regard to the balance of industrial advantage in the present circumstances, the maintenance so far as possible of the work of Junior Technical Schools takes the first place and that of National Certificate courses the second place. If the industrial efficiency of the Junior Technical School would be seriously damaged by the transfer of a teacher to work under B (industrial upgrading courses for skilled workers and army technicians) or C (industrial training courses for the Ministry of Labour) the case will need special consideration.[13]

One partial solution was the employment of aliens: 'the supply of teachers is at present so limited in practically all subjects that we can hardly object to the appointment of an alien'.[14] With friendly aliens (Belgian and Dutch allies for example) there was no problem, but enemy aliens (refugees from the enemy) faced certain restrictions. They could not teach on radio courses - which was an advantage to JTSs. Yet neither could they teach in JTSs where war work was being done somewhere else in the same (usually technical college) building without special permission of the Board, which was only exceptionally given. In practice a number of aliens had already started teaching in technical schools before the war, and since Home Office control had been 'a trifle erratic' there was no means of knowing who or where they were.[15] Women teachers also filled the gaps. At Luton JTS Building School half the members of staff were women graduates.[16]

The children having departed the JTSs, their valuable equipment still remained for other purposes. Training courses of various types were run.

Men and women from the forces were trained in engineering, making and repairing equipment, cooking and radio 'and other work of a highly skilled, and often very confidential nature'. Ministry of Labour trainees also studied there and some forces personnel took courses in vocational training to fit them for civilian life. As well as training, the schools immediately after Dunkirk, 'played an important part in production work, mainly producing work which needed great skill and accuracy such as jigs and gauges'. This was chiefly in the immediate crisis, but as soon as possible the schools returned to their priority training work. It may be that there was a greater concern to evacuate the London JTSs than any other form of schooling precisely so that their valuable premises and equipment could be used for these urgent adult purposes. R. A. Butler reported to the Cabinet that 40,000 army tradesmen were training in technical colleges, many inevitably using JTS facilities.[17]

The war led to a greater appreciation of JTSs. One of the reporters for the Nuffield Survey noted that 'the war has increased the demand from the intelligent parent for entry to the pre-industrial Junior Technical School course . . . the demand from industry for the boy with a sound pre-industrial vocational training has increased under war time conditions.'[18] The wartime demand for all kinds of engineers and technicians placed a premium upon the JTS boy. A London Juvenile Employment officer found that 'skilled tool makers have always been in great demand and are now rarer than ever',[19] such that a lad's starting wages had risen from 14s. a week to £1 or 25s. This heightened appreciation was also reflected in the private sector as various engineering firms began their own works schools for their juvenile workers in 1942 and 1943.[20]

The Board was accordingly very willing to approve schemes for the expansion of JTSs in response to parental demand. For example at Bristol in 1940 reorganization of some central and other schools created two large junior technical and commercial schools, expanding this form of education from 100 pupils to 660.[21] Luton, finding a greater number and higher quality of applicants to the JTS, asked permission to double the intake on the grounds that 'under the present emergency conditions with the heavy demands on the engineering industry an increased supply of Junior Technical School boys in two years time may be most valuable.'[22] The Board was happy to approve this and shortly afterwards a further expansion for a large Building School. These extensions expanded the pupil provision from 60 to 330. Canterbury, likewise, finding 100 applicants (50 of high intelligence) for 24 first year places was allowed to double its intake.[23] This contributed to a general nationwide expansion during the war years. No figures were collected during the war but in 1937–8 there were 242 schools with 29,590 pupils and this had risen to 324 schools with 59,918 pupils by 1946.

III

JTSs also seized the opportunities of the war to diversify their activities, seeking new areas of service to the war effort. The Board was happy to support this too. A Board official noted 'more and more it seems that LEAs and principals are being encouraged to experiment'.[24] Just before the war it was evident that there were problems in the recruiting and training for the rapidly expanding aircraft industry. The Board proposed that 'the technical schools of the country might make a substantial contribution towards solving it.'[25] No specialist aeronautical courses seem to have resulted and in any case the schools were soon to be evacuated. But the suggestion signalled that in time of war the JTSs might be targeted to even more specific objectives.

Nursing was a good example. The General Nursing Council allowed some subjects - anatomy, physiology, hygiene - to be examined before entry to hospital training. The Board accordingly suggested that 'it is therefore urgently desirable that pre-nursing courses should be established as soon as possible in suitable secondary and technical schools.'[26] Canterbury JTS established a nursing course in 1942 with a third of the curriculum devoted to domestic science and science for nursing.[27] Textiles too received attention. Many Lancashire technical colleges had well equipped textile departments but few students during the war. The Cotton Board, concerned about the lack of recruits, urged Lancashire LEAs to create junior textile schools. They were created as departments in JTSs at Blackburn, Oldham, Bolton and Salford, 'but did not attract pupils readily'.[28] The memories of the depressed cotton industry in the interwar years and the more evident and glamorous opportunities in engineering in wartime clearly shaped motivations.

The war also gave a new urgency to agriculture. The destruction of allied shipping importing food forced Britain back on her own resources. Rationing, the Land Girls and 'Dig for Victory' were inevitable responses. A greater attention to agricultural education was another. A pioneer model opened during the war was a JTS attached to Llysfasi Farm Institute, near Ruthin, Denbighshire, opened in 1942.[29] The JTS section took boys at 13, both day and boarders. The work consisted of general education with science related to farming matters from plant growth to farm machinery. There was a strong emphasis on the practical side, with the boys caring for 120 cattle, 1,000 sheep and horses, pigs and poultry on 700 acres. Metalwork and woodwork were essential crafts for farm maintenance. The purpose of this was to train not the ordinary agricultural worker but the boy who would be likely to rise higher to managerial level. R. A. Butler visited the school with approbation. Another initiative was the pre-agricultural course at Canterbury JTS. On their Barton Court estate they dealt with fruit with 3 acres of orchard, glasshouse, rabbit, poultry and piggery work reflecting Kentish agriculture.[30] The Kent LEA also started a similar course at Maidstone JTS.

Hardly had these schools started than they received a douche of discouragement from Lord Luxmoore's Committee on Post War Agricultural Education.[31] Luxmoore noted the Kent schools and Llysfasi but concluded disappointingly that 'we do not think there is any place for separate junior technical schools in agriculture; indeed we are opposed to any attempt at vocational training before the age of 15.' They preferred having gardens in all schools and some 'fur and feather' care but not specific rural studies schools with vocational agricultural education before the school leaving age. One of his committee, the Hon. Mrs R. J. Youard, disagreed with this. In a very sensible dissenting Minority Report she argued that as JTSs already operated successfully from the core studies of engineering and construction there was no reason why other JTSs should not have biology and the life sciences as a core. She imaginatively saw that this would not be narrow but could lead to a range of occupations from agriculture to nursing. Curiously, another of Luxmoore's committee, Dr Thomas Loveday, Vice Chancellor of Bristol University, seems to have changed his mind within the year. He chaired yet another committee on education and agriculture in 1944 and endorsed the desirability of a Rural Junior Polytechnic and JTSs providing agricultural courses.

The operation of Llysfasi, Canterbury and Maidstone remained unaffected by the polarization of attitudes represented by Luxmoore, Loveday and Mrs Youard. They fulfilled a commonsense wartime need. After the war the Kent schools continued but Llysfasi JTS closed, due to a shortage of building materials rather than to any policy change by the LEA which wished to keep it. The notion of the agricultural JTS did not develop. In the 1950s A. G. Gooch an HMI notably keen on technical schools, regretted that 'the development of agricultural courses for pupils of genuine Secondary Technical calibre has so far regrettably been negligible.'[32]

One area of JTS activity which was greatly stimulated by the demands of war was building. The Blitz destruction in industrial cities and the suspension of normal building during the war years suggested that there would be a considerable surge in construction in the postwar years. The Ministry of Works and Buildings had set up a committee on education and training in the building industry in autumn 1941 which suggested that building courses be added to existing JTSs.[33] The Board considered that the number of additional recruits who would be required by the building industry would be 'extremely large' and that there was 'no danger of over-production of Junior Technical School pupils even if the numbers of schools is very greatly increased'.[34] The existing output of 500–600 a year was 'negligible' as the Board considered an output of 10,000 a year absorbable and necessary. The Board urged the establishment of three-year courses 'since experience shows it is the work done in such schools which is likely to make the most effective contribution to the needs of the [building] industry'.[35] A lad who had taken a two-year JTS course would be able to enter the first year of the National Certificate Course in Building or the second year of a Trade Course in Building Subjects. Or one who had finished a three-year JTS course could enter the second or third years respectively of these higher courses. However the Board recognized that in existing circumstances three-year courses would be 'impossible of achievement in many places' and so two-year courses would continue to predominate.

In 1943 a Government report calculated that the building industry would require a labour force of 1 ½ million men. It noted that JTS building courses had increased substantially and that 'it is intended that it [the JTS] should become the main channel of entry to apprenticeship.'[36] In June of the same year the Building Apprenticeship and Training Council was formed under Sir Malcolm Trustram Eve and with H. B. Wallis of the Board. Their first report in December 1943 was enthusiastic about JTS courses for building and recommended that employers should give preference to ex-JTS boys who had undergone this pre-employment education when selecting apprentices.[37] By 1943 institutions providing or proposing to provide junior full-time courses for building were as shown in Table 5.1. Lancashire and Yorkshire with large urban areas were far in advance of other counties, Liverpool and Sheffield (whose Chief Education Officer was W. P. Alexander) were especially keen on this development. As a result pupils in JTS building courses rose to 4,000 by March 1944.

The Board was prepared to go to unusual lengths to stimulate this

Table 5.1 *Junior technical schools for the building trades, 1943*

	A Boys to enter the building industry	B To enter one of the constructive industries	C Junior Departments painting, decorating plastering
Lancashire	18	9	2
Yorkshire	18	2	6
London	3	-	1
Other counties	69	15	20
Total	108	26	29

Source: ED 135/3 Junior schools of building, 14 Apr. 1943.

development. For example Southampton, which had suffered heavy destruction, itself proposed a large and expensive JTS in 1942. The Board quickly approved it although it ran counter to two existing Board policies. It was a rare (unique?) case of a new school approved in an *evacuation* area. Yet as a Board official jotted, 'the national urgency for the establishment of such courses might be sufficient reason.' Nor did they object to the proposal that the JTS could lead up to a course at the Southampton University College - something they would not have countenanced in the 1930s.[38] Furthermore, to ease the flow of teachers to these new courses, the Board on 15 March 1944 granted powers to LEAs to transfer men aged 34 and over from building into teaching in JTSs.[39] The irony of this was that by the later stages of the war there was difficulty in placing in employment lads leaving JTS building schools.[40] There was a large transfer of skilled building labour from some parts of the country to war-damaged areas, a lot of building in some areas and none in others. However it was admitted that these 'very abnormal conditions' would be only temporary. Indeed so. This considerable development of JTS building courses was one of the great achievements of wartime education and played a crucial role in the provision of a labour force for postwar reconstruction.

IV

The war and the prospect of an expansion of secondary technical schools after the war stimulated a concern for the training of technical teachers. The negative situation of the prewar days was well expressed in a letter to the Chief Inspector. 'Though for years we have agreed upon the urgency of training teachers for posts in Technical Schools I cannot remember any definite action being taken' beyond some part time courses for engineering teachers in Birmingham and London.[41]

An HMI, Miss B. B. Briant, began to stir things up. She could find no teacher in Berkshire qualified to teach dressmaking (an important wartime housewifely skill) in schools. She accordingly organized courses taught by a Miss Browning from a local firm. These were held at Reading University in the face of opposition from an apathetic Chief Education Officer. However Miss Browning herself could get no training. She might have gone to Chelsea Polytechnic but could afford neither to give up her job nor the travel costs for part-time study.[42] The outcome of the persistence of Miss Briant and Miss Browning was the Board's instruction to LEAs in 1943 that they should provide financial assistance for fees, travelling and maintenance for technical teacher training.[43]

In 1944 with the end of the war in sight there was very positive thinking in favour of training for technical teachers. C.I. Elliott discussed the matter with S. H. Wood and Gilbert Flemming, 'they came to the conclusion that any course . . . should be based on the supply of teachers for the technical (secondary) schools'. This seemed to Wallis a shift in concern more towards training for technical school teachers of children rather than lecturers in technical colleges.[44] Further discussion with Sir Gilbert Flemming (the new Permanent Secretary) confirmed this, 'from what he told me the idea is that we should concentrate primarily on the training of persons who are prospective teachers in the Technical (Secondary) Schools and will be responsible for the more purely technical subjects.'[45] Flemming regarded this as an important issue. He saw that there would be more technical work in secondary schools as well as in technical high schools, 'a Regional Committee was investigating the possibility of providing training for recruits for this type of teaching at Manchester'.[46] It was agreed that Manchester would be 'a natural centre for a permanent scheme of training for persons who will go into the Technical Schools'.[47]

The war also prompted optimism about the future possibility of staffing technical schools after the war. A research team from Nuffield College Oxford, interviewing workers in Swindon, found 44 men in industry, working at GWR, Armstrong Whitworth and Vickers who were interested in switching careers from industry to teaching after the war. Two thirds of them had industrial experience and were keen to teach technical and scientific subjects to adolescents. Their motives were usually a highly idealistic belief in the importance of education for the future of the nation. G. D. H. Cole concluded 'there is little doubt that a considerable flow of teachers from industry would be started as soon as the war is over'.[48]

The effect of the war was not so negative as might have been feared at the outset. It was undeniable that the evacuation resulted in an unavoidable deterioration in the quality of training for pupils taught in rural church halls rather than their fully equipped home schools. Also 24 technical college buildings, many of which must have contained JTSs, were destroyed or severely damaged by enemy action. Yet on the positive side the enhanced role of the JTSs in building and temporarily in agriculture and the greater concern for teacher training arose from the war. Above all the war brought a greater awareness of the importance of science and education from the university boffin down to the JTS pre-apprentice. This practical experience together with the favourable attention paid to the JTS in the debate about educational policy that preceded the 1944 Education Act augured well for the technical school as it entered the postwar years.[49]

CHAPTER 6

Policy and the Technical School from Spens to the Butler Act

It takes a long time for sense to penetrate the wooden heads *of Old England.*

H.B. Wallis to R.A. Butler 27 September 1941
(underlining by Butler)[1]

I

While the war was in progress, and in the months before, a long debate was taking place about the future shape of the educational system and the place of the technical school within it. This began with the Spens Report in 1938 and culminated in the Butler Act in 1944.

From 1937–8 in the year leading up to the publication of the Spens Report, Board of Education officials crystallized their views about post-primary education and technical schools which foreshadowed those of the report itself. R.S. (later Sir Robert) Wood, one of the influential shapers of the 1944 Act noted that there was a growing feeling that there was an excessive provision of secondary education of the academic grammar school type. Yet schools other than grammar schools were regarded very much as poor relations, 'hence the agitation to bring the Junior Technical School more into line with the Secondary School'.[2] Wood deplored that too many people thought that the main objective of secondary education was 'to educate a few more people out of their class, thereby actually strengthening instead of diminishing class distinctions'. This was an interesting implied attack on the social attitudes of Morant, Bryce and Webb and other 'ladder of opportunity' men of the 1900s when the new grammar and junior technical schools had been created. It looked forward to more egalitarian aspirations of the 1940s. In Wood's view there were too many children in grammar schools – 500,000 in 1937 compared with 20,000 in 1914, in spite of a decline in the child population. The result was some 30 per cent of pupils in grammar schools who were not of the capacity to benefit from such academic education and who were consequently entering jobs inappropriate for grammar school boys.

This view was confirmed by Dr Innes, the Director of Education at Birmingham. He too found large numbers of his grammar school boys leaving prematurely. Yet there was no similar reluctance to stay the course at JTSs because the pupils were better motivated and the vocational nature of the course meant 'that the pupils would be advantageously placed at the end'. Innes 'looked for any further expansion in the direction of a wider provision of schools on Junior Technical School lines'.[3] The views that were forming in the Board were that there should be technical high schools admitting at 11+, the old 'junior' nomenclature should be dropped, that saturation point had been reached with grammar schools and an expansion of technical schools was the way forward.[4]

This was the context of opinion within which Sir Will Spens presented his report on secondary education and technical high schools in 1938.[5] Sir Will Spens (1882–1962) had succeeded Sir Henry Hadow as Chairman of the Consultative Committee in 1934. He was well disposed towards scientific and technical matters. In the 1890s he had been educated at Rugby School, a pioneer in science education among the public schools, and he had gained a 'First' in Part I of the Natural Sciences Tripos at Cambridge in 1903. He had been Master of Corpus Christi College, Cambridge, since 1927, where R.A. Butler was one of the Fellows he had appointed.

Since the mid-1930s Spens and his Consultative Committee had been receiving evidence strongly in support of technical schools. The ATTI impressed on him the keenness of students, their links with industry, the desirability of expanding these schools and lowering the age of entry to 11.[6] The technical college principals deplored that secondary education was too related to professional and black coated occupations and not enough to industry and commerce. They urged a new 'technical secondary' school as an antidote.[7] If the 'producers' of technical education could be expected to be enthusiastic yet the 'consumers' were no less so. The British Association for Commercial and Industrial Education enthused,

> there is probably no type of school in the whole system of English education whose reputation for the accomplishment of its defined aim stands higher than that of the Junior technical School . . . [and] . . .

there is little doubt that an increase in their number is desirable.[8]

This impressed Spens who became a keen advocate of technical schools. Whereas Spens noted that Hadow had given only a 'brief mention' to the schools, Spens himself devoted at least 45 pages to them. He found in the schools he visited 'an atmosphere of vitality, keenness and happiness' that impressed him.[9] But he went beyond the usual praise for he wanted the schools to evolve into something more and saw them as a key area of future development. To eradicate the difference between them and academic secondary grammar schools, Spens proposed that the junior technical schools should be turned into technical high schools - 'We are now unhesitatingly recommending the establishment of Technical High Schools which shall have complete equality of status with grammar schools'.[10] To remove the problem of the 'double break' entry ages to the old JTS he proposed that both the new technical high schools (THSs) and the grammar schools should have a common age of recruitment at 11+ with the same selective examination. He also proposed that a foreign language, preferably German rather than French, should be allowed in THSs.[11]

Parity with the grammar school would also be evident through a fee system which should be the same in both grammar and THS.[12] He envisaged that THSs should still be housed in technical colleges to facilitate common use of machinery and facilities.[13] Indeed Spens would have been aware that unit costs in JTS were often higher than those in grammar schools. To have free standing THSs in independent buildings would have proved very expensive and with fees the same as in grammar schools (as Spens proposed) this would have been a strong disincentive for LEAs against creating THSs. Spens also proposed a School Leaving Certificate for the THS, awarded on the basis of internal examinations but endorsed by the Board of Education. This too removed another status disability of technical schools *vis-à-vis* grammar schools. He envisaged an upper age limit of 16 for the THS, whence pupils would move into industry or to a higher technical course at a technical college. He did not contemplate sixth forms in THSs. There was still the assumption that THS products should get into productive work rather than embark on an ever extending conveyor belt to more academic and less practical studies. Yet he did not rule out that 'a few of these schools may in course of time develop the equivalent to a sixth form.'[14]

Spens also tackled the question of the more specialized form of JTS. He liked the trade schools teaching furniture-making, silversmithing and so forth, and wanted them to continue with an age of entry at 13+ or 14+ after sufficient general education. The steady demand for their products in established trades especially in London gave them a justification and effectively regulated their size. He also approved the continuation of JCSs and home training (domestic science) schools for girls, provided that they retained an age of entry at 13 and did not reduce to 11 like the THS.[15]

Radical as this was, the most pregnant part of the Spens Report was his suggestion that there were too many grammar school pupils and that authorities with more than 15 per cent of their secondary pupils in grammar schools 'should consider whether the supply of this particular form of secondary education is in any way excessive'. If so 'it may be found desirable, in appropriate circumstances, that some of their grammar schools should become schools with a strong technical bias' - in practice they should be converted to technical high schools.[16] Spens was clearly reflecting ideas which had been the subject of debate within the Board by R.S. Wood and others in the discussions of 1937–8.

Board officials subjected the Spens Report to critical scrutiny in the first six months of 1939. In their discussions they raised six points of reservation about the technical high school. First they calculated that the increased cost in salaries of converting JTSs to THSs and reducing the age of entry to 11+ would be £900,000 a year.[17] Second, they welcomed the suggestion that the leaving age of the THS should be 16 but feared that the pressures of industry would force it down as firms would be keen to recruit potential high quality technicians at a younger age.[18] Linked with this was a disappointment that Spens had not envisaged sixth forms for THSs. Sir Percival Sharp in particular thought that THSs should not be truncated at 16 but should go on until 18, he expressed doubt 'whether Technical High Schools because of . . . the absence from them of a sixth form, would secure entrants of satisfactory quality in industrial areas'.[19] The technical HMIs also had doubts about Spens's view that THSs should be departments in technical colleges. They thought that they should be in separate buildings 'because of the status attached to independent premises'.[20]

The chief reservation, however, derived from the strong reverence for the secondary grammar school and the implied suspicion that the THS would encroach on its role. The Secondary School Advisory Committee took a high moral line that the grammar school had 'inherited a fine tradition based on the principles of disciplined study . . . very high prestige in public estimation'. Not surprisingly they thought that the general adoption of the THS 'would be unnecessary because most of the functions will in future be able to be carried out in a secondary school'.[21] It was also feared that separate THSs would actually 'prejudice the very desirable movement towards the widening of the secondary school curriculum'.[22] Assistant Secretary Griffith Williams used the opportunity to unburden himself of some frank feelings. He deplored that there was an unfortunate impression around that the grammar school had been too academic. He cautioned against correcting this academic bias and against those who 'are naturally inclined to seize on Technical High Schools and new Regulations as nostrums for all our problems'.[23] Spens's pregnant page 322, suggesting that there were too many grammar schools and that some should be converted to technical schools, found no support in this quarter and this was ultimately to prove significant.

Finally, as the grammar school had its defenders against the new THS, so too did the old JTS. This was the standpoint of E.G. Savage and H.B. Wallis who observed, 'We feel no enthusiasm for the substitution of a Technical High School for a Junior Technical School which is doing good work.'[24] It was clear that reservations about the THS did not always derive from coolness about technical education as such. For some enthusiasts like Savage the JTS was not something to apologize for or tolerate as a stepping stone to something better. It had its own justification which was not to be enhanced by turning it, in effect, into a technical grammar school.

Sir Maurice Holmes, the Permanent Secretary of the Board, summed up the discussions coolly,

> While the Committee had obviously no enthusiasm for the institution of Technical High Schools on a large scale, he thought that they would not cavil at the experimental conversion in suitable cases of existing Junior Technical Schools into Technical High Schools.[25]

He was even cooler in his digest of the discussion:

> the Committee were very lukewarm indeed towards the recommendation of the Spens Report on this matter (Technical High Schools). The point was made that Technical High Schools would in large measure be unnecessary if the curriculum of secondary schools were widened on the lines suggested in that Report.[26]

Holmes was in fact rather unfair in his summary. Some of the objections to Spens had arisen not from opposition to the THS but from a belief that Spens had not claimed enough for them - sixth forms, independent sites, a guaranteed high leaving age. Holmes was already siding with the G.G. Williams pro-grammar school position and its slight regard for the THS. The Board view was that few if any cases of new THSs would be approved at the moment. It would be a matter of considering proposals for converting JTSs into THSs. Holmes, Wallis and others agreed to discuss this further after the holidays. But after this August 1939 vacation the outbreak of war intervened. So the discussion fed less into immediate administrative changes than into the stream of thinking that was to flow towards the 1944 Act.

II

If the outbreak of war held up developments, yet the threatening advent of war gave a stimulus to technical education in 1938–9. War concerns and the Spens Report impelled a strong secret movement to raise the profile and funds for technical education generally and the JTS in particular. In March 1938 Savage was already warning about Britain's lagging behind the Continent, and in July he attended the 1938 International Conference on Technical Education in Berlin. He returned very concerned:

> there is no doubt . . . that Germany is far and away ahead of us in the provision of technical schools . . . our capacity at the moment is very much inferior to a country which may be our serious rival in peace or enemy in war.[27]

He impressed his master at the Board, Lord Stanhope, who found his comment on Berlin 'alarming', and throughout the summer of 1938 Stanhope, Sir Thomas Inskip of the Committee of Imperial Defence, Oliver Stanley of the Board of Trade (but formerly President of the Board of Education) and Ernest Brown of the Ministry of Labour were writing to each other urging the importance of technical education. It was achieving greater importance in widening Government circles.

It had been difficult to expand technical education in the late 1930s because LEAs were spending on the Hadow reorganization and preparing to raise the school leaving age to 15 after the 1936 Act. Moreover central government, which provided 50 per cent of the cost of building, was busy with rearmament. Expenditure on all matters not to do with raising the school leaving age had slowed down.[28] Yet Robert Wood pointed out that technical education should not be a neglected trade-off for rearmament but was intimately linked with it. There was an urgent need to prepare boys for industry 'immediately to assist by vocational training the progress of the rearmament programme . . . for this purpose we can safely do our best to secure an increase in the number and size of Junior Technical Schools.'[29]

Lord de la Warr, the new President of the Board, took this point and referring to 'Germany, our main competitor on all fronts' suggested that the Exchequer should enable the Board of Education to raise its contribution to capital expenditure from 50 per cent to 75 per cent.[30] Sir John Simon, the Chancellor, demurred and likewise refused proposals to match pound for pound contributions from private employers.[31] Undaunted pressure was kept up by de la Warr and Oliver Stanley through the midsummer of 1939. Then between May and July, as war drew even closer, the arguments struck home and the Treasury relented and made available an extra £150,000 - though some £215,000 would have been needed to move to 75 per cent grant.[32] The Chancellor of the Exchequer, Sir John Simon, seems to have been changing his mind about budgets and public expenditure as the war drew nearer. He reflected in retrospect that the demands of war changed the approach to national finance from being merely a balancing of accounts and imposing taxes, 'it is a potent means to the desired end and its main purpose is to make the best use of the productive resources of the country for winning the war'.[33] This new attitude was consonant with the releasing of this extra £150,000. De la Warr's rearguard action had paid off but within a few weeks war had broken out and the issue was shelved. But this movement of 1938–9 had served its purpose in heightening awareness of technical education. The torch was to be taken up and passed to Butler by subsequent initiatives.

III

With the outbreak of war, Board of Education civil servants evacuated to the Branksome Dene Hotel, Bournemouth. They continued to think about the shape of education after a war they expected to win. The three most important figures were G.G. Williams, head of the secondary branch, William Cleary of the Elementary and H.B. Wallis of the Technical. Williams believed in the virtues of the grammar school and academic selection. He was a friend of Sir Cyril Norwood and a frequent visitor to the Headmasters Conference, he was 'steeped in grammar and public school traditions'.[34] William Cleary, by contrast, advocated the multilateral school. H.B. Wallis, who carried the flag for the technical school, was a much less influential figure than Williams or Cleary and this is thought to have perpetuated the inferior status of the JTS and proposed THS. Noel Annan suggests that Wallis, 'responsible for technical education, was not their equal and therefore technical schools died at birth'.[35] Sir Maurice Holmes inclined to Williams' view, as he had in the debate about the Spens Report.

Attitudes crystallized in the 'Green Book' of 1941.[36] This was prepared by 'some officers of the Board' and represented their 'personal views and suggestions' for discussion. As regards the JTS, they noted the tiny proportion of children over 11 in JTSs, some 27,000 or 1.4 per cent of the total.[37] They proposed the raising of the school leaving age to 15 and the division of secondary education into secondary modern schools with a leaving age of 15+, secondary technical schools with leaving at 15 or 16 and grammar schools with leaving at 16–18. Most important, the officials came to the view that the double break entry into the JTS - which they had been defending in the 1920s and 1930s - was no longer necessary. Indeed they wanted a fairly common education between the ages of 11 and 13 in all three types of secondary school. They recognized that equality between all three types of post primary education 'can never be secured either in fact or in the public mind until the same administrative machinery is made applicable to all alike'. Beyond the leaving age they wanted a return to the Fisher idea of the compulsory day continuation school for one day a week between the ages of 15 and 18.[38] This foreshadowed several features of the 1944 Act and represented a willingness to bring the technical school into other forms of secondary education.

The Green Book was welcomed by the technical colleges, schools and principals, though they preferred a structure by which all pupils were transferred from junior to modern schools at 11 and thence to grammar or technical schools at 13 with most remaining in modern schools. Wallis could see no sense in grammar school pupils going to modern schools first but still believed in 13 as the appropriate age of entry to a technical school. But neither of these views was to influence the 1944 Act.

The Green Book was presented in June 1941 to Herwald Ramsbotham, the then President of the Board of Education. He was succeeded by R.A. Butler in the next month, 20 July 1941. Butler wrote to Churchill indicating his intentions and priorities, 'there is, first, the need for industrial and technical training and the linking up of schools closely with employment' and Churchill replied approvingly.[39] Butler took this seriously. He had just asked H.B. Wallis for an explanation of the technical school system which Wallis provided[40] along with two key memoranda setting out the Technical Branch view and which influenced Butler's receptive mind on the issue.[41]

Wallis pitched in enthusiastically, 'I take it that there will be general agreement that Junior Technical Schools have been a success.' He thought that they should be kept specific in purpose and not 'generalised' (Butler wondered what this meant) to imitate the broader education of the secondary schools. On the other hand they should not be too narrow either, 'we want good and adaptable recruits to an industry not to a trade within it'. He noted that there was a large amount of evening technical work in mining, textiles and footwear and wondered whether such industries might not benefit from some JTS pre-employment training. He also thought that JTSs would be suitable for agriculture and Butler thought this worth considering. Butler was not originally greatly in favour of JTSs. In September 1941 he wrote

> I am not convinced that we can or should introduce a series of new Technical *Schools*. But there is a strong case for developing secondary schools with a technical bias, then putting the products at 16 into industry with an obligation in the case of apprentices to attend technical *colleges*.[42]

However, Wallis reinforced his advocacy of the technical school with a further memorandum after Butler had taken office and which the President read and annotated carefully.[43] Wallis told Butler that 'it is common ground that the provision of Junior Technical Schools should in their new form of Technical Schools be *greatly extended*'. Butler underlined the last two words in red pen as was his practice with things which especially interested him. Technical schools provide the 'higher grade of craftsman and of those who pass from the workshop, often through the drawing office to positions of responsibility as foremen, submanagers and so on'. Trade schools were appropriate for London but mostly JTSs trained '*young people for an industry rather than for a more specialised occupation*' (Butler's underlining again). The British system created the 'adaptable recruit', capable of '*horizontal* mobility' between branches of the same industry. Butler liked that. As the age of apprenticeship was rising, so staying on at technical schools could be extended to 16. Moreover more pupils in JTSs would result in more use of technical colleges during the day rather than merely at night. Butler appreciated this point too. These were the kind of positive ideas about technical schools which Butler was receiving and largely agreeing with in his first year in office.

The further education of the new President in the importance of technical schools was powerfully reinforced in February 1942. Several officials, R.S. Wood, E.G. Savage, H.B. Wallis and Sir Frank Tribe, sought to modify the natural academic élitism of the former Fellow of Corpus into yet more appreciation of the importance of the technical sector. They deplored 'the present system under which the abler brighter children are selected from the elementary schools at the age of 11+ and put into secondary schools diverting this ability almost entirely to the professional, clerical and office occupations'. This had deprived manufacturing industry of talent, a loss which the country could not afford. They emphasized their point that the education system 'has concentrated almost entirely on the elite or potentially elite with too little regard to the needs of the rank and file'.[44] The point struck home and Butler marked this in red. They regretted that the JTS had not developed very far and stressed that the JTS 'undoubtedly provides a training much better adapted to subsequent industrial employment than the normal School Certificate course of the grammar school'. Butler marked this in red also.

This was a remarkable exercise in the education of the new President. His whole academic background would have made him incline to public and grammar schools with little knowledge or a sympathy for the technical, manual education of non-academic teenagers for industrial jobs. Wallis, Wood and others kept before him the claims of industrial education against academic élitism and he seems to have been receptive to them.

IV

Another influence on Butler was his great Parliamentary Secretary James Chuter Ede. Chuter Ede was Labour MP for South Shields and a former teacher himself. Nobody in Butler's entourage had such a practical experience of education. It certainly sounded as though Butler needed it. At their first meeting Butler had 'not yet grasped the difference between elementary and secondary' which did not restrain him from proposing a 'larger measure of reform which he hoped to introduce'.[45] In his conversations with Butler and officials at the Board Ede emphasized the need for practical, technical education. He told Butler that 'we had to reserve them (pupils) from the extraordinary prevalent fallacy that the most skillful craftsman was the inferior socially of the most influential clerk'[46] and 'we must avoid sending all our brighter children into the academic stream'.[47] He had similar conversations with R.S. Wood on 16 October 1941 and 1 April 1942. However Chuter Ede did not believe in the JTS as the best solution. He wanted technical education either diffused through all types of secondary schools or ideally provided in multilateral schools.[48] When R.S. Wood told him that the evacuated civil servants of the Board in Bournemouth were inclining to the idea of the 'secondary school polytechnic' Ede was pleased: 'I said they were an inevitable development'.[49] A few months later in discussion with Butler and Sir Maurice Holmes he was quite explicit, 'as far as technical education was concerned I hoped the JTS work would be done in the secondary school and not in a separate school'.[50] Ede's view was to be crucial in the rewording of the Education Bill.

V

In October 1941 the Conservative Party set up a Central Committee on Post War Problems, to report on political, social and economic problems created by the war. This had various sub committees and in January 1942 Butler set up the Educational Sub-Committee under the chairmanship of the publisher Geoffrey Faber. Their first two reports on *Educational Aims* and *A Plan for Youth*, both published in September 1942, were not relevant for technical education. The third report on *The Statutory Education System*, published in January 1944, was arguably the best.[51] This was very keen on JTSs. It claimed that 'an expansion of the Junior Technical Schools to an extent far beyond anything envisaged in 1939 must surely be a central part of the immediate post-war programme' for

> not until this expansion is sufficient to enable the Junior Technical Schools to take their full share in post primary education, alongside the fully reorganised senior (or modern) schools, shall we be in a position to say that the machinery of post primary education is properly assembled.

The JTS was an 'immediate and urgent need'. Faber re-emphasized this to Butler shortly after: 'the wishes of the committee are clear. There must be a great increase here and the technical schools must come to rival the grammar schools'.[52]

The Committee was also proposing to publish a report specifically on technical education. James Pitman, a former Treasury civil servant, was working on it, but the resulting draft was unsatisfactory. Pitman tried to argue that 'culturalists control the educational machine' and this had stifled vocational education and the JTS in particular, which he deplored! There was a kernel of truth there, but H.B. Wallis advised Butler that Pitman was masking thin research behind an 'ill informed' and 'virulent attack' and was ignorant of developments in the field since 1902.[53]

Butler was relieved that Pitman's report 'has been blown skyhigh' by the Committee and it was never published.[54] Yet the strong messages that Butler was receiving from his sub-committee in the good sense of Faber's third report, and even in the extremes of Pitman's, was that JTSs were totally worthwhile, had been held back and should be expanded.

VI

Another influence on Butler came from outside, from Nuffield College, Oxford, and the activities of the socialist economist G.D.H. Cole. Nuffield had set up a Social Reconstruction Survey from February 1941 with Cole as Chairman and Director.[55] This had groups of investigators reporting on the effects of the war on educational services. But he also ran a series of conferences of privately invited academics, industrialists, civil servants and others to discuss policy issues relevant to postwar reconstruction. One of the most important of these was on industry and education, and it inevitably had views about technical schools.

Cole's meetings referred to JTS matters from time to time. In particular, at a meeting on 27 June 1942, E.G. Savage told them about the virtues of the JTS, and Paley Yorke reminisced about early engineering schools in which he was a pioneer. This clearly impressed Cole who concluded: 'We must learn a culture appropriate to the twentieth century . . . Junior Technical Schools had a part to play.'[56] This was the more remarkable in that the Left and the WEA in particular had a long tradition of scepticism and hostility to the JTS, but the schools were favourably presented to the conferences.

This carried through to the Report arising from the meetings. In this Cole said that 'We look forward to a very great development' of JTSs. He took a rather soft interpretation of their purpose downplaying their occupational and craft preparation role and playing up 'a wide instruction in mathematics and basic science'.[57] But he emphasized the need to '*raise the prestige of high manual skill*' and welcomed the 'proposal to create *Technical High Schools*' (more of Butler's interested underlining in both cases). Butler was more impressed by Cole's activities than one might have expected. The Board officials regarded Cole as an interfering busybody, Cyril Norwood had quarrelled with him and complained to Butler about him.[58] Yet Butler's father-in-law, Samuel Courtauld, who was a Visiting Fellow at Nuffield, attended Cole's meetings and told Butler of their 'interesting discussions', a compliment Butler relayed to Cole.[59] Moreover Samuel Courtauld at this time was advocating the state responsibility for running technical schools to replace the industrialists' former responsibility for the old apprenticeship system.[60] Butler clearly read and annotated Cole's report with interest and its favourable comments about technical schools would have reinforced similar signals he was receiving from within the Board.

VII

Butler seems to have been increasingly converted to the idea of the JTS. Although he praised technical education in general terms he made no specific reference to the JTS in speeches after his appointment as President on 20 July 1941. But on 27 March 1942 he attended and spoke at a BACIE Conference on recruitment and training for industry.[61] Butler's own introductory speech was rather general but he heard virtually all subsequent speakers praise and emphasize the importance of the JTS in the strongest terms. W. Davis of the building industry told him that 'the recruitment into the industry of youths . . . will come in the main through our Junior Technical Schools', another speaker called for 'an enormous expansion development of Junior Technical Schools' and the new JCS in Bristol was lavishly praised.

This seems to have been something of a turning point in Butler's mind, since in the next year from October 1942 to October 1943 he not only started referring to JTSs but advocating them forcefully even to unreceptive audiences. At the meeting of the Union of Lancashire and Cheshire Institutes at Wigan in October 1942 he deplored the tiny (8,000) output of the JTSs and the unnecessary length of apprenticeship and told his audience 'there will have to be a considerable extension . . . of the numbers of pupils passing through their Junior Technical Schools'.[62] He repeated much the same in speeches later that month to the Federation of Education Committees for Wales[63] and to the Institute of the Plastics Industry.[64]

In addressing businessmen in the cotton industry he became even more forceful. Theirs was an industry of poor and declining technical education matching feeble economic performance. He told them

> in the reconstructed system of education which will be established after the War there will, it is certain, be room for a greatly increased provision of Junior Technical Schools . . . we should surely have a thoroughly effective scheme of Junior Technical Schools in the main centres of Lancashire . . . the constellations of Junior Technical Schools shall sparkle and gyrate.[65]

This last bit of lyricism may have been intended to uplift the grey Manchester businessmen who were the custodians of the failing fag-end of a once great industry. He urged them to become better acquainted with JTSs and placed before them the comparison with the building and engineering industries where the JTSs had been so successful in providing a young labour force. He continued his theme in a speech in Birmingham later in the year and even, more surprisingly in a lunchtime lecture at St Paul's Cathedral.[66] It is without doubt that between 1942 and 1943 Butler had changed from being indifferent to or simply ignorant of JTSs to being their keen supporter and advocate.

R.A. Butler had inherited the Spens Report and the Green Book but he felt the need for an investigation of his own. Accordingly in 1941 he asked Sir Cyril Norwood to look into the secondary school curriculum and examinations. Norwood was a notable headmaster of Bristol Grammar School, Marlborough and Harrow before becoming President of St John's College, Oxford. He had no particular experience of technical schools. But long before being approached by Butler he had already expressed views which suggested a sympathetic understanding of their role. He reflected that 'all education is vocational in reference to life', teaching for specific occupations was quite appropriate, more boys ought to have their practical abilities developed 'by more extended teaching of handicraft'.[67] He also, rather surprisingly, thought that the standard of mathematics and science in public and grammar schools was too high to be of use to most pupils.[68] Very much an academic Establishment figure, Norwood harboured some rather radical opinions and a sympathy with other less academic traditions.

The setting up of Norwood's committee affronted Sir Will Spens. He went to see Butler in 'great alarm' concerned that Butler's commission to Norwood was an indication that he regarded that Spens Report of 1938 and his whole chairmanship of the Consultative Committee had been inadequate.[69] The emollient Butler smoothly reassured his seething, icily autocratic former Master but the tensions resonated. Sir Walter Citrine told Butler that Norwood's re-opening of Spens was unnecessary[70] and the Secretary of Norwood's committee wondered whether the rivalry of Spens and Norwood 'is so great that the course of education is likely to suffer'.[71] This was the serious point behind these tensions of *amour propre.* So committed was Spens to the technical school that there was a danger that bad feeling might damage this concept and policy. Fortunately Norwood and Butler were sufficiently broad-minded not to let this happen.

Norwood seems originally to have taken a narrow view of his task as largely concerned with grammar schools.[72] However, Board officials of the Technical Branch met Norwood to describe the role of the JTSs to him and their role in building and engineering.[73] Norwood anyway could scarcely neglect the JTS as he received a flood of opinion from interested parties. There were those who were hostile or who regarded the JTS as irrelevant. These included those in favour of multilateral or comprehensive schools, notably the TUC.[74] At the other pole were a number of grammar school masters who saw no need for technical schools since all their work could be absorbed by grammar and modern schools.[75] In the middle were others happy with Spens tripartism and the separate JTS.[76]

The strongest submission received by Norwood was from the psychologist and Director of Education for Sheffield, Dr. W.P. Alexander.[77] He was the psychologist who perhaps most firmly believed in the existence of the 'practical or technical factor' in mental capabilities. In his view there was not only general intelligence (g) but in some this was specifically combined with technical ability (F) and this was 'the justification of a case for the creation of Technical Secondary Schools' to cater for gF types. Moreover he was unusual in his view that this ability was detectable at 11 or younger. Finally he stressed that this technical ability was not inferior to academic ability. The difference between grammar schools and technical schools on the one hand and modern schools on the other was one of *degree* of ability. The difference between the grammar school and the technical school was one of *type* of ability within the same level. This certainly needed saying, and Alexander's submission was one of the strongest and best-argued pieces to influence Norwood. It is sometimes said that Norwood, unlike Hadow and Spens, took no psychological advice for his report.[78] Certainly Cyril Burt (who was in Aberystwyth at the time) was not invited and took no initiative to express a view. Norwood himself took psychology seriously as

a subject. In the late 1930s he would refer Harrow boys to the National Institute of Industrial Psychology for vocational guidance tests.[79] In the end it was Alexander's psychological justification of the JTS which influenced Norwood and was translated into a policy recommendation.

The officials around the Norwood Committee were also clarifying their views. R.S. Wood saw this as an opportunity to develop the JTS.[80] R.H. Barrow, the Secretary of the Committee was clear that there had to be at least two distinct types of school, 'the good old Grammar School' and a technical and/or commercial school, since technical studies could not be absorbed into grammar schools without destroying their nature.[81] A pretty firm anti-multilateral position was commonly held, not least by Norwood himself who had endured two hours with the abrasive Sir Percival Sharp who 'spits on multilateralism, having been to America.'[82]

Accordingly the Committee began to hammer out its views. They liked the Spens term 'Secondary Technical School' since 'such nomenclature would bring technical education and modern schools into parallel with existing so called secondary schools'.[83] They rejected multilateralism.[84] They saw the drawbacks of technical school entry at 13 but agreed that '13 plus was to be regarded as the right age for entry to Technical Schools'.[85] They wanted the retention of separate high status technical schools and were receptive to Chief HMI Elliott's view that such schools should not be made into pale reflections of grammar schools 'so losing their specific character which depended on close touch with industry'.[86]

Sir Cyril's Report of 1943 accordingly took a most supportive view of the technical school.[87] He divided human intelligence into three types - the academic, mechanical and concrete. The mechanically inclined boy 'has an uncanny insight into the intricacies of mechanism . . . the knowledge and its application which most appeal to him are the control of material things'. Accordingly such children should have a curriculum 'directed to the special data and skills associated with a particular kind of occupation . . . it would thus be closely related to industry, trades and commerce in all their diversity'. So they advocated three types of schooling - the grammar, secondary technical and secondary modern - with 'parity of esteem' between them.

In the secondary technical school they proposed a lower school of 11+ to 13+. This would overcome the old problem of the different age of entry between the technical school and other forms of secondary education, but also meet the objection of premature technical specialization at ll. They reaffirmed the aims of the technical school 'to give a training for entry into industry and commerce at the age of 16+ to meet the demands of local industrial conditions'. But they envisaged also that technical schools could lead to advanced work in technical colleges and universities. They also approved of commercial education in technical and commercial schools.

Norwood handed on to Butler a strong endorsement of the tripartite structure, grammar–technical–modern. Yet the great value of the Report was that, in spite of the suspicions of Spens, Norwood so strongly backed the technical school as part of this triad. He did so partly on commonsense psychology and Alexander's views on the existence of technical faculties of mind. Cyril Burt responded critically suggesting that the mental types Norwood believed in could not be detected for selection at 11.[88] Burt's biographer suggests that he was 'actuated by pique'[89] because of Norwood's neglect of Burt's view. It was indeed perverse for Burt to approve of Spens and disapprove of Norwood.

The real danger of Norwood lay elsewhere. One of his categories of intelligence was the 'concrete'. This is sometimes taken as a euphemism for children who were 'dense' or 'thick'. In fact it was a term in serious academic psychology of the time and Norwood may have learnt of the terms 'abstract' and 'concrete' through Alexander's work to which the latter referred in his submission to Norwood.[90] The problem was that Norwood's description of the concrete intelligence, with its emphasis on the practical, was insufficiently distinguished from the technical. The result was that in turn the justification of the secondary modern school became insufficiently distinctive compared with the technical school. This was to prove a factor undermining the specific role of the technical school in the postwar years.

VIII

Throughout 1943 the Education Bill went through 14 drafts and it is interesting to see how junior technical schools were provided for as they evolved.[91] In the first draft of 24 February 1943 JTSs were actually specified for the only time. Local education authorities had to ensure

> that there shall exist for their area an adequate supply of Junior Technical Schools, that is to say, schools for providing secondary education of a technical or commercial character for senior pupils who are expected to continue their full time education until they attain the age of sixteen years.

In Butler's annotation the word 'junior' was put in brackets. Accordingly in this first draft Butler had been prepared to accept the idea that the Act would make JTSs a mandatory form for the provision of technical education. However at this point Chuter Ede intervened. He did not like the specific reference to differentiated types of schools including the JTS. He wanted something more generalized and discretionary. So on the same evening, 24 February 1943, he devised a new wording. LEAs were to provide

> secondary education of sufficient variety of type as to secure sufficient choice of studies suitable to the ages, abilities, aptitudes and requirements of the pupils, including at appropriate stages, practical technical or commercial instruction . . .[92]

Sir Maurice Holmes agreed with this the next day and the day after that, Friday 26th, Butler, Holmes, RS Wood and other officials - but not Ede - met to approve a new wording based on Ede's changes. This was that LEAs should provide 'schools for providing for senior pupils education of such variety of type as to secure a choice of studies and practical courses suitable to the ages, abilities, aptitudes and requirements of the pupils'.[93] Ede in turn approved this the next Monday, 1 March.

Consequently in the second draft of 24 March there was no reference to junior technical schools specifically but some key words, 'practical training . . . as is appropriate for him in view of his age, aptitudes and requirements' made their appearance. The later famous phrase 'ages, abilities and aptitudes' already devised by Ede in February 1943 did not appear in print until the eleventh draft of 1 October 1943. All this crystallized into the core of the subsequent Act, Clause 8(1) of the fourteenth draft of 26 November 1943. This required LEAs to provide pupils with 'opportunities for education offering such variety of instruction and training as may be desirable in view of their different ages, abilities and aptitudes . . . including practical instruction and training appropriate to their retrospective needs'. Accordingly LEAs were not obliged to establish JTSs - as the first draft would have had them do. But the wording of Clause 8(1) gave discretion for those who wished to do so. The Act made JTSs permissable but not mandatory; the perhaps surprising point is that the latter was once contemplated.

In the spring of 1943 Ede was already telling Butler and others that 'I did not think many new Junior Technical Schools would be established. The Secondary Schools (whether modern or academic) would have practical and technical sides to them'.[94] Ede's changing of the first draft had made this a possible solution. Ede's dislike of tripartitism was curiously tied up with his dislike of Sir Robert Morant whom he regarded as a 'thug'.[95] There was no doubting Ede's commitment to technical education but his removal of the reference to the JTS from the Act made possible the decline of the form after 1945. His attitudes and his power were a root of the postwar assumption that technical education could be adequately provided in other secondary schools and especially in future comprehensive schools.

IX

In July 1943 the White Paper *Educational Reconstruction* was published as a preparation for the Act.[96] It presented the junior technical schools in a favourable light. It found them praiseworthy - 'their success has been remarkable' – in spite of the handicap of the recruitment age of 13. It hoped that they would develop more rapidly with altered conditions and a uniform age of entry at ll. The Paper was clear that too many able children were attracted to the academic education of the grammar school which overshadowed other types of secondary schooling. By contrast 'too few find their way into schools from which the design and craftsmanship sides of industry are recruited . . . some means must be found of correcting this bias'. The Paper had had little to say of technical school education but that had been encouraging.

The Commons debate on the White Paper was more disappointing for technical school advocates. R.A. Butler praised the schools.[97] He thought that there were too few of them (379) 'that figure is far too low and it is our desire to see these junior technical schools as constellations surrounding the new technical colleges which we hope will be built up in our great cities and which will be the universities of industry'. However this visionary flame did not ignite the rest of the debate. Butler said that Chuter Ede, his Parliamentary Secretary, would say more of JTSs later in the debate, but oddly he never did. The only other three speakers to refer to them did so sceptically, deploring the early specialization and materialism they feared would characterize these schools.[98] Thelma Cazalet-Keir, who was one of them, was a 'progressive' Conservative who unusually favoured comprehensive schools and so shared some of the Left's suspicions of premature technical schooling'.[99] 'It would be fatal if we were to turn out a generation of children who were experienced in the radio and the internal combustion engine but had not a real feeling for the humanities' intervened Mr Linstead of Putney piously. The Commons debate gave Butler no support over technical schools.

Nor did the Lords, who had no interest in the matter with the exception of Lord Selborne, Minister of Economic Warfare. He deplored the 'great dearth of technical schools' which had resulted 'in starving our industries of that skilled craftsmanship which used to be the glory of Old England', and called for less emphasis on academic education and more prestige for the craftsman.[100] He was repeating themes he had recently expressed in the debate on problems of youth in the previous February.[101] But he was an honourable exception.

The White Paper and the subsequent Parliamentary debates were a disappointment to technical education enthusiasts. The four-year plan for education after the war was concerned with raising the school leaving age, yet neglected technical education. Officials expressed 'disappointment and apprehension at the deferment and inadequacy of the provision for technical education proper'.[102] It was deplored that only £100,000 had been allocated to the whole of technical education in the White Paper.[103] H.B. Wallis pointed out that this small sum included JTSs as well and that this was due to Treasury pressure.[104] R.S. Wood agree that the impression had been given that technical education was a low priority in postwar plans. It prompted Butler defensively to assert that he was going to press forward with technical schools in the postwar rearrangements.[105]

The Parliamentary debates on the Education Bill of 1943 and the subsequent 1944 Act had virtually nothing to say on technical schools specifically. Chuter Ede referred to 'the school with a strong technical side' and Mr Silkin wanted assurances that technical schools would not be inferior in status to grammar schools.[106] That was about it. Nobody else referred to them nor did the Lords debate. The Act itself framed the educational system in very general terms. There were merely to be 'three progressive stages to be known as primary education, secondary education and further education'. What secondary education was to consist of was left to LEAs so long as it was appropriate to the 'different ages, abilities and aptitudes' of the children.[107]

It is now well appreciated that the 1944 Education Act was not solely the brainchild of R.A. Butler assuming office as President of the Board of Education in July 1941.[108] It was the product of a long evolution of policy from the evidence gathered by Spens in the late 1930s through to the Act itself. Secondly much of the work, the drafting of memoranda, debating and clarifying issues and lobbying was done by the Board officials - Maurice Holmes, G.G. Williams, R.S. Wood, H.B. Wallis and the Inspector E.G. Savage -with the last three especially pressing the claims of technical schools. This is not to belittle the role of Butler - and his annotating red pen - who had to win over Churchill and the House of Commons, nor his Parliamentary Secretary Chuter Ede whose role is now better recognized as crucial. Butler's personal role was much more concerned with the religious issues of the Act. But it is clear that in spite of little public attention paid to them in the Commons debates of 1944 the technical schools received a disproportionate amount of private, favourable discussion behind the scenes. There were reasonable hopes that in the postwar years the technical schools would take their place as part of a genuinely tripartite structure. But this was not to be.

CHAPTER 7

Change and Decay, 1945–1960s

I do not have a clear idea of the importance of these schools
Sir David Eccles, 20 December 1954[1]

it is therefore now pretty clear that not only do technical schools not yet enter into the picture in most cases but that they never will
Ministry of Education to G.L. Payne, *c*.1960[2]

I

The Education Act of 1944 did not specify or require any particular form of secondary education since it was always intended that this should be left to the discretion of local education authorities.[3] Butler himself was rather inclined to the comprehensive school. He was keen to leave this option open in the White Paper of 1943 and the Act, and when comprehensivization became general in the 1960s he welcomed it as 'an improvement on the original tripartite divisions'.[4] Yet at the end of the war the assumption, following Spens and Norwood, was that LEAs would devise combinations of grammar, secondary modern and technical schools - the tripartite system.

The implementation of the 1944 Act brought about changes in the old JTSs. They were renamed secondary technical schools which made them unambiguously part of the secondary education system and removed the lower status overtones of 'junior'. More importantly the contentious age of entry was at last reduced from 13 to 11. So the two- or three-year course, 13 to 15 or 16, was replaced with a four- or five-year course, 11 to 15 or 16. Pupils now entered the secondary technical school after the 11+ examination and such schools need no longer feel the disadvantage (as in the 1930s) that potentially good entrants had already been creamed off to the grammar school two years earlier.

The new Ministry of Education (which replaced the Board in 1945) explained the options in its first pamphlet, *The Nation's Schools*. It suggested that there was no case for increasing the intake into grammar schools. They had over-expanded in the interwar years, yet a quarter of their pupils left before the age of 16 and 40 per cent of their 16-year-olds did not take School Certificate. The grammar schools were over-producing the clerical, black-coated workers and not those going into productive manufacturing industry. 'On the other hand', they thought, 'there is without any doubt ample scope for a very substantial increase in the provision made for secondary courses broadly described as technical.'[5] *The Nation's Schools* took a high view of technical schools, devoting four pages to them, compared with two and a half pages each to the grammar school and the secondary modern.

Equally influential was Lord Eustace Percy's report on Higher Technological Education in 1945 which likewise accorded an important role to the secondary technical school. Since the 1930s Percy had been an advocate of JTSs providing a flow of technology students to technological universities[6] and he pressed this argument in the more receptive atmosphere of the postwar years. He praised the emergence of the secondary technical school out of the old JTSs and hoped that they would gain equal status to the grammar schools. He said,

> an important contribution to industry's needs should come from students from the Secondary Technical Schools who proceed to Colleges of Technology. Indeed this new avenue to higher education is an essential part of the plans necessary for supplying to industry in future a steady flow of recruits of high quality.[7]

In early 1946 Ministry officials clarified their views about the new secondary technical schools in the light of *The Nation's Schools* and the Percy Report. Antony Part, one of the keenest supporters of the STS, raised some of these issues with Sir Robert Wood the new Permanent Secretary.[8] Part especially respected Wood as one of the few officials genuinely keen on technical education. The age of entry was still a problem. Eleven-plus had been taken as the age of entry to the new STS though psychologists still did not believe it possible to select children until 13. Part was also concerned that 85 per cent of old JTSs were in Technical Colleges and it was undesirable that this continue. The new STSs needed to be separate schools in their own right especially since they now accommodated young children for whom the more adult atmosphere of the technical college was inappropriate. Thirdly the JTS had been especially related to the engineering and construction industries and Part wondered whether they could not be more related to other industries like textiles and motor cars. Wood replied, 'Yes, experiment.'

The much more ambitious conception of the STS that was being entertained by the Ministry was revealed in other issues explored. Part asked whether they wanted STSs to develop sixth forms with appropriate examinations. Wood replied 'Yes - with Universities.' And when Part suggested that 'there are likely to be quite a few boys who after attending a Secondary Technical School, will hope to go on to University' Wood agreed. A concomitant of this would be the need for more graduates in STS staff. Finally Part drew the conclusion that the schools would have to be larger, with three stream entries to justify the expensive machinery and staff. Indeed Part thought that STSs ought to be 750–800 pupils in size.[9] Part was concerned that the STS should not merely be 'a sort of hotted up JTS with what is in effect a preparatory department'.[10] This was the new concept being pushed by Antony Part with Sir Robert Wood's agreement - much larger, genuine secondary schools with their own buildings, 11+ entry, establishing links with a wider range of industries, with sixth forms, graduate staff and preparing to expand the nation's supply of university graduate scientists.

The Nations Schools (1945) was followed by a sequel *The New Secondary Education* (1947)[11] This later pamphlet was written in the Ministerial period of office of Ellen Wilkinson (3 August 1945-10 February 1947), who approved it, and issued by her successor George Tomlinson. This too presented a lengthy favourable view of the technical school emphasizing their new buildings and broad education. Presaging the future it suggested that bilateral technical grammar schools may be the way forward. With encouraging enthusiasm the 1947 re-write suggested optimistically and prematurely that the new secondary technical schools were 'an important factor in the development plans of the local education authorities'. But were they?

Local education authorities were required to devise development plans for the implementation of the Act. Joan Thompson analysed 111 of these plans and from these we can see the relative importance of the new technical school in the thinking of the LEAS (see Table 7.1). It was already evident that technical schools were to be a very minor part of the tripartite structure. They were to be about half the number of schools and pupils as grammar schools and only about a seventh of those in secondary modern schools. Another tiny sliver of technical school activity was to be provided in grammar-technical schools and rather more in so called technical-modern schools. But these hybrids were to prove no substitutes for the pure form. It was

Table 7.1 *Local education authority plans for implementing the 1944 Education Act*

Type of school	In county council plans		In county borough plans		In all 3 development plans including London	
	Schools (%)	Places (%)	Schools (%)	Places (%)	Schools (%)	Places (%)
Grammar	16	14	15	14.5	15	13
Technical	5.5	7.5	11	9.5	7	7.5
Modern	58.5	55.5	61.5	56	56	51
Grammar Technical	3.5	3.5	1.5	1.5	2.5	2.5
Technical Modern	9	9.5	7.5	8.5	8.5	8.5
Grammar Modern	2.5	3	0.5	1	2	2
Comprehensive	4	6	3	7	5.5	12.5

Source: Joan Thompson, *Secondary Education Survey* (London, 1952). This analysis incorporates and extends her earlier survey *Secondary Education for All* (London, 1947).

well said that 'the system which evolved after 1945 was virtually a bipartite one because LEAs displayed little enthusiasm for establishing technical schools'.[12]

Nor were the early Labour Ministers of Education especially keen on the secondary technical school. Ellen Wilkinson came to office (1945–7) with few ideas about education. She accepted the tripartite system, yet was sceptical of secondary technical schools as a separate stream, 'the idea of boys building pig sties or making beehives and wheelbarrows and of girls doing laundry work or catering infuriated her'.[13] She increasingly thought of bilateral arrangements of technical streams in grammar schools to ensure flexibility and generosity of secondary education. Her successor George Tomlinson (1947–51) evinced no special interest in secondary technical schools and shared the same reservations about too much vocational education in schools.[14] He specifically disapproved of using the extra year 'to provide vocational courses of a narrow kind'.[15] He himself had left school at 12 or 13 to go to work in a cotton mill and knew the stultifying effect of the premature encroachment of employment on the young developing mind. The Ministers of the 1940s should not be criticized too much. They were rightly concerned with raising the school leaving age, getting more teachers and temporary buildings. It was not a period in which the cause of school technical education received any great enthusiastic push from the top.

II

The crucial debate and decision about STSs came about under Sir David Eccles in 1955. He had become Minister of Education in October 1954 and shortly after, in December, he raised the issue of the role and future of the STS.[16]

Although he had no clear idea about the schools when he began, he asked the pertinent questions. There was a shortage of trained craftsmen and engineers and he wondered what role the STS could play. He was puzzled that only 5 per cent of schoolchildren went to such schools, a proportion 'so low that it shows this to be a national problem which calls for a policy that directs action beyond the boundaries of many authorities'. He queried what lay behind this figure of 5 per cent, 'if some such proportion was right 25 years ago when industry was less complicated and took more apprentices how can it be right today?' He also questioned whether a technical school needed to be separate or whether they could be combined with modern or grammar schools. He guessed that children from low cultured backgrounds but with some practical abilities could do well in technical schools, 'this is one reason why technical schools attract me'. In this way Sir David Eccles initiated the debate with his officials.

Some insight into David Eccles's state of mind at this time may be gained from a series of questions tabled for him to help him to clarify his views.[17] He thought that 25 per cent was too high a proportion going to selective grammar and technical schools. He accepted the Spens suggestion that some grammar schools could be converted to technical schools. Yet he did not know whether it was desirable for grammar schools to develop technical sides or whether separate technical schools should be encouraged - this last had important resonances for the future.

The debate began early with a contribution by A. G. Gooch, the HMI most notably keen on the STS. He surveyed the familiar (though not to Eccles) reasons for the rise of the JTSs and their prewar problems and indicated that the Inspectorate did not favour bilateral technical-modern schools. He gave an interesting snapshot of the state of the STSs in the early 1950s based on a survey of 71 of them. Only 14 per cent had their own buildings and only 32 per cent had sixth forms. Yet 53 per cent were doing GCE work and 60 per cent were teaching languages, usually French. In this time of transition 70 per cent of classes were still being admitted at 13 and 30 per cent at the new age of 11. Eccles having been well briefed, the debate began in earnest in the New Year 1955 with a barrage of memoranda in January preliminary to a Minister's meeting in February. All were agreed on the need for more technical education at the secondary level but the issue was whether to do this by developing secondary technical schools or by incorporating this work into that of grammar schools.[18] The two attitudes began to polarize.

Arguing in favour of the bilateral grammar-technical school were D.H. Morrell, Toby Weaver and A. R. Maxwell Hyslop. Those for the STS were Antony Part and HMI A. Bray. Morrell took a subtle line.[19] He argued that there had been a confusion since the Butler Act between 'ability levels' and 'aptitude types'. That is to say people of the same aptitude may display it at quite different ability levels. Similarly people of the same ability and intelligence might manifest it in quite different aptitudes. The technical school had been regarded as 'essentially an aptitude school' and the root problem had been that the technical aptitude had been regarded as indicative of a lower level of ability than the academic. Morrell then embarked on a logical path which impressed Eccles. If STSs attracted first rate ability then this is what grammar schools already did. So if grammar schools were not providing for those with first rate ability who also had an aptitude for technology then they should be encouraged to do so, since it is not desirable for technologists to be educated 'divorced from the liberal tradition of the grammar school course'. If on the other hand the STS was offering lower level courses than those of the grammar school then they should be done in modern schools. He concluded 'I suspect that this (the STS) will prove to be a side turning. The main road seems to me to be the development of a wider range of courses, biased towards particular subjects in both grammar and modern schools'. Toby Weaver shared this view.[20] He agreed that Britain needed more craftsmen and engineers but this should not be at the expense of 'the humanities'. He deplored the divorce between technology and the humanities that separate grammar and technical schools embodied. He concluded, as Morrell had done, 'cannot the answer be found in a liberalised and technologised grammar school whether or not it is organised or labelled as a grammar technical bilateral?'.

The defence of the STS lay chiefly with Antony Part.[21] He argued that the separate STS was desirable on two grounds. Firstly the grammar school was not good at technical education. The grammar school tradition was in the arts, pure science and the professions producing 'cutters up of the cake and not enlargers of it'. Secondly, scarce industrial teaching staff needed to be concentrated in STSs; it was not available to be spread around hundreds of grammar schools. Part's programme (already indicated in his memoranda in 1946) was to increase STSs, have more sixth form and GCE work and to relate to them a wider range of industries. HMI Bray strongly supported Part. Technical schools made boys industry-minded, 'we know that almost 100 per cent of the old JTS pupils entered industry . . . and we can assume that had those pupils been successful in the grammar school entry at 11+ they would most likely have gone into some other occupation'.[22] He was right, as the figures in Table 4.12 suggest.

The Permanent Secretary, Sir Gilbert Flemming, pulled all this together for his Minister with a bias towards the grammar technical school.[23] He thought that the case for separate STSs depended on the industrial backgrounds of particular localities but the STS could not be relied upon as the main source of technologists. The grammar school was already there and could be brought up to date. The Minister and his officials then had a debate at the end of February in which the foregoing arguments were again rehearsed.[24] Eccles weighed up the views and came to the conclusion that the bilateral grammar technical school and not the STS was the way forward. He may also have been influenced by the Federation of British Industry view which was also that 'the bilateral grammar technical schools appeared the happy solution'.[25] Antony Part's clear and courageous defence of the STS had evidently become a minority view, but in hindsight he was probably right.

Sir David made his policy very clear in a speech to the NUT at Scarborough in April 1955.

> Everyone is agreed that what technical schools teach is valuable and likely to grow more so in the modern world: but there is no agreement as to the extent to which this education should be given in separate schools. My conclusion is as follows: the pioneer stage in technical education is over; the experience has been so great a success that we ought now to distribute technical courses over as many schools as possible . . . The technical schools we have today are doing splendid work and long may they flourish. There will be rare cases where the local need is so strong as to call for a new technical school, but I hope the general policy will be to distribute technical courses over as many courses as possible.[26]

In the light of this LEAs reasonably began to wonder whether to pursue STS policies that would be regarded as 'rare cases' rather than part of 'general policy'. This firm Ministerial steer was more precisely reinforced by various questions which Toby Weaver intended to pose to LEAs.

> Would you not do better to enlarge your grammar schools by the addition of technical courses? . . . If you are sure that there is room for a separate technical school, does your proposal make sense in the light of the industrial background and traditions of the neighbourhood? . . . Are you sure that a grammar technical school would not provide a better chance of attracting a fairer share of the abler boys into technical courses?

These questions sounded deliberately biased and Weaver admitted that they were 'loaded slightly in favour of bilateral grammar schools'. LEAs were intended to receive a strong Ministry message that the STS was not favoured and the grammar technical school was preferred.[27]

One body that was most concerned about this shift of policy was the Association of Headmasters of Secondary Technical Schools. Their position prior to the debate was quite clear. They considered that 'wherever possible secondary technical education should be provided in secondary technical schools. In areas where it is not possible, bilateral grammar technical schools should be provided.'[28] Sir David received a deputation of STS headmasters on 5 December 1955.[29] He sought to reassure them that he valued their achievements but he wanted grammar schools and technical schools to draw closer together. The fundamental point that emerged was the Minister's frank admission that 'he was strongly opposed to the organisation of secondary education into three tiers' since this would result in STSs being the poor relations of the grammar school and deprive the modern schools of the chance of building up attractive courses. The implication was evident. Eccles did not believe in a tripartite structure and certainly not in comprehensives, but in a dual structure of grammar schools and secondary moderns with technical subjects being catered for at different levels in each.

One or two things are remarkable about this shift of policy, one of the most important of the postwar years. Eccles moved with remarkable rapidity from a state of almost total ignorance to a very firm policy view within the short space of two months. Moreover he had never visited a secondary technical school to see something of their work. The Cabinet never discussed the matter, or indeed any educational matter at all in the whole of Eccles' period as Minister of Education.[30] This may account for the odd feature that the Conservative Party manifesto later in 1955 claimed that 'to prepare for the increasing opportunities of the modern world we need all three kinds of Secondary school, grammar, modern and technical'. Yet David Eccles no longer thought that.[31] Finally this policy became an especially long-lived and hence deeply entrenched one since David Eccles was Minister of Education for five years in two phases between 1954 and 1962, the longest tenure of the postwar years. There was no doubt of David Eccles's commitment to technical education in general but the STS was not to be a major distinctive part of it.[32]

Just how entrenched this policy decision against the STS had become was evident a few months later. The Ministry debated a variety of worries about technical education in which the STS would have had a vital role to play. For example there was far too high a failure rate of candidates taking the Ordinary National Certificate since only about a half of entrants passed in the early 1950s.[33] Also Sir Gilbert Flemming, the Permanent Secretary, thought that technical colleges were 'cluttered up with too much low level work', though (with uncharacteristic unclarity) he wanted to extend and improve it.[34] There was agreement that the grammar schools and modern schools were not producing the technologists Britain needed.[35] What is extraordinary in hindsight is that the development of the secondary technical school would have been an obvious contributory solution to all these problems - failure at ONC, too much low level work in technical colleges, lack of technologists produced by grammar schools. Yet such was the strength of the 1955 decision not to promote the technical school that it received no mention, still less discussion, in this raising of issues later in the same year.

A curious paradox began to emerge from the mid-1950s under David Eccles and Lord Hailsham. Great emphasis was placed on higher technical education. The Colleges of Advanced Technology were created and it was planned to spend £70 million on a great expansion of technical education in the period 1956–61. Yet the STS was to be kept constrained. The general principle was followed that the proportion of 13-year-olds in grammar and technical schools, taking existing and projected schools together should be between 15 and 25 per cent.[36] From this point, 1955–6, an increasing enthusiasm for higher technological education was countermatched by a diminished willingness to accord any important role to the secondary technical school.[37]

This view was certainly held and expounded by the National Advisory Council on Education for Industry and Commerce under Sir Ronald

Weeks, the Chairman of Vickers. The emphasis was on technical colleges developing more advanced work and transferring 'elsewhere' the junior work. By setting the imagination on a 'Royal College of Technology', which never came into being, they diverted attention from the technical schools. Whereas Percy in 1945 had a strong sense of technical schools feeding talent into advanced technical colleges this was not so with Weeks. By 1956 Weeks's views reflected those of Eccles. STSs for him had a role 'where suitable courses are not already available in grammar schools'.[38] Moreover there was a dangerous 'softening' of the hard vocational edge of the STS. In Sir Ronald's view technical education 'must not be too narrowly vocational' and 'a place must always be found in technical studies for liberal education'. The STS was seen as having a role only where there was no grammar school and even then its formerly distinctive education was to be liberalized to become more like that of the grammar school.

The STS continued to fade in the policy statements of the late 1950s. In the major White Paper on Secondary Education in 1958 the STS received scarcely a mention save that 'advanced technical courses may be concentrated in separate technical schools or provided in grammar schools'.[39] Why *advanced* one wonders? The whole tone was to make the STS sound unusual, highly specialized and isolated, its work just as well done by the grammar school. Lest the STS retain the belief that it still had a special role, it was warned sternly that no type of school should regard its activities as 'a fixed and self-contained territory into which no other must enter'. In 1959 David Eccles returned to the Ministry and his new important statement on technical education oddly, but predictably, contained no reference whatever to STSs.[40] So diminished had the technical schools become that when an American scholar enquired about them at this time he received an admission of brutal frankness from the Ministry, 'it is therefore now pretty clear that not only do technical schools not yet enter into the picture in most cases but that they never will'.[41] The consequence was that STSs fell from a peak of 324 in 1946 down to 291 by 1952 and then from its second peak of 302 in 1955 (the year of Eccles' decision) steadily down to 184 by 1964. This decline was in spite of 63 new STSs having been built between 1945 and 1960.[42]

In the early 1960s, with Sir Edward Boyle as Minister, the STSs seemed to vanish from Government thinking altogether, even from roles which were intended to be specifically theirs. Boyle's views had been made quite plain to headmasters of STSs. He refused to see any

Table 7.2 *Technical education of Members of Parliament, 1951–66*

	Technical education of Members of Parliament			
	1951	1955	1964	1966
Technical college	10 (1.6%)	15 (2.4%)	31 (4.9%)	41 (6.5%)
Secondary technical school or JTS	6 (0.9%)	2 (0.3%)	4 (0.6%)	5 (0.6%)
Total MPs	625	630	630	630

Source: A. J. Jenkinson, 'The technical education of Members of Parliament', *Vocational Aspect*, 17 (1965) no.37 (summer) and 18 (1966) no.40 (summer).

special role for STSs but praised science teaching 'throughout the whole range of our secondary schools'. He wanted more general education alongside the technical, and thought that success lay with the 'articulate with general know-how' rather than with those 'who are content to be thoroughly expert.'[43] It was at one with a certain softness of attitude to expertise and vocationalism found in the prosperous years of the 1950s and early 1960s. It was quite different from the attitudes of Percy in the 1940s. Indeed at this time Percy deplored the 'sickly distaste for vocational education' which had grown up since his active days.[44] The STSs were the losers in this change of climate. As Boyle later said 'the schools are not sub-assembly lines processing material for industry' and 'the schools do not need to ape the technical colleges'.[45]

It has been argued that the STS received little support in Parliament largely because so few MPs in the 1950s and 1960s had any first-hand experience of technical education, as A.J. Jenkinson has shown (see Table 7.2). While more had been to technical colleges, very few had been to JTS or STS. These were preponderantly Labour members which meant that they were impotently out of office for most of this time and in any case increasingly ideologically committed to comprehensive schools.

III

As policy turned against the secondary technical school in the mid-1950s so there was an increasing awareness of problems for which such schools would have been a solution. There was concern that too many children especially of the working class were not benefiting from the highly academic education of the grammar school and were leaving early. Whereas the semi- and unskilled made up 20.9 per cent of grammar school pupils yet they made up only 7.3 per cent of sixth forms.[46] Leaving at the earliest opportunity, even these highly intelligent young people were rejecting the seemingly pointless impracticable academicism of the grammar school. The Crowther Report of 1959 precisely identified the issue,

> the grammar school has a single type of curriculum. In many individual instances these boys and girls would have done better in a technical school where the practical subjects have a high place in the work of the ablest as well as the least able pupils.[47]

Crowther was keen on the secondary technical school, he called for an 'alternative road' to the academic education of the grammar school and welcomed the development of sixth forms in technical schools. Crowther's Committee included Dr H. Frazer, the Headmaster of the Leicester Gateway School and Dr (Sir) Peter Venables of Birmingham College of Advanced Technology (CAT) who were both notable advocates of secondary technical schools. It was ironic that Crowther's inquiry had been set up by Sir David Eccles in March 1956. It reported to his successor Geoffrey Lloyd in July 1959, but by October Sir David had returned for his second term as Minister. The Crowther Report awaited him. Yet in spite of Crowther's advice the technical schools continued to diminish during this second term, from 269 to 255 between 1959 and 1962.

The Early Leaving Report and Crowther had been concerned that many grammar school boys might have been better off in technical schools. But studies of the 1960s suggested that this would have been so for many secondary modern pupils also. In Sheffield 39 per cent of secondary modern boys wanted skilled jobs - electrician, motor mechanic, plumber and so forth - precisely the type of occupations that the STS would have led them to. Yet only 14 per cent actually succeeded in entering these careers. Conversely 18 per cent of boys ended up in the kind of dead end jobs the STS was intended to save young people from. Moreover the ethos of the secondary modern was much less relevant to working life than the STS; M.P. Carter found for Sheffield that 'to many children the values of school had always appeared irrelevant to life as it is actually lived . . . school itself appeared to some children as futile'.[48] So it was in East London where secondary modern education was felt by too many pupils to be 'dull and uninteresting'.[49] What was valued, and more of it would have been valued more, was the technical vocational side of the curriculum. This was especially since a half of their output went into skilled trades but a quarter into semi- and unskilled work. STS education would have raised the former and lowered the latter figure. Peter Willmott considered that a much more career oriented curriculum would have improved East London secondary moderns in the 1960s - in practice something nearer the STS.

Misallocation to grammar and secondary modern schools of pupils who would have been better catered for in STSs was matched in seriousness by the lack of flow of apprentices into industry. The Carr Report warned of the 'serious shortage of skilled workers in the 1950s' and that the 'present intake into craft apprenticeship is inadequate'.[50] He recommended the starting of pre-apprenticeship courses but had no word to say about STSs as having any role in this problem. What is remarkable in (not very long) hindsight is that all these concerns of the 1950s - the wasting of technically inclined young people in grammar and modern schools and the lack of flow into apprenticeship and skilled labour would have been met by an expansion and encouragement of the STS. Yet policy refused to see a connection between the two and mistakenly hoped that grammar and modern schools would answer the need.

IV

Whether secondary technical schools were to flourish or not depended not only on attitudes in Whitehall, but equally on those of the LEAs. Here many local authorities were frankly set not on developing STSs as a part of the tripartite system but on absorbing old ones as streams in other kinds of schools. For example in London the postwar educational reconstruction plan had been approved in July 1944 and its principles were firmly multilateral - the future replacing of grammar, central and technical schools eventually with large comprehensive high schools. Immediately after the end of the war was too soon for costly rebuilding on these lines but in the 1950s the long term plans were put into effect. For example the Borough Road Polytechnic JTS, one of the first, was transferred to a secondary modern school. Two secondary technical schools were absorbed into the new comprehensive school in Kidbrooke Grove. By 1961 London had 59 comprehensive and 21 grammar schools, yet only 5 secondary technical schools remained of that proud London tradition of JTS and trade schools.[51] A commentator who deplored the absorption of the secondary technical schools in London observed presciently, 'they will of course lose their identity as schools and this will be the ultimate fate of all the secondary technical schools'.[52]

The pseudonymous local authority of 'Townley' in the South East of England began the postwar years with tripartite assumptions.[53]

But by 1949 the authority prepared schemes of modern-technical and grammar-technical schools on the grounds that the 11+ could distinguish grammar and modern pupils 'but was no indicator of suitability for a technical course'. If the grammar and modern scholar types could be distinguished, then allowing them into technical courses would be more flexible than a tripartite structure. It was the policy of the Chief Education Officer and became 'Townley's' Conservative policy for the 1950s. The blunt politics of the situation were that the Conservatives were concerned to defend the grammar school and to resist the comprehensive at almost any cost. This was in accord with Conservative central government policy. Sir Edward Boyle recalled that 'defending the top grammar schools in their existing form seemed an absolute "must" for the government at that time'.[54] Their defence of the grammar school did not extend to all parts of the tripartite structure. 'Townley' was an authority very amply supplied with grammar schools with about 30 per cent of children attending them. In this situation there was little talent left over for secondary technical schools and no motive to create them to reduce the numbers going to grammar schools. Labour likewise had no wish to defend the tripartite system, they wanted comprehensives. With neither Left nor Right deeply committed to tripartitism the loser was the separate technical school.

So it was also in Leicester which had a proud tradition of technical school education at the Gateway School - now a municipal museum. In their 1946 plan to implement the 1944 Act they proposed three more STSs providing 16 form entries of technical school accommodation for the city as a whole. In the 1952 revised plan they cut out two of the proposed technical schools. The LEA was increasingly doubtful about the possibilities of assessing and identifying special aptitudes at 11 and they were uneasy about the rigidities of the tripartite structure, preferring to encourage 'each type of school to provide as varied a curriculum as possible'. By 1961 even the Gateway School had ceased to be categorized as 'technical' and had become one of the grammar schools of the city.[55] In the West Riding of Yorkshire at the end of the war about 3,000 children attended JTSs in the county and its county boroughs. This did not change into the mid-1950s, and plans to build a new STS were abandoned in 1955. On the contrary, the existing technical schools were to be converted to grammar schools providing technical instruction. Various influences lay behind this - David Eccles's change of policy in 1955 signalled from the centre, an awareness of the difficulties of detecting technical aptitude at 11 and advice from industrial firms that they preferred generally educated youngsters rather than those with specific technical training.[56] Such changes evident in London, 'Townley', Leicester and the West Riding were repeated across the country, and Gary McCulloch has shown similar developments in Wolverhampton, Wigan and Doncaster at this time.[57]

A root of the problem was the urgent desire of parents and local authorities for grammar schools. Spens thought that grammar schools had over-expanded in the first third of the century. Parents preferred grammar schools because they led to clerical and white-collar occupations and not to manufacturing. Behind this was the belief in the superiority of office work, the 'preference for the black coat of the office over the boiler suit of the workshop'. Behind that in turn was not merely snobbery but the experience of the 1930s that industrial employment was associated with insecurity, 'in bad times the man at the bench is stood off more quickly than the man at the desk'.[58] If the Ministry and the LEAs were ambivalent about genuine tripartitism, so too were parents. The Ministry in 1951 observed that

> the implications of the 1944 Act are lost upon many parents. Authorities are subject to strong pressure to admit children who are unsuited to a grammar school course to what may appear to parents in some cases to be the only true secondary school available.[59]

There was no doubt that the STS was regarded very much as second best choice among parents, all classes of whom strongly preferred the grammar school. F. M. Martin in 1954 found the disposition of preferences as shown in Table 7.3. Barely a fifth of all fathers actually wanted their children to go to STSs. Those with the greatest inclination were the skilled workers, but nevertheless twice as many even in that group preferred the grammar school. For the professional middle classes the technical school was barely more acceptable than the secondary modern; for both the acceptability was negligible. This also related to the low preferences for going to technical college or entering an apprenticeship, the next stages to which the STS would normally have led. All social classes massively preferred university or professional training with the technical route as very much second best. Parental preference and prejudice was accordingly a great weakener of STS development.

V

Another problem causing difficulties for the STS was the lack of clarity

Table 7.3 *Parental preferences for different types of school, 1954*

Father's occupation	Number	Percentage of parents expressing a preference for Secondary modern	Grammar	Secondary technical	Other	Don't know or no preference
Professional	104	1.9	81.7	3.8	10.6	1.9
Clerical	104	4.8	77.8	9.6	2.8	4.8
Supervisory	255	9.1	60.7	19.2	2.7	8.2
Skilled	630	16.9	48.2	23.0	0.8	10.9
Unskilled	309	23.9	43.4	19.4	1.0	12.3
Total	1402	16.0	54.1	19.1	2.1	9.6

Source: F.M. Martin, 'An enquiry into parents' preferences in secondary education' in D.V. Glass, *Social Mobility in Britain* (London, 1954, reprint 1966) pp. 163, 172.

about the purposes of the new secondary modern schools. This had already been presaged in the Norwood Report in 1943. Whereas 'academic' and 'mechanical' abilities were fairly self evident and well defined, 'concrete' was by no means clear. *The Nations Schools* (1945) which was supposed to explain the tripartite system, added further confusion by suggesting that the purpose of secondary moderns was to provide 'meaning and enjoyment of life' for those whose work would not demand any measure of skill and knowledge. This patronizing nonsense provoked an outcry against the pamphlet at the Labour Party Conference and led to its replacing by the sequel *The New Secondary Education* (1947). The depiction of the secondary modern in the 1947 pamphlet was even more fatuous. Here it was envisaged that it would cater for a wide range of abilities from 'the intelligent', those with 'a

Table 7.4 *Parental preferences for post-secondary education, 1954*

	Preferred post-secondary education or training (%) Professional	Clerical	Supervisory	Skilled	Unskilled
Technical college	7.4	2.4	14.2	9.5	17.1
Apprenticeship	2.5	4.7	7.1	8.2	7.5

Source: F.M. Martin, 'An inquiry into parents' preferences in secondary education' in D.V. Glass, *Social Mobility in Britain* (London, 1954, reprint 1966) pp. 163, 172.

practical bent' through to 'backward children'. The reader might wonder why the first should not be in grammar, the second in technical and the third in some kind of special schools rather than all together in the one school whose purpose no one could define satisfactorily. It was quite evident that the function and clientele of the secondary modern school was not being thought through in the mid-1940s.

Crucially there was confusion about the relation of the secondary modern school to the STS. A leading influential enthusiast for secondary moderns at this time was Chief Inspector Elliott. He justified them at length for their work in crafts, woodwork, printing, navigation and industrial science, and their bias towards technical education.[60] This was an odd argument justifying one part of the tripartite system in so far as it could mimic and overlap the functions of another. The most popular explanation of the 1944 Act was the cinema film *The Children's Charter* (1944) and this took the same line. Here too the depiction of secondary modern schools with workshops was barely distinguishable from that of technical schools. The dangers of this unclarity were twofold. It almost deliberately fostered the idea in the public mind that there was little need for a distinctive technical school stream since their work could be done as well in secondary modern schools. Secondly, it reinforced the image that practical workshop work, undertaken by 11+ 'failures' was something inferior to the academic work of the grammar schools.

A further factor undermining the credibility of the STS was that psychologists and educational administrators no more believed in the possibility of selecting pupils for STSs after 1945 than they had for JTSs in the 1930s. After surveying a whole gamut of mechanical, spatial judgement and other psychological tests, R. Edgar admitted that

> the only conclusion to be drawn up to the present (1946) is that none of the tests gave a clear indication of the existence of ability of the kind it was hoped they would show . . . they are in effect tests of commonsense and experience rather than of special abilities.[61]

Cyril Burt held to his view that

> it is not possible at the age of 11+ to distinguish by the use of psychological tests between those pupils who would benefit most from a secondary technical school course and those who would profit most from a grammar school course.[62]

Only W. P. Alexander, the psychologist and then Chief Education

Officer of Sheffield believed in the existence of technical aptitudes in young children and their detectability.

This clearly presented problems for Chief Education Officers who genuinely wanted to develop STSs. Alexander (Sir Alec) Clegg, Director of Education for the West Riding of Yorkshire consulted four psychologists (including Cyril Burt) about the feasibility of selection for STSs at 11. They convinced him that it was impossible.[63] J. H. (Sir John) Newsom, the Chief Education Officer of Hertfordshire also concluded that it was too difficult to decide which intelligent children should go to the grammar school or the STS.[64] The Chief Education Officer for Wigan, Reese Edwards, although keen on technical schools, came to the view that it was not possible to get accurate scores of general 'g', verbal 'v' or practical 'f' ability.[65] Accordingly 'it does not appear that any distinct and separate ability for technical education actually exists'.[66] Southampton also came to the same view.[67] The HMI chiefly interested in this matter, A. G. Gooch, summed up his experience of inspecting LEAs: 'no Authority has ever given serious weight to special aptitude tests in the selection of pupils for technical courses either at 11 or 13'.[68] In practice scarcely any LEAs used tests recording special aptitudes in selection for STSs in the 1940s.[69] This was in accord with the central Ministry view which was quite bluntly that there was no evidence that 'special abilities' could be assessed accurately at 11 or at 13, 'and in any case the relation of special abilities to the various technical courses is by no means clear'.[70] This was a kiss of death for the STS. If such special technical abilities did not exist or (which came to the same) they were undetectable then there was little point in having a specific stream of schools to cater for them.

Moreover the STS was not helped by any positive support from industry. We have seen that in the interwar years enthusiasm for the JTS was patchy across a range of industries, though they were most valued in the construction and engineering industries they served. In the postwar years industrial opinion as represented by the Federation of British Industry (FBI) was cool. They strongly preferred the public and grammar schools as the major sources of recruitment. The STSs they ignored or equated with the inferior secondary modern schools.[71] The FBI in any case preferred a more generally educated boy, the 'right type' which academic schools provided and saw little value in a more vocational element in the curriculum. It was at one with an increasingly 'soft' attitude to vocationalism in the 1950s evident in the statements of the National Advisory Council on Education for Industry and Commerce and Sir Ronald Weeks and the FBI and other reports on arts graduates in industry in the 1950s.[72] Gary McCulloch concludes sadly that 'while the secondary technical schools were stagnating and in many cases dying for lack of attention and resources, the industrial sector to which they were committed refused to recognize or encourage them in an active way'.[73]

The failure to develop the tripartite system resulted in only a small proportion of pupils attending secondary technical schools. Sir Peter Venables pointed out that in 1952–3 there were seven times as many pupils in grammar schools as in secondary technical schools and nearly 17 times more in secondary modern schools. This curious ratio 1 : 7 : 17 was hardly a true tripartite system and 'the ratio provokes grave doubts as to whether this is a proportion appropriate to the needs of a commercial and industrial nation'.[74] But even this small proportion was swallowed up by the advent of the comprehensive school. This was the final factor leading to the downfall of the STS.

The idea of the comprehensive school had grown in the 1930s and for many groups on the Left it became the preferred form.[75] Spens recommended LEAs to experiment with it and Chuter Ede and Butler were in favour of it. There were some early pioneers: Windermere in 1945 and Anglesey in 1949 with Kidbrooke School in London as the first purpose built comprehensive in 1954. They grew steadily under the Conservatives in the 1950s. But with the return of Labour in 1964 Anthony Crosland issued his Circular 10/65 (12 July 1965) requesting LEAs to make comprehensive schools the normal pattern within five years. This led to a surging development of comprehensives not checked by Margaret Thatcher's reversal of Crossland's policy by Circular 10/70 in 1970. We can see the reciprocal relationship of the rise of the comprehensive and the extinguishing of the STS in Table 7.5. From very trivial levels in the early 1950s the proportion of pupils in comprehensive schools overtook those in technical schools between 1958 and 1959. The sharp growth was evident after 1965 and was not held up by Margaret Thatcher's Circular in 1970. Reciprocally the already low levels of technical school pupils rapidly shrank to the negligible, both absolutely and relatively, after 1965.

There was inevitably a direct relationship between these two developments. London, for example, had been 'inordinately proud' of its JTSs yet 'in time they were to be absorbed in the comprehensive schools'.[76] The 21 of 1924 had shrunk to 5 by 1961. Indeed two technical schools had been absorbed into the creation of Kidbrooke, the first London comprehensive, in 1954. In Walsall they had a JTS from 1929, planned

Table 7.5 *Pupils in technical and comprehensive schools, 1950–85*

	Pupils in technical schools in England and Wales	As a percentage of all pupils in maintained secondary schools in England and Wales	Percentage of pupils in comprehensive schools
1950	72,449	4.3	0.5
1955	87,366	4.6	0.8
1958	97,485	4.1	3.1
1959	99,224	3.8	4.1
1960	101,913	3.7	4.7
1965	84,587	3.0	8.5
1970	43,700	1.4	30.7
1975	18,049	0.5	64.3
1980	11,327	0.3	82.2
1985	2,502	0.06	85.0

Source: Calculated from figures in Brian Simon, *Education and the Social Order 1940–1990* (London, 1991) pp. 583-5.

to have two from 1945 but in 1947 created bilateral schools which then became comprehensives absorbing the old JTS.[77] Chelmsford STS, which with 900 pupils was one of the largest in the country, became part of Chelmer Valley Comprehensive in 1975. These were but particular examples of an inexorable trend. By 1966 even the Association of Teachers in Technical Institutions favoured comprehensive schools and saw no role for the STS in the structure of technical education.[78]

VI

The diminishing number of STSs that remained fought a rearguard action by making high claims for their status. Various presidents of the Association of Heads of Secondary Technical Schools heartened their fellows. A. B. Moffatt in 1958 rightly thought that Government was paying too much attention to the 'top heavy creation of technological research colleges' and ignoring the need for technical schools. In his view grammar schools should focus on the humanities while secondary technical schools should be their status equivalents for science and economics. For him the STS was to be 'the foundation stone of our education system'.[79] In 1961 E. Semper stressed the need for the STS to be an 'Alternative Road' (a Crowther phrase) to the grammar school and that 'the role of the secondary technical school is fundamentally that of working out what general education should be in a technological society'.[80] The next year Dr H. Frazer praised the postwar development of the technical school and its 'sense of purpose' as 'the success of the 1944 Education Act'.[81] This was not merely rhetoric for behind the fine words the STSs were sharply changing their status in practical ways.

Firstly, the STSs became larger. In 1920 the average size of school was 131 pupils, in 1930 it was 114 pupils but by 1950 it had risen to 240 and by 1960 to 406. This was a response to various pressures.[82] The rising birth rate at the end of the war meant that the number of 11-year-olds rose from 533,000 in 1952 to 812,000 by 1958. In addition the raising of the school leaving age to 15 increased the size of all secondary schools by an extra age cohort. The STSs also expanded at the other end as their former entry age of 13 was reduced to 11. Moreover the STSs were increasingly likely to have their own purpose-built premises by 1945. JTSs were usually in larger technical colleges. They occupied empty space during the day since most college students attended in the evening. In the 1950s day release apprentices increasingly used colleges during the daytime, competing for accommodation with the STS pupils. Furthermore with the reduced age of entry it was regarded as even less appropriate for 11-year-olds to be educated in the same environment as adult apprentices. These pressures tended to move the STSs out into their own buildings. These in turn were likely to be larger since it was more economical to build for a few hundred than one hundred children, especially with expensive equipment.

The STSs also came to be more like grammar schools. For example, it is surprising that consistently through the 1950s 1.2 to 1.9 per cent of the staff of secondary technical schools were teaching classics. It is not many, but it is amazing that they were there at all. The motive was clearly to enable able pupils to go to Oxford and Cambridge where Latin was an entrance requirement. More striking, from 11 to 14 per cent of secondary technical staffs in the 1950s were teaching modern languages. Also from 1951 there were consistently more teachers of English in these schools than of mathematics and science - in contrast to the 1940s. This was especially odd in schools which were supposed to be oriented to science and technology but which in the 1950s were beginning to take on more of the liberal characteristics of the grammar school. This convergence of the STS with some of the more academic characteristics of the grammar school aroused unease among some observers. One perceptively feared that 'unless some strong effort is made to keep the

Table 7.6 *Secondary technical school pupils taking 'O' and 'A' level examinations*

	Boys	Girls	Total
Pupils taking 'O' levels in			
1951	2201	755	2956
1955	6789	3663	10452
1959	11056	5690	16746
1963	12980	7531	20511
Pupils taking 'A' levels in			
1957	881	399	1280
1959	1334	433	1767
1961	2140	700	2840
1963	2496	685	3181

Source: G. F. Taylor, 'Selection for junior and secondary technical education', *Vocational Aspect*, 20 (1968) no.47 (Autumn) pp. 330, 331.

secondary technical school different from the grammar school, it can easily slide into the academic rut, whereby its own potentialities will remain unrealised and its *raison d'être* unfulfilled'.[83]

The changed status of the STS was also evident in the increasing entry of their pupils for national external examinations. This had been discouraged in the interwar years on the grounds that it would divert JTS curricula from local needs. In the concern to match the grammar school these considerations were left behind. G. F.Taylor has shown that the total number of STS pupils taking 'O' level rose (see Table 7.6), as did those taking 'A' levels. Again, this seemingly desirable development aroused suspicion. An STS headmaster recalled

> It became necessary to introduce the School Certificate Examination into these schools. We felt some misgivings in doing so. The syllabuses, devised by university boards for grammar school pupils, were often too academic in outlook. The time needed to work for a group of certificate subjects might mean a reduction in the time available for that valuable practical work. There was a real danger that the technical school course would lose its characteristic flavour of realism and vocational stimulus. By substituting the examination incentive, we might easily turn these schools into duplications of the grammar schools and destroy their *raison d'être*.[84]

There was some indication of this in the kind of 'A' levels being taken by STS pupils in 1958.[85] The leading ones, mathematics (637), physics (538) chemistry (336), were clearly desirable in helping to produce the scientists of the 1960s. Yet this was indistinguishable from the work of the grammar school. It was disappointing that only 153 were taking engineering drawing (a third of those taking physics) which suggested that the STS, by imbibing some of the academic values of the grammar school, was contributing to the dangerous bias - too many pure scientists; too few engineers. It was also sad to see traditional JTS subjects – woodwork (30 candidates), metalwork (27), needlework (13), cookery (10) – relegated to minimal significance. These hands-on crafts so essential for entrepreneurship in important industries like building, fashion, hotel and catering were being lost in the drive to emulate the grammar school. As Dr Frazer of the Gateway School, Leicester, put it 'the focal point of the STS used to be its workshops but it has moved to its laboratories and its library'.[86]

This 'A' level work was done in sixth forms in STSs, themselves a new feature of their raised status. The Crowther Report was keen on STSs developing this work and found that of 270 such schools 133 (almost half) had sixth forms, the average size being 21.[87] Crowther had hoped that STSs would develop sixth forms sufficiently distinctive to attract pupils from other secondary schools. However the spread of subjects actually been done in STS sixth forms at this time (to which we have just referred) suggests that they were not sufficiently distinctive from grammar schools. The sixth form activity now partly accounted for 40 per cent of STS staff being graduates.[88] It also contributed to both a relative and absolute decline of STS pupils going directly into jobs from 15,948 to 12,120 between 1950 and 1959 and a sharp rise of those proceeding to higher education from 19 to 229. At Chelmsford STS, for example, whereas only one boy had gone to university before 1961 yet 40 a year were doing so by the early 1970s from a sixth form which had been built up from around 30 to over 200 over the same period.[89]

There was also an evident raising of the status of the occupations followed by technical school pupils. Thelma Veness found in 1956 a fairly traditional output from technical schools (see Table 7.7). Yet the output from Cray Valley Technical High School in 1962 revealed the higher - rather grammar school - level at which

Table 7.7 *Careers of pupils from technical schools, 1956*

	Percentage of output	
	Boys	Girls
Apprentices	55.4	14.8
Clerical	30.3	78.7
Professional	8.9	-
Forces and police	5.4	-
Nursing	-	1.6
Distribution	-	4.9

Source: Thelma Veness, *School Leavers* (London, 1962) p.66.

STSs now operated. Of their 32 boys leaving the sixth form in that year[90]

> 16 entered universities to read physics, mathematics, chemistry, metallurgy, engineering, geography, economics, social studies.
> 8 entered colleges of advanced technology to read for engineering degrees or the Dip. Tech.
> 3 entered colleges of agriculture, architecture and aeronautics.
> 1 entered a teacher training college.
> 4 entered scientific civil service, technological or medical laboratories, commerce.

The high proportion studying science and engineering in universities and CATs, and the fact that only one was entering teacher training was a cause for satisfaction. Boys who left Cray Valley at 16 or 17 with Ordinary Level certificates took up the following occupations: engineering apprenticeships, banking, insurance, printing, engraving, advertising, army, navy, air force, merchant navy, journalism, surveying, pharmacy, metal refining, management courses in building and tent-making, paint technology, dentistry, catering, and clerical work. This too appeared useful and productive.

The STSs, to avoid being absorbed into grammar or other schools, were seeking to become like grammar schools themselves. The pity was that the secondary technical schools had a special ethos biased towards industry which the grammar school did not have. Indeed there was the fear that technically minded boys in grammar schools would be diverted into pure science and the professions whereas 'in the technical schools the boys are directed towards industry'. Moreover secondary technical schools were linked with technical colleges which in turn had the direct links with local industry and firms which grammar schools did not. Merely debasing secondary technical schools to technical streams in grammar schools 'is likely to result in such technical streams being technical only in name' for 'the two atmospheres cannot properly be developed side by side in the same institution'.[91] A receptive observer of the time noted that technical schools 'savoured of the working world' and 'had a unique flavour which no alternative type of school could hope to acquire'.[92] A technical headmaster also warned that 'there is a unity of purpose in the technical school to which it owes its success, but this unity cannot easily be obtained in a dual purpose establishment'.[93] There were many claims at this time that the ideals and atmospheres of the grammar and technical schools were so different that the latter would be destroyed by absorption into the former. There were in fact 25 so called grammar-technical schools in 1957, the last year they were specified as such. The interesting assumption was that the culture of the grammar school was so powerful that it would dominate that of the technical school, not the reverse. The warnings were correct but remained unheeded.

Accordingly the movement to create a thriving secondary technical sector, which Spens had hoped for, was stifled in the postwar years. This failure had implications far beyond the 1950s and 60s and the STS sector itself. It lay near the heart of England's educational defects and declining economic performance in the postwar years.

CHAPTER 8

Why This Matters

the absence of a tier of technical schools comparable with those found on the Continent and in Japan is the single biggest failure of British post war educational policy

Financial Times, 9 May 1990

This unfortunate story of the technical schools has played its part in Britain's poor economic performance since the war, which is illustrated by the figures in Table 8.1.

In GDP per man year Britain was overtaken by France, Germany, Italy and Japan between 1955 and 1975. Also Britain's share of world exports of manufactures sharply declined from 25.5 per cent to 9.3 per cent between 1950 and 1975 when it was overtaken by France, Germany and Japan. Alford calls it a 'particularly sad story of a relative decline for a once dominant trading nation'.[1]

There is a host of reasons for this and a library of books explaining them. Education plays a contributory role and is no more a total explanation than any other. But near the heart of Britain's industrial deficiencies lies a chain of problems which starts with the paucity of pupils inclined to science, technology and industry produced by the schools. It ends with the under-production of skilled and practically capable labour at different levels. Had the well-springs of the technical schools been retained, things might have been different. This final chapter is devoted to exploring these interconnections.

I

In the 1950s the proportion of 'A' level students taking mathematics and science rose to 64.5 per cent by 1960. This suggested a satisfactory flow from schools helped on by the glamour of 'big science' engineering in the 1950s - the record-breaking jet planes and the nuclear power stations. But in the 1960s the 'Dainton Swing' (identified by Sir Frederick Dainton), reversed, with a swing in preferences to the arts and to a greater extent to the social studies and away from

Table 8.1 *Postwar average annual growth of GDP in selected trading nations*

	Average annual percentage growth of GDP					
	1950–55	1955–60	1960–64	1965–69	1969–73	
UK	2.9	2.5	3.1	2.5	3.0	
France	4.4	4.8	6.0	5.9	6.1	
Germany	9.1	6.4	5.1	4.6	4.5	
Japan	7.1	9.0	11.7	10.9	9.3	(GNP)
USA	4.2	2.4	4.4	4.3	4.4	

Source: B. W. E. Alford, *British Economic Performance 1945–1975* (London, 1988) p.14 citing Sir Alec Cairncross and D. T. Jones.

mathematics and science.[2] By 1963–4 UCCA (Universities' Central Council on Admissions) found that all university places in arts and medicine had been taken up but 10 per cent of places in science and technology remained unfilled.[3]

This shortage of science and technology students prompted the new universities of the 1960s to rely heavily on the humanities and social studies in their urgent concern for rapid growth. Technology places would have been too expensive to provide and difficult to fill. Indeed in 1969 more than 1,500 university places remained unfilled, mostly in science and technology.[4] Grammar and secondary modern schools were producing only an inadequate and constricted flow of potential technologists since, unlike the technical schools, this was not their chief aim. This also threw the new supposedly technological universities off course. They had been notable technical colleges upgraded to Colleges of Advanced Technology in 1956 and elevated to university status in 1966 and 1967. Their Principals told Robbins in 1963 that they intended to have 65 per cent of their places in technology, 15 per cent in science and 10 each in social science and the arts. This proved disingenuously optimistic given the decline of the feeder technical schools. They were unable to get students to fulfil this programme, and by 1974 only 43 per cent of the students were in technology (22 per cent fewer than intended) and 32.8 per cent in social studies and arts (12.8 per cent more than intended).[5]

If the technological universities were diverted from their intentions, so too were the polytechnics. They were the next tranche of technical colleges below those designated as CATs and technological universities.

Table 8.2 *Distribution of students in polytechnics in the 1960s and 1970s*

	Percentage distribution of students				
	Engineering & technology	Science	Social admin. & business	Language & lit.	Arts
1965–6	43.9	14	26	0.6	1.6
1968–9	32.8	13.2	34.2	0.9	1.5
1974	20.4	17.4	36.9	------ 15.0 ------	
1978–9	-------- 33.9 --------		30.4	------ 20.0 ------	

Source: For 1965–6 and 1968–9: J. Pratt and T. Burgess, *Polytechnics, a Report* (London, 1977) p.77. For 1974: Sir Peter Venables, *Higher Education Developments: the Technological Universities* (London, 1978) p.295. For 1978–9: Alan Matterson, *Polytechnics and Colleges* (London, 1981) p.67.

In 1992 they too have been accorded university status. But in the 1960s and 1970s they embarked upon a 'policy drift' of expanding with a view to becoming universities. Since this expansion was hardly possible with technology students it involved a shift of the polytechnics' activities away from technology.

In a sense the polytechnics could hardly be blamed for responding to a student demand driven market. Since there were scarcely any STSs providing their natural clients, so the polytechnics trawled the rich shoals of arts and social studies students along with other institutions of higher education. The polytechnics were also playing their own game of aiming at university status. It was significant that all 30 polytechnics elevated to being universities in 1992 were delighted to embrace the title 'university'. Only one retained the term 'polytechnic' in its title (Anglia Polytechnic University). All the rest jettisoned any titular hint of their connection with matters technical. This is an interesting cultural contrast with Germany where the great Technische Hochschulen of the nineteenth century have proudly become Technische Universitäten.

The lack of science and technology students coming from schools continues to distort the pattern of studies (see Table 8.3).

The consistent disparity remains between the industrial sciences (for which the STSs would have been relevant) and the arts. Not only do science and technology departments have difficulty in attracting a scarce supply of students but there is concern about the inferior quality of technology departments and universities. In the 1989 Universities' Funding Council (UFC) assessments of research, 8 technological universities could muster only one excellent department among them

Table 8.3 *'A' level entrants in industrial and arts subjects, 1991, 1992, 1993*

'A' level entrants in industrial subjects for which STSs would have provided students (% of total)

	1991	1992	1993
Technology	1.2	1.2	1.5
Art & design	4.5	4.6	4.8
Science	0.8	0.8	0.8
Chemistry	6.4	5.8	5.6
Physics	6.2	5.7	5.1
Mathematics	10.8	9.9	8.9
Computing	1.2	1.3	1.3
	31.1	29.4	28.0

'A' level entrants in arts subjects (% of total)

	1991	1992	1993
History	6.3	6.4	6.3
English	11.4	11.9	12.1
Classics	1.1	1.1	1.1
Social sciences	8.7	9.6	10.4
French	4.4	4.3	4.1
German	1.5	1.6	1.5
Geography	6.1	6.2	6.4
General studies	7.5	7.3	7.5
	47.0	48.4	49.4

Source: The *Independent*, 20 Aug. 1992, 19 Aug. 1993.

(Pharmacy at Aston) but 14 poorly rated departments. Of the poorly rated departments in technological universities two each were in civil engineering, chemical engineering, electrical engineering and chemistry and one each in physics and computing - the very subjects in which technological universities should have been claiming and achieving excellence. And, it may be said, the very subjects for which a sector of technical schools would have been providing students. This assessment of the technological universities is considerably inferior to that of the 'new' universities with 12 excellent and only 4 poorly rated departments.[6]

The lower quality of the technological universities is also evident from the UFC grant allocations of 1992 based on research performance.

Table 8.4 *Universities Funding Council grant allocations, 1992*

New universities (%)		Technological universities (%)	
Warwick	17.0	City	12.5
Essex	16.0	Surrey	9.7
East Anglia	14.5	Bath	8.8
York	13.7	Loughborough	3.5
Lancaster	10.9	Bradford	3.0
Sussex	9.7	Aston	2.0
Kent	8.1	Salford	0.8
		Brunel	– 3.0
Average	12.8	Average	4.6

Note: English average 12.1%.
Source: *The Independent*, 25 Feb. 1992.

II

This low status and performance of technology education relative not only to the humanities but also to the pure sciences has had deleterious effects on manpower formation and use. The Robbins Report criticized the fact that in the 1950s British universities taught too much pure science in proportion to technology. In 1959 first degrees in technology in Britain as a proportion of first degrees in science and technology were only 36 per cent compared with 65 per cent in Canada, 68 per cent in Germany, 49 per cent in the USA and 48 per cent in France.[7] It was normal for advanced industrial countries to have a technology–science degree balance of about two-thirds to one-third, or half and half. Britain's ratio of one-third to two-thirds was perverse and peculiar and reflected both the lower status of technology and the difficulties of getting technology students.

The knock-on effect of that was that Britain was also unusual in having a lower proportion of engineers and a higher proportion of natural scientists than other countries, as Merton Peck has shown (see Table 8.5). Peck concludes that 'no other country trains as engineers such a low proportion of its total professional manpower'. He also rightly identifies a root cause, 'British secondary school education is too limited and inflexible to permit much of an immediate increase in the supply of engineers'. In short it lacks the secondary technical school stream producing such manpower. This in turn has led to too

Table 8.5 *Relative proportions of engineers and scientists in UK and elsewhere in the 1960s*

	Percentage distribution of engineers and scientists		Percentage of total engineers and scientists in industry
	Engineers	Scientists	
UK	54	43	55.6
USA	71	25	73.9
France	67	21	76.1

Source: Merton J. Peck, 'Science and Technology' in Richard E Caves (ed.) *Britain's Economic Prospects* (Washington and London, 1968) p.451.

many scientists researching and too few engineers producing. The low use of engineers in research and our dependence on pure scientists also accounts for Britain's poor research and development pay-off.[8]

All these features: the Dainton swing against science, the lack of an adequate flow of young technological talent into the technological universities and polytechnics, the drift of both of them away from productive technology towards the liberal arts, the imbalance and arts bias of 'A' levels, the empty places in science and technology departments, the low ratings and grants of technological universities and the under-production of engineers in proportion to scientists - all were pathological signs of the failure of the education system to catch and nurture young technical talent and pump it onwards. It was all very well for educationists in the 1940s and 1950s to argue that grammar schools or modern schools could amply provide this talent by having technical streams or sides. But in practice the policies of David Eccles and Cyril Burt and others have not worked, as the preceding passages show.

The policy-maker whose clear vision would most have alleviated these problems was Lord Eustace Percy, the Conservative President of the Board of Education. As early as 1930 he envisaged a system in which young people would pass from JTSs through to technical colleges which would become part of higher education. This, he hoped, would be a genuine alternative counterpart to the grammar school-university track.[9] He was still advocating this in the 1950s. He wanted 'a parity between two educational "ladders", one leading through the secondary school to the university, the other through the senior and technical schools to the college of technology'.[10] But it was not to be. The neglect of the

Table 8.6 *Percentages of 18-year-olds in non-higher technical and vocational education in the 1970s*

Germany	(1979)	51.8
Switzerland	(1976)	48.9
Denmark	(1977)	30.3
France	(1979)	6.7
UK	(1976)	5.7

Source: *Policies for Higher Education in the 1980s* (OECD, 1983) p.105.

technical schools has led to distortions in higher education and beyond, and we suffer the consequences.

III

However, Britain's problems lay not only in higher education but in the production of technicians. The low levels of British 18-year-olds in non-higher technical and vocational education in the 1970s were notorious (see Table 8.6). The German comparison is illustrated in Table 8.7. The very low levels of apprenticeship and vocational education and the excessive numbers going into work or to the dole without training were a British peculiarity the retention of the STS would have worked against. This in turn has led to a lower proportion of the British labour force having vocational qualifications than its rival German counterpart. As S. J. Prais has shown, the percentage of the labour force with vocational qualifications in manufacturing industry compares badly with the figures for West Germany (see Table 8.8). The scandalous residual result has been that two-thirds of the British labour force had no qualification compared with only a third of the German. The working population qualified in engineering and technology is 40

Table 8.7 *Destination of 18-year-olds in Britain and West Germany, c. 1980*

		Full time general education	Full time vocational education	Apprenticeship	Work or unemployed
W.Germany	(1980)	25	18	50	7
Great Britain	(1977)	32	10	14	44

Source: Sidney Pollard, *The Development of the British Economy 1914–1980* (London, 1983) p.408, citing Ian Jones.

Table 8.8 *Percentage of British and West German labour forces holding vocational qualifications*

		University degree (%)	Intermediate (%)	None (%)
Britain	(1974–8)	3.3	28.7	68.0
W. Germany	(1978)	3.5	60.8	35.7

Source: S.J. Prais, 'Vocational qualifications of the labour force in Britain and Germany', *National Institute Economic Review*, 1982.

per cent lower in Britain than in Germany.[11] The difference lay not at university level but precisely at this intermediate level which the STS would have fed into. As P. J. A. Landymore stresses it is 'poverty in middling skills and qualifications' which has dragged us down. This was also the popular perception. In 1987 over a third of the British population regarded Britain as worse than most at industrial training.[12] They were probably right.

Since the system without STSs was not producing sufficient qualified people, one consequence has been shortages of skilled labour even in times of depression. Derek Aldcroft notes that 'skill shortages have been an endemic feature of post-war Britain. Every upturn in the business cycle has been accompanied by complaints of shortages of skilled labour'.[13] For most years in the 1970s 20 per cent of firms experienced skill shortages rising to over half in the early 1970s and just under half in the late 1980s. Most tellingly the numbers qualifying each year in Britain in the 1980s as mechanical fitters, electricians and building craftsmen were only a half to one-third of the corresponding numbers in Germany. So that, absurdly, two-thirds of firms in the Building Employers' Confederation reported difficulty in recruiting carpenters and bricklayers[14] - a mainstay output of the neglected and abandoned old JTSs.

How little the constrained JTS and STS were allowed to contribute to the stock of skill may be seen by comparing their output as a proportion of the skilled labour force (see Table 8.9).

If the entire output of the technical schools had still been working in 1961, theoretically possible if improbable, they would still have made up only 8.5 per cent of those specific occupations they were intended to supply. They would have made up only 2.9 per cent of the entire occupied population of 23,639,000 in 1961. These proportions are far

Table 8.9 *Cumulative output of technical schools, 1911–61*

	(*a*) Lower professionals and technicians, foremen and inspectors, skilled manual	(*b*) Cumulative output of JTS and STS	(*b*) as % of (*a*)
1911	6,405,000		
1921	6,530,000	17,492	0.2
1931	6,669,000	78,517	1.2
1951	7,266,000	454,285	6.2
1961	8,081,000	687,380	8.5

Source: A.H. Halsey, Trends in British Society since 1900 (London, 1972) p.113, Table 4.1, related to estimates of the output of JTS/STSs, calculated from *Annual Reports* of the Board and Ministry of Education.

too low. It is interesting to note that the occupational levels classified in (*a*) were 34.9 per cent of the total occupied population in 1911 and 34.1 per cent in 1961. If the technical schools had been genuinely a third part of a tripartite system educating about a third of children then this would have been in line with the proportions of technician, skilled labour, etc. in the workforce. Having only 3 per cent of children in such schools producing only 8.5 per cent of this labour group falls far short of what was desirable by any criterion.

Not only was formal skill training lost with the abandonment of the technical school but also a strongly pro-industrial ethos superior to that of the grammar school. Thelma Veness found that when boys from different schools wrote imaginary future life stories three quarters of technical school boys wrote accounts in which work was the dominant theme, compared with 41 per cent of secondary modern and 44 per cent of grammar school boys.[15] Secondary technical boys were more work-minded, regarded themselves as already starting their careers, nearly two-thirds regarded ambition as a good thing, thought work was the way to get on and looked forward to National Service as a rewarding experience. Here was a reservoir of keenness, positive attitudes oriented towards industry, which the nation to its cost undervalued in the 1950s and 1960s and allowed to be dissipated. This abandoning of the technical schools and their keen young pupils is an unremarked but important part of that 'decline of the industrial spirit', that undervaluing of technology and industry which G. C. Allen characterizes as the 'British Disease'.[16]

There was also a more subtle point for the national psyche. Technical school work entailed a rigorous schooling in precision, in getting things right and making things work. Woodwork joints must fit and hold, gears must mesh and drive, a mechanical drawing is not an impression. Nothing in the essay writing or even language translation of the grammar school exacted this rigour. Grammar school mathematics did so but without having to carry through to testable marketable utility. The grammar school developed the capacity for abstract thought, imagination, a capacity to spin arguments - right, wrong or partial - in inconclusive areas. It is doubtful whether industry has benefited from allocating the very ablest children to a form of education inculcating these broader habits of mind and only 3 per cent to the unforgiving disciplines of getting things right and making things work.

The neglect of technical school education has been in accord with and part cause of a most dangerous drift in the British economy since the war, what Bacon and Eltis have called 'too few producers'. It has been a curious feature of the labour force in Britain 1961–75 that 41 per cent of it has been in non-industrial employment (excluding agriculture). This was considerably higher than in other major industrial countries.[17] Britain employs far too many people in non-productive non-market occupations. Conversely there were disproportionately few with hard technical vocational qualifications actually producing and making anything. Although Bacon and Eltis do not draw the point, a higher proportion of the population educated in technical schools would have provided the labour force for that productive manufacturing they extol. It would also have worked against the excessively general arts education which has contributed to the trends they deplore.

The relative lack of well-qualified people in manufacturing has also contributed to Britain's low productivity which has underlain our low growth up to the mid-1980s. Stanislaw Gomulka regards educational factors, notably the low status of technical education, as a factor in this. The low productivity was linked with low value added, such that by 1975 one tonne of German mechanical engineering exports were worth 60 per cent more than a representative tonne of British mechanical engineering exports.[18] Low technical education begat low productivity and added value and all resulted in low economic growth.

IV

The technical schools have been stifled by a set of English cultural attitudes. The first of these was the English reverence for liberal education. This was the belief that the purpose of education was the

Table 8.10 *Changes in industrial output per man for UK, USA and West Germany, 1920s to 1970s*

	Percentage changes in industrial output per man, annual averages		
	Period I	Period II	Period III
	1920/5–38	1947/50–60	1960–74
UK	1.8	2.5	3.5
USA	2.0	2.5	3.4
Germany	2.6	5.1	4.7

Note: Period I: UK 1924, USA 1920, Germany 1925 to 1938
Period II: UK 1947, USA 1946, Germany 1950 to 1960
Period III: 1960 to 1974

Source: Stanislaw Gomulka, 'Britain's slow industrial growth – increasing inefficiency versus low rate of technical change' in Wilfred Beckerman, *Slow Growth in Britain* (Oxford, 1979) pp. 173, 188–9.

development of the intellectual and moral qualities of the gentleman and not training for specific occupations and vocations. That, if it came at all, came after the liberal education provided in public school and Oxford and Cambridge. This liberality (which did not imply breadth) was inculcated by the narrow study of classics and mathematics. The difficulty of these subjects was supposed to 'cultivate' the mind which could then subsequently apply itself to other matters in service of the state, church or professions. But for its nineteenth-century advocates, from Edward Coplestone to J. H. Newman, J. S. Mill and Matthew Arnold, the purpose was 'culture' and 'cultivation'. The Victorian grammar school took over this idea from the public schools and Sir Robert Morant's post-1902 municipal grammar schools perpetuated this ideal for a slightly lower social class. These values were still strong in the post-1944 grammar school. The preferences of parents (and hence LEAs) for what Morant had foreseen as a pseudo public-school education undermined Morant's other dream of the technical school. The Left, R. H. Tawney and the WEA had their own tradition of liberal education which was hostile to technical schools. The value system conveyed by the grammar school elevated the academic over the technical and suggested that doing and producing were inferior to thinking and administrating. The assumption carried through to future occupations where it was manifest in the over-reverence for the doctor and the lawyer (and formerly the Victorian clergyman) and the undervaluing of the engineer. Eustace Percy as early as 1930 saw that 'the besetting sin of our nation has been the superstition of the "liberal professions" . . . it may well prove disastrous to us'.[19] The excessive prestige for liberal education (perhaps especially the grammar school) and the liberal education professions, with the consequent relegation in importance of doing, producing and entrepreneurship, have been a psychological weakness sapping Britain's position as an industrial manufacturing nation. The technical schools were at odds with this cultural bias and tried in a small way to change it. But they were ultimately vanquished by it.

Secondly, another influence on policy in the 1950s and 1960s was the debate over C. P. Snow's *Two Cultures*. This was published in 1959 and expanded ideas raised by Snow earlier in 1956.[20] Snow's argument was that Britain was too divided into two self-contained cultures, the artistic and scientific. He called for a greater interpenetration of each - a greater awareness of science by humanities students and vice versa. Few would disagree with that. But a danger of the reception of Snow's argument was that by attacking educational specialization it encouraged the dilution of scientific and technical studies with contextual human studies. Snow called for 'men whom we don't yet possess (who) need to be trained not only in scientific but in human terms'. It added to the softening of the concept of technical education evident in the attitudes of Ronald Weeks and Edward Boyle. It reinforced suspicions of the technical school as something too narrow, specialized and vocational. It also authenticated the policy that such studies should only be pursued in conjunction with other forms in the grammar or comprehensive school. The Snow arguments, intended to bring a wider awareness of science into all education, may have had the unfortunate effect of making the separately specialized technical school unacceptable.

A third cultural attitude to which the technical school fell victim was the preference for seeing education as an agency of social mobility and social justice rather than a servant of industry.[21] This was well recognized at the time. Edward Boyle recalled that in the 1960s

> there were two traditions in the Department (of Education): the social justice tradition, wanting to widen opportunity, giving people the greater opportunity to acquire intelligence, and the technical college tradition - education for investment, education for efficiency. They were described in the early 1960s . . . as the dialectic within the office.[22]

The desire for social advancement and entry into the professions shaped the preference of middle-class (and would-be middle-class) parents for the grammar school over the secondary technical school. This shaped LEAs' motives in the 1940s and 1950s. In the 1960s the desire to remove the exclusiveness of middle-class grammar school privilege, and extend its virtues to all, informed the Left's concern to expand the comprehensive schools. In both phases hope was vested in the grammar school and then the comprehensive to deliver social mobility or equity. When such considerations predominated, the technical school was pushed into a marginal position and with it the needs of industry.

V

The demise of technical schools has left Britain without a stratum of education which most of our industrial competitors retain. As regards Germany we have seen that their nineteenth century development of trade schools influenced the origins of the JTS in England. The Germans have retained a divided system.[23] After the Grundschule primary education (ages 6-10) the Gymnasium takes a fifth of children for academic education (ages 10-19). The Realschule (ages 10-16) takes another quarter for more vocational education which will lead them to the technical college. More distinctively the Hauptschule (ages 10-16) provides vocational technical education which leads either to the technical college or direct to work for on-the-job and day-release training in the Berufsschule. The Hauptschule pupils also spend part of the week in an Ausbildungszentrum or apprenticeship centre mixing with apprentices, which they themselves will soon become.

German companies spend £7–8 billion on vocational training and in 1984 German firms provided over 700,000 apprenticeships and 97 per cent of school leavers not proceeding further were placed in one. In contrast with England, only a small minority of pupils attended Gesamtschulen or comprehensive schools. Far from going over to a comprehensive system, the Germans have retained a system with types of schools related to aptitude types with a strong vocational technical sector.

The Japanese 6–3–3–4 system begins with six years in an elementary school, three years each in a junior and senior high school followed by four years at university for the ablest. The sharp division comes at 15 when children proceed either to senior high school *en route* for university or to the vocational school. The vast majority, 96 per cent, actively continue into one of these schools beyond 15. The vocational schools take about two thirds of post-15 pupils. They maintain the pupils' science and mathematics studies and focus on engineering, draughtsmanship in specific trades, pottery, building and so forth as appropriate.[24]

In France in the 1950s the system included elementary education to 11 then followed by the academic *lycée* or the technical *école nationale professionelle* or the *école primaire supérieure* - the nineteenth-century technical school which had influenced Morant. From 1967 French pupils were separated into practical and academic streams between 13 and 15. Roughly a third of each year group were switched into vocational schools, the three-year *collège d'enseignement technique*, preparing for traditional craft trades. At a higher level the *lycée technique* leads after four or five years to the technical baccalauréat. This was the kind of technical grammar school which Spens would have wanted but which Britain was abandoning at the time. In 1985 the baccalauréat professional was introduced to raise the standard of technical schooling.

The same may be noted of Holland which has types of technical school from 12 or 13, the *Hogere* and *Lagere Technische Schools* which so impressed Crowther. There is no need to elaborate this further. Britain abandoned the separate technical school. Yet major industrial rivals Germany, Japan and France, plus various other similar societies like Holland, Belgium and Norway, retained separate specialized secondary technical schools which fed directly into their skilled labour forces. They lie behind the Sony and Panasonic electronics, the BMW and Renault cars and much else which British consumers enjoy, to the devastation of our balance of payments.

VI

With the decline of the secondary technical school sector it was assumed that science and technology would be adequately dealt with in the existing secondary schools. This was far from the case, since a series of well-meant initiatives failed to meet the need.[25] The Nuffield Foundation Science Teaching Project began in 1962 but it became evident in the 1960s that it was primarily concerned with pure academic science to the neglect of applied science, technology and engineering. Nuffield was in fact working in a direction quite contrary to the declining technical schools and was diverting attention from applied to pure science. In 1965 the Schools Council Project in Technology (SCPT) began and tried to redress the balance by emphasizing the importance of crafts. But it became the centre of a tangled clash of interest groups and individuals around the basic issue of how far schools should be teaching traditional science and how far applied crafts and technology as the old technical schools did. The SCPT, trying in many ways to carry the banner of the technical school ideals, found itself bitterly attacked by the pro-science Association of Science Education's Action Group and several others. A Schools Science and Technology Committee was created in 1968 but relations between it and the SCPT were a 'major source of anxiety and discord'. The SCPT had virtually finished by 1972 and the optimistic urgency about school technology in the 1960s had dwindled by the 1970s. The tensions between groups and personalities betrayed the national interest as did the Department of Education and Science (DES) which remained aloof. Nothing effective was devised to replace the vanished STS. Accordingly the historians of this dismal story concluded that 'despite major efforts there has been no "technological revolution" in the schools'.[26]

It might be argued that STS activities have been effectively carried on by other developments both outside as well as inside the school. But this would hardly be true either. On the contrary, the failure to develop a technical school sector has resulted in a whole series of stop-gaps and substitutes of questionable value.[27] The Youth Opportunities Programme (YOP) was introduced in 1978 to give jobless school leavers work experience through tuition and practical work studies. The short training 'had very little merit' other than providing cheap labour to employers. This was replaced in 1983 by the Youth Training Scheme (YTS). But training remained low level, many left prematurely and the scheme was 'little short of a disaster', partly due to the lack of pre-vocational training and education in schools. Here was a vicious circle. Without STSs, schemes like YTS were needed to fill the gap, yet the latter failed for lack of the schooling which the STS had provided. The YTS was replaced in 1990 with Youth Training (YT) 'too loose and unstructured' and only dealing with 2 per cent of the labour market. For those failed by youth schemes a parallel gamut of adult initiatives awaited. In 1972 the Training Opportunities Scheme (TOPS) provided short courses for unemployed adults but too short and lacking skill depth. This was replaced in 1988 by Employment Training (ET) but 'too often . . . of low quality standard'. Yet more organizations overlay these. In 1986 the National Council for Vocational Qualifications (NCVQ) was to rationalize and evaluate the plethora of courses and qualifications while the Training and Enterprise Councils (TECs) from 1990 were to be employer-led bodies to assess local training needs and assume responsibility for seeing that they were met. In spite of this shoal of 'initiatives', some might say gimmicks, Derek Aldcroft finds that 'no comprehensive and coherent programme of training of good quality' was created. How much of all this would have been necessary if its recipients had been provided with a proper technical school education some years earlier?[28]

Perhaps in recognition of what has been lost with the STS, there has been a recent concern to get technology back into the classroom. In 1983 the Technical and Vocational Initiative (TVEI) was started with the aim of offering pupils from 14 to 18 a more vocationally oriented curriculum.[29] This provides funds for projects in schools, usually in technology, information technology and crafts like catering and horticulture. It arose from Sir Keith Joseph's proper concern to produce technicians in schools and its former director is certain that it has increased technology in schools, especially for girls. This is an area of hope. Hope might also have been placed in the introduction of technology into schools through the National Curriculum in 1990. Unfortunately a recent authorative survey of this by Professor Alan Smithers finds that 'technology in the National Curriculum is a mess' and that the attempt 'to give making and doing their proper place in education seems to be foundering'.[30] This is because what 'technology' was supposed to be has become too diffuse, encompassing information technology, art, home economics and business studies down to 'generalised problem solving without a specified knowledge base'. Thus the development of skills in actually producing anything has been devalued. Smithers disdainfully points out that drawing or describing what a desk tidy might look like has become an acceptable substitute for actually making one, and he rightly deplores the loss of the secondary technical school which would have obviated these problems.

The nearest the system has come in recent years to replacing the old technical school has been the creation of the city technology college (CTC). These were announced by Kenneth Baker, the then Secretary of State, on 7 October 1986. There were to be 20 pilot colleges to 'offer a curriculum with a strong emphasis of technological, scientific and practical work, business studies and design'.[31] It was explicit in Mr Baker's mind that the CTCs would revive some of the values of the older form. In talking of the CTCs later he reflected that it was 'a great pity' that the secondary technical school had not been developed after the 1944 Act.[32]

The CTCs were to have many distinctive characteristics. They are schools for the 11–18 age group and the curriculum is to be strongly biased to science and technology. The schools were to be independent of the LEAs but were to be run by trusts. They would charge no fees and it was envisaged that business sponsors would substantially meet the costs of their building. To facilitate this, the City Technology Colleges Trust was established under Sir Cyril Taylor in May 1987. Its task is to co-ordinate private business money and DES funds and acts as a broker bringing together projects, sites and sponsors. The running costs would be met by per capita funding direct from central government. Unlike grammar schools, the CTCs were not supposed to select their pupils academically but to take them from a wide ability range, though taking account of their commitment to the particular studies of the schools. The staff were to be employed directly by the governors of the schools who would set their own salaries, independently of national, trade union agreed, scales and somewhat above them. Finally the schools were normally to be located in cities ideally to provide special opportunities for the deprived youth of the inner city. The CTCs were accordingly seen as attacking a number of problems as seen by the Conservatives of the 1980s. Most obviously they were to redress the neglect of technology (rather than science) in the existing school system and correct that imbalance wherein technical matters were seen as second rate to academic. As such they would be a new weapon in British manufacturing industry's fight back against the recession of the early 1980s and international competition. Secondly the CTCs were an attack on comprehensive schools which were already being undermined by the falling rolls of fewer pupils. Poor and unpopular comprehensives might be forced to close by the competition of a privileged nearby CTC. Linked with this the CTCs were an implied criticism of the local education authorities since they were outside their control. The LEAs had failed to develop technology effectively in the grammar and comprehensive schools and had neglected to develop the technical school since 1944. They were not to be trusted. Even less so were 'looney left' LEAs with curricula more related to influencing pupils ideologically than preparing them for the world of work. The CTC would combat these trends, though now LEAs can run their own CTCs. Fourthly, the CTCs would help to address the problem of the inner city and its deprived and discontented youth which had erupted in riots in 1980. Finally the CTCs would bring industry to a sharper awareness of its responsibilities for the education of its future workforce as they were asked to provide the capital funds for the establishment of the schools.

The CTCs began to be created slowly. The first was Kingshurst CTC, Solihull, which opened in September 1988 in a secondary school which was due for closure. Hanson plc acquired the 125-year lease on the school for £1 million and thus became the first industrial sponsor of a CTC. It attracted much favourable attention under its dynamic head, Mrs Valerie Bragg. A visitor noted 'there are 80 computers for word and information processing . . . there are dishes on the roof for beaming satellite television programmes, fridges, freezers, cookers, microwaves, kilns, brazing hearths and computer controlled lathes'.[33] The teachers were encouraged to think of themselves as high status 'managers' and 'executives' wearing suits and ties, working long hours for personally negotiated performance related pay. There was a glamour in all this which the old JTS and STS never had. After Kingshurst came Djanogly College, Nottingham supported by Harry Djanogly, a textile entrepreneur who put up £1 million. This opened a year after Kingshurst in September 1989. In the same month Macmillan CTC opened in Middlesborough, supported by BAT Industries and others. Four more followed in 1990 in Bradford, Gateshead, Dartford and Croydon. Of particular interest was that Gateshead was intended to have a distinctive evangelical character and was supported by a motor retailing group. Particularly imaginative is Richard Branson's proposal for a CTC for the performing arts in recognition that pop music, television and the theatre are highly technical industries in which Britain has an acknowledged excellence.

In spite of these bold initiatives the CTCs have not been uniformly welcomed. Contrary to expectation many leading firms have declined to support the CTCs, notably Shell, Imperial Chemical Industries (ICI), British Petroleum, J. Sainsbury. 'The CBI is sceptical, the Industrial Society outright opposed, of 1800 firms approached just seven have responded positively' within nearly three years.[34] Sir John Harvey Jones, then of ICI, considered them too expensive and not enough 'bang for the buck'.[35] The above firms are notable supporters of education outside the CTC sector. But the reciprocal unease is that large sums spent on CTCs by Hanson, BAT, Dixons, Forte, W.H. Smith, Virgin might be better spent on technology through the state sector.

The initial failure of industry to finance the CTCs forced the Government to step into the breach. Now sponsors are expected to meet not 'all or a substantial part' but only 20 per cent of the capital costs. The taxpayers' commitment has accordingly been raised. Up to 1990 private sponsors had put £17.25m into CTCs, but central government £59.93m and LEAs £55.69m.[36] What was intended to be a massive injection of private sector industrial funds has had greater public spending implications than envisaged. This is especially galling to hard-pressed LEAs which regard CTCs as a massive diversion of funds better used for technology in existing schools in the deprived state sector. It is pointed out that government capital expenditure per pupil in the CTCs in Bradford, Gateshead, Croydon and Dartford was £6,484, yet only £78 per pupil in all the other 1,218 schools in these areas.[37] Both government and private industry money channelled into the CTCs might, it is argued, more usefully have been spent on improving technology teaching and equipment in comprehensive schools.

Not only is money diverted but also talent. The shortage of science and technology teachers is exacerbated by these especially attractive schools. Likewise there is the fear that creaming off pupils with technical aptitudes from comprehensive schools will reduce the latter to secondary moderns. A more surprising argument concerning the intake of CTCs is that it remains too narrowly working class. Geoffrey Walford found that a half the intake into Solihull CTC came from the skilled (49 per cent) manual class and only 1 per cent from professional and managerial background. This was very similar to the old JTS/STS. He concludes, 'it cannot be said that the middle class have made any significant inroads into the CTC'.[38]

Yet the chief criticism of the CTC is that there are so few of them. The Government had wanted 20 CTCs by 1990 but by 1993 only 15 exist. This is as nothing compared with the 324 technical schools at their peak in 1946. They have stimulated one or two LEAs to start their own (non-CTC) technology schools, notably the pioneer Chaucer Technology School in Canterbury in 1990 and one in Lincoln in 1992. Even so it would take many years and vast expense to recreate even that small technical school sector which used to exist and was dissipated in the 1950s and 1960s. The CTC should be valued and extended as the best attempt to resurrect the old concept of the JTS and the STS. The policy of merely incorporating technology teaching into existing schools has not been successful. What is needed is some powerful demonstration that the technical school can be not only worthy and useful but even prestigious and glamorous. This is necessary to woo the public mind from the dangerous enchantment exercised by the liberal education of the grammar school with its emphasis on pure science, the humanities and professions. Special privileges given to the development of a CTC sector might just bring about that change in a way the JTS had no hope of doing. The tragedy is that the CTC has emerged from radical Right policies in the Conservative Party and accordingly meets understandable resistance from the Left. At least the Left is more consistent, it always has disliked technical schools. Conservatives conveniently forget that it was Conservative educational policies in the 1950s which undervalued and destroyed the old technical schools they would now wish to resurrect. The Conservatives are getting back on track as regards the technical school. It would be a pity if some returning Labour Government destroyed the CTCs out of aversion for some of the ideology which helped create them, throwing out the technological baby with the anti-LEA, anti-comprehensive bathwater.

VII

Britain's problems came home to roost in the summer of 1992 when it was contemptuously forced out of the Exchange Rate Mechanism by the strength of the Deutsche Mark. This was not the fault of the Bundesbank or of speculators but the long term deep seated weaknesses of British manufacturing industry. Behind this lie weaknesses of policy both in the economy and the educational system. There has been an addiction to the 'quick fix' and the 'soft option' in both when what was needed was a long steady building up of a culture of *Technik* which Sir Montague Finniston called for in 1980.[39] This he defined as the capacity 'to devise technical and economic solutions to practical problems'. It is a third culture which should rank alongside the humanities and the sciences. For the 'technical' should not merely be a sub-section of the 'scientific' or a second rate handmaid to it. Although Finniston does not draw the point there would have been no better way of inculcating this culture than having a third of schoolchildren going to secondary technical schools as part of a genuine tripartite structure of secondary education. The alternative strategy of hoping that grammar and modern schools would take the task on board has been a failure. A society like Britain with 81 universities and only 15 city technology colleges betrays grotesque inadequacies and imbalances that mirror its economic deficiencies.

The problems continue. The National Institute of Economic and Social Research rightly and perpetually reminds us that 'it is the lack of training to craftsman-level – rather than the lack of university graduates – that forms the principal deficiency in Britain's education and training system.'[40] In a telling study of the teaching of practical subjects in Britain and the Continent the superiority of the latter is evident. Germany, Holland and Switzerland especially emphasize practicality, accuracy of measurement, quality of finish and actually *making* something. Moreover this craft training is also intended to inculcate moral qualities – reliability, responsibility, the fulfilment of duty. British practice, which used to be similar to the Continent has diverged from these older traditions. In Britain emphasis has moved to individual projects on broad themes with 'written evaluations' being given a high importance and actual skill and quality of finish a subordinate role.[41] The feeble British performance at school knocks on to the higher level. It is hardly surprising that in 1987 France awarded three times as many qualifications to engineering craftsmen and technicians as Britain did. Germany awarded more than four times as many (134,000).[42]

From September 1993 technology becomes compulsory in state schools for 14–16 year olds. Yet there are still grounds for unease. In the view of Bierhoff and Prais there is till too much emphasis on 'identifying human needs', planning, organizing and evaluating, i.e. 'paperwork of the intellectualised kind'. There is still too little on using tools and equipment for Making (which as an 'Attainment Target' bears a capital 'M'). The number of materials with which pupils will work is reduced. Moreover short courses may be introduced in e.g. business studies, music and economics, further reducing the focus on making things. Bierhoff and Prais find this still much inferior in practicality to Continental practice and conclude that 'there is thus still a long way to go before we can be confident that secondary schools in Britain are doing all that could be expected of them to provide a foundation for the skills needed in a technically-advanced economy'.[43] Nor are teachers and parents happy.[44] Headteachers complain of shortages of staff and workshops, they are suspicious of 'technology' as an ill-defined subject, they find that university engineering departments do not want it, prefering mathematics and physics, they fear that as a compulsory subject it will crowd out a foreign language or art and music. Whether these fears prove well founded or resolvable is for the future. But the whole unsatisfactory situation is the bitter legacy of the abandoning of the JTS/STS tradition in the 1960s.

In the wake of a continued decline in science and technology 'A' levels in 1993 and hundreds of science places at the universities remaining unfilled for that year's entry, Mr Patten announced another initiative in September. It was clear that the CTC was not fulfilling the hopes placed in it. Only 15 schools had been created and, since business sponsors had only come forward with £35 million, this had resulted in £120 million of public funds being spent on only 15,150 pupils. In this context on 27 September 1993 Mr Patten announced the provision of £25 million to be earmarked for grant maintained or voluntary aided schools which adjust their curricula to be more like CTCs, with 60 per cent of their studies in science and technology. Business sponsors are to have seats on governing bodies in return for a 'substantial' – around £100,000 – investment in a school and they are expected to maintain a commitment to their school for between five and seven years. Mr Patten hopes that some 200 schools of this nature will be created over the next few years. The plan has already met the predictable criticism that it is channelling funds to the few which should be used to enhance science and technology teaching throughout all secondary schools. At its worst it is seen as no better than a bribe to induce schools to opt out of LEA control to receive these benefits. One can only hope that the scheme enjoys more success than some of its predecessors. It is yet another attempt to revive something of that JTS/STS tradition so disastrously abandoned in the post-war years.

Would that we could go back to the cold night on 24 February 1943 when that honourable man James Chuter Ede altered the original clause 7 (c) of the draft 1944 Education Act. By deleting the specific reference to junior technical schools he sealed their fate as surely as Sir David Eccles was to do in 1955. These are among the most fateful decisions influencing Britain's postwar experience. We need to recover these schools, or something like them. We also need to be rather less reverential of education for its own sake and less suspicious of hard-edged vocational training for the young. So may we hope to revive the capacities and prestige of making and producing, of converting 'know-how' into 'can-do'. Otherwise we shall remain a third rate economy moving in the slow lane of a two speed Europe on its inexorable path of relative decline.

Notes

CHAPTER 1 An Edwardian Problem

1 Reginald A. Bray, *Boy Labour and Apprenticeship* (London, 1911) p.159.
2 Corelli Barnett, *The Audit of War* (London, 1986); Martin Wiener, *English Culture and the Decline of the Industrial Spirit 1850–1980* (Cambridge, 1981); Julia Wrigley, 'Technical education and industry in the nineteenth century' in B. Elbaum and W. Lazonick, *The Decline of the British Economy* (Oxford, 1986).
3 Reese Edwards, *The Secondary Technical School* (London, 1960); Michael Sanderson, 'The Missing Stratum, the Problem of Secondary Technical Education in England 1900–1960s' in Gabriel Tortella (ed.) *Education and Economic Development since the Industrial Revolution* (Valencia, 1990); Bill Bailey, 'Technical education and secondary schooling 1905–1945' in Penny Summerfield and Eric Evans (eds) *Technical Education and the State since 1850* (Manchester, 1990); Gary McCulloch, *The Secondary Technical School, a Usable Past?* (Lewes, 1989).
4 M.W. Kirby, *The Decline of British Economic Power Since 1870* (London, 1981) pp. 139, 149.
5 Michael Sanderson, *Educational Opportunity and Social Change in England* (London, 1987) p.135.
6 G.R. Searle, *The Quest for National Efficiency* (Oxford, 1971); A.L. Friedberg, *The Weary Titan, Britain and the Experience of Relative Decline 1895–1905* (Princeton, 1988).
7 Harry Hendrick, *Images of Youth, Age, Class and the Male Youth Problem 1880–1920* (Oxford, 1990).
8 Alexander Paterson, *Across the Bridges or Life by the South London River-Side* (London, 1911) p.119.
9 C. V. Butler, *Social Conditions in Oxford* (London, 1912) p.53.
10 Spencer J. Gibb, *The Problem of Boy Work* (London, 1906) p.7.
11 R.A. Bray, 'The apprenticeship question', *Economic Journal* 19 (1909)

p.408.

12 Spencer J. Gibb, *The Boy and His Work* (London, 1911) pp.11–12.

13 C. B. Hawkins, *Norwich, a Social Study* (London, 1910) pp. 42–3, 65.

14 Butler *Social Conditions in Oxford*, p.55.

15 Paterson, *Across the Bridges*, pp. 126–7.

16 R.H. Tawney, 'The economics of boy labour', *Economic Journal* 19 (1909) p.527.

17 J. O. Dunlop, *English Apprenticeship and Child Labour* (London, 1912).

18 1909 XXXVII CD 4499 *Report of the Royal Commission on the Poor Law*, vol. I, pp. 407–11, 630.

19 Arnold Freeman, *Boy Life and Labour* (London, 1914) pp. 227–8.

20 Professor S. Chapman in 1909 XVII Cd 4757 *Report of the Consultative Committee . . . Continuation Schools* (A.H.D. Acland) vol. I, p.176.

21 G. A. N. Lowndes, *The Silent Social Revolution 1895–1965* (Oxford, 1969) pp. 3, 4, 61.

22 Michael Sadler, *Report on Secondary Education in Liverpool* (London, n.d. (1904)) p. 156.

23 Butler, *Social Conditions in Oxford*, p.165.

24 Paterson, *Across the Bridges*, pp. 65, 68.

25 Gibb, *The Boy and his Work*, pp. 84–5, 88. Also Gibb, *The Problem of Boy Work*, p.44; Spencer J. Gibb, *Boy Work, Exploitation or Training?* (London, 1919) p. 146; J. J. Findlay (ed.) *The Young Wage Earner and the Problem of his Education* (London, 1918) p.45; W. R. Lawson, *John Bull and his Schools, a Book for Parents, Ratepayers and Men of Business* (London, 1908) pp. 19–21, in the same vein.

26 Eglantyne Jebb, *Cambridge, a Brief Study in Social Questions* (Cambridge, 1906) p.148.

27 1909 XVII Cd 4757 (Acland) vol. I p.456.

28 Paterson, *Across the Bridges*, p.164.

29 Freeman, *Boy Life and Labour*, pp.126–7; E.J. Urwick (ed.) *Studies of Boy Life in Our Cities* (London, 1904) p.285.

30 Clarence H. Creasey, *Technical Education in Evening Schools* (London, 1905) p.*v*.

31 Sadler, *Report on Secondary Education in Liverpool*, pp. 64, 125.

32 Gibb, *The Problem of Boy Work*, p.37.

33 Hawkins, *Norwich, a Social Study*, p.197.

34 Keith McClelland, 'The transmission of collective knowledge: apprenticeship in engineering and shipbuilding 1850–1914' in Penny Summerfield and Eric Evans (eds) *Technical Education and the State since 1850* (Manchester, 1990); Paul Robertson, 'Technical education in the British shipbuilding and marine engineering industries

1863–1914', *Economic History Review*, (1974) May.

35 William Knox, 'Apprenticeship and deskilling in Britain 1850– 1914', *International Review of Social History*, 31 (1986) pt. 2; C.V. More, *Skill and the English Working Class 1870–1914* (London, 1980).

36 N.B. Dearle, *Industrial Training* (London, 1914) pp. 351–5.

37 J. G. Cloate 'The boy and his work' in Urwick (ed.) *Studies of Boy Life in Our Cities*, p.115.

38 Jebb, *Cambridge, a Brief Study*, p.79.

39 Cloate 'The boy and his work' p. 115.

40 Bray, *Boy Labour and Apprenticeship*, p.210.

41 Dearle, *Industrial Training*, p.45.

42 Hawkins, *Norwich, a Social Study*, p.197.

43 William Calderwood in 1917–18 XI Cd 8512 *Final Report of the Departmental Committee on Juvenile Education in Relation to Employment*, (J.J. Lewis) vol. I p.69.

44 More, *Skill and the English Working Class 1870–1914*, pp. 203–4.

45 John Springhall, *Coming of Age: Adolescence in Britain 1860–1960* (Dublin, 1986) p.173; Hendrick, *Images of Youth*, Ch. 4 on unease about the social life of the working-class young.

46 John R. Gillis, 'The evolution of juvenile delinquency in England 1890–1914', *Past and Present* (1975) May.

47 Stephen Humphries, *Hooligans or Rebels? An Oral History of Working Class Childhood and Youth 1889–1939* (Oxford, 1981) pp. 94–6; Geoffrey Pearson, *Hooligan, a History of Respectable Fears* (London, 1983) Ch. 4.

48 Humphries, *Hooligans or Rebels*, p.45. Vic Amey born 1896.

49 Cloate 'The boy and his work' in Urwick (ed.) *Studies of Boy Life in Our Cities*, pp. 108–10, and Alex Paterson, *Across the Bridges*, p.119, make this point.

50 Ald. J. R. Heape, Chairman of Rochdale Technical School Sub–Committee in *Report of the Mosely Educational Commission to the United States of America* 1903 (London, 1904) p.207.

51 Lady Florence Bell, *At the Works, A Study of a Manufacturing Town* (London, 1907) pp. 146–62.

52 Hoshimi Uchida, 'Japanese technical manpower in industry 1880–1930' in Howard Gospel (ed.) *Industrial Training and Technological Innovation* (London, 1991) p.114.

53 C. R. Day, 'Education for the industrial world, technical and modern instruction in France under the Third Republic 1870–1914' in R. Fox and G. Weisz, *The Organisation of Science and Technology in France 1808–1914* (Cambridge, 1980).

54 1897 XXV C 8447 *The French System of Higher Primary Schools* (R. L. Morant); Michael Sanderson 'French influences on technical and

managerial education in England 1870–1940' in T. R. Gourvish and Y. Cassis (eds) *Management in the Age of the Corporate Economy*, forthcoming.

55 Lewis Flint Anderson, *History of Manual and Industrial School Education* (New York, 1926), a useful near-contemporary account.

56 *Report of the Mosely Educational Commission to the United States of America* 1903.

57 L. R. Klemm, *Public Education in Germany and the United States* (New York, 1914); F. W. Roman, *The Industrial and Commercial Schools of the United States and Germany* (New York, 1915); M. E. Sadler, *Continuation Schools in England and Elsewhere* (Manchester, 1908) are good contemporary accounts. Also Klaus Harney, 'The emergence of the technical school system in Prussia' in Ian Inkster, *The Steam Intellect Societies* (Nottingham, 1985).

58 R. H. Best and C. K. Ogden, *The Problem of the Continuation School and its Successful Solution in Germany* (London, 1914). Best was a Birmingham brass and light fitting manufacturer who had made a comparative study of his trade in Birmingham and Berlin. He visited Kerschensteiner in 1910. Ogden was a Fellow of Magdalene College, Cambridge, and was the translator of Kerschensteiner's work. Kerschensteiner wrote an introduction to this book. R. F. Cholmeley, *Secondary Education in England* (London, 1913) Appendix I 'Munich as a model', pp. 140–3.

59 Edwin G. Cooley, *Vocational Education in Europe, a Report to the Commercial Club of Chicago*, vol.I (Chicago, 1912) p. 138, 140, 133, 108.

60 *Memorandum on the Place of the Junior Technical School in the Educational System*, Board of Education pamphlet no.83 (1930) p.8.

61 C. K. Harley, 'Skilled labour and the choice of technique in Edwardian industry', *Explorations in Economic History*, 11 (1974).

CHAPTER 2 A Solution: The Junior Technical School, 1905–1918

1 W.P. Welpton, *Primary Artisan Education* (London, 1913) p.8.

2 1909 XVII Cd 4757 *Report of the Consultative Committee on Attendance at Continuation Schools* (A.H.D. Acland) p.107; J.J. Tobias, *Crime and Industrial Society in the Nineteenth Century* (London, 1972), pp.249–52; J.S. Hurt, *Outside the Mainstream* (London, 1988).

3 G.W. Tracey, 'The origin and growth of scientific instruction, science classes under the Science and Art Department 1853-1870', *Durham Research Review*, 21 (1968) Sep.

4 G.A.N. Lowndes, *The Silent Social Revolution*, 2nd edn (Oxford, 1969) p.45.

5 Ethel M. Hogg, *The Polytechnic and its Founder Quintin Hogg*

(London, 1904, reprint 1932).

6 *Memorandum on the Place of the Junior Technical School in the Educational System*, Board of Education pamphlet no.83 (1930) pp.9–10.

7 1898 XXIV C8943 *The London Polytechnic Institutions* (Sidney Webb) p.65.

8 *Kent Education Committee Special Report on Higher Education in the County of Kent* (London, 1906) pp.38, 40, 46, 48, 228.

9 J. Lyon, 'Engineering apprenticeship and education in Bolton 1900–1914', *Vocational Aspect*, vol. 15 (1963) no. 32 (Autumn).

10 *Memorandum . . . Junior Technical School*, Board of Education pamphlet no. 83 (1930) p.10.

11 T.A. Spalding, *The Work of the London School Board* (London, 1900) p.162.

12 1909 XVII Cd 4757 (Acland) pp.106–7.

13 Olive Banks, *Parity and Prestige in English Secondary Education* (London, 1963); E. Eagelsham, *From School Board to Local Authority* (London, 1956); A.M. Kazamias, *Politics, Society and Secondary Education in England* (Pennsylvania, 1966) are valuable accounts.

14 Meriel Vlaeminke, 'The subordination of technical education in secondary schooling 1870-1914' in Penny Summerfield and Eric Evans (eds) *Technical Education and the State since 1850* (Manchester, 1990) for a more critical view of Morant.

15 1904 LXXV Cd 2172 *Regulations for Evening Schools, Technical Institutions and Schools of Art and Art Classes*, 1 Aug. 1904–31 Jul. 1905, pp.7, 22.

16 1905 LIX Cd 2574 *Regulations for Evening Schools*, p.8.

17 *Memorandum on the Place of the Junior Technical School in the Educational System*, Board of Education pamphlet no. 83 (1930) p.10.

18 *Junior Technical Schools*, Board of Education pamphlet no. 63 (1928) p.11.

19 A.E. Evans and J. Wilson, *The Association of Teachers in Technical Institutions, the First Half Century 1904–1954* (London, 1955).

20 *Report of the Consultative Committee . . . Technical High Schools* (Sir Will Spens) 1938, p.270.

21 ED 10/272 Nuffield College Social Reconstruction Survey, sessions 27 Jun. 1942. J. Paley Yorke.

22 ED 22/57 Junior technical schools, 1 Jun. 1914.

23 Welpton, *Primary Artisan Education*, pp.243–4.

24 *Report of the Consultative Committee . . . Technical High Schools* (Sir Will Spens) 1938, p.270.

25 ED 12/419 Report of HM Inspectors on the London Junior Technical Schools for Boys, 31 Jul. 1928; Stuart Maclure, *One Hundred Years*

of London Education 1870–1970 (London, 1970) p.95.

26 Apprenticeship and Skilled Employment Association, *Trades for Boys and How to Enter Them* (London, 1912) pp.188–9.

27 ED 24/1849 Draft memorandum on junior technical schools, 23 Mar. 1916.

28 *Trade and Domestic Training for Girls*, Board of Education pamphlet no.72 (1929).

29 ED 24/1849 Letter, L.A. Selby-Bigge to Major Ernest Gray, 20 Jul. 1914.

30 ED 77/206 Report of HM Inspector on the use made of the workroom of a London County Council school by the Boys Department, 4 Dec. 1911.

31 ED 24/1849 Draft memorandum on junior technical schools, 23 Mar. 1916.

32 ED 22/57 Proposals of HMIs on curriculum of trade schools, 1 Jun. 1914.

33 T.M. Pugh 'Working girls and trade schools' in J.J. Findlay (ed.) *The Young Wage Earner and the Problem of his Education* (London, 1918) p.144.

34 D.W. Thoms, *Policy Making in Education, Robert Blair and the London County Council*, Education Administration and History Monograph no. 10 (Leeds, 1980); Andrew Saint, 'Technical education and the early LCC' in Andrew Saint (ed.) *Politics and the People of London, the London County Council 1889–1965* (London, 1989).

35 N.B. Dearle, *Industrial Training* (London, 1914) p.310.

36 Gladys Carnaffan, 'Commercial education and the female office worker' in Gregory Anderson (ed.) *The White Blouse Revolution, Female Office Workers since 1870* (Manchester, 1988).

37 J.J. Findlay (ed.) *The Young Wage Earner and the Problem of his Education* pp.159-61.

38 ED 22/52 Junior day commercial schools, 5 Aug. 1910.

39 ED 24/1412 Memorandum of the relation of junior technical schools to central schools, 29 Nov. 1918.

40 ED 22/39 Memorandum, WCF to HMIs, 29 Jul. 1911.

41 ED 22/55 Memorandum, Visits to works, 1 Aug. 1912.

42 ED 22/55 Memorandum, 12 Dec. 1912.

43 ED 22/55 Memorandum, 20 Dec. 1911.

44 1913 L Cd 6919 *Board of Education Regulations for Junior Technical Schools in England and Wales* (1913).

45 *Survey of Technical and Further Education*, Board of Education pamphlet no.49 (1926) p.19.

46 ED 24/1849 Letter, Selby-Bigge to Major Ernest Gray, 20 Jul. 1914.

47 ED 24/1849 Private memorandum by Selby-Bigge, 7 Jan. 1918.

48 ED 24/1849 Letter, Selby-Bigge to Spurley Hey, 13 Mar. 1918.
49 L.A. Selby-Bigge, *The Board of Education* (London, 1927) p.55.
50 ED 10/151 National Association of Inspectors of Schools, 23 Mar. 1934.
51 H.A.L. Fisher, *An Unfinished Autobiography* (Oxford, 1940) pp.91,96 'I had no desire to alter the system'.
52 H.A.L. Fisher, *Educational Reform, an Address at the University of Manchester 26 September 1917* (Manchester, 1917) p.12; H.A.L. Fisher, *Educational Reform Speeches* (Oxford, 1918) pp.xv, 23–4, 96.
53 ED 24/1412 Memorandum on the relation of junior technical schools to central schools, 29 Nov. 1918. A private memorandum in H.A.L. Fisher's own hand.
54 8 and 9 Geo 5 Chapter 39 *An Act to Make Further Provision with Respect to Education in England and Wales*, 8 Aug. 1918.
55 ED 22/56, 16 Jul. 1913 and ED 22/87, 1 Aug. 1913, Junior technical schools application for recognition.
56 *Junior Technical Schools*, Board of Education pamphlet no.63 (1928) p.15.
57 ED 22/57 Junior technical schools, memorandum, 1 Jun. 1914. This was compiled by a small committee of Inspectors.
58 ED 22/56 Memorandum, 3 Apr. 1913.
59 ED 35/1814 Minute, Dr E.R. Edwards 16 Mar. 1907.
60 C.T. Millis, *Technical Education, its Development and Aims* (London, 1925) pp.130-1; C.T. Millis, 'Junior technical schools their status and position', *Education*, 15 Apr. 1921. Millis was Principal of Borough Polytechnic Institute, 1892–1922, whose junior technical school after the 1905 Regulations became one of the largest in the country by the early 1920s.¯
61 1917-18 XI Cd 8512 *Final Report . . . Juvenile Education in Relation to Employment* (J.H. Lewis) vol. I p.20, vol. II p.14.
62 Richard Inwards, *William Ford Stanley, His Life and Work* (London, 1911) pp.41–2, 51–66.
63 Ibid., p.81. Letter, Sir William Crookes to W.F. Stanley, 12 Mar. 1907.
64 ED 24/1849 List of recognised junior technical schools, 1916.
65 ED 12/50 Suggestions for manual instruction in public elementary day schools, Feb. 1902, and Note, 1 Jun. 1908, E.K. Chambers to M. Holmes.
66 Rev. H.S. Pelham, *The Training of a Working Boy* (London, 1914) pp.30–1.
67 A.P. Newton, *The English Elementary School* (London, 1919) Ch. VIII.
68 ED 12/50 Manual instruction in secondary schools, circular 547

(1908).

69 ED 12/211 G.A. Baxendall, Report on engineering in secondary schools, 1 Oct. 1914.

70 ED 22/57 L.A. Selby-Bigge sending to HMIs copies of letters from the War Office to General Officers Commanding, 14, 17, 19 Aug. 1914.

71 ED 22/57 Memorandum, L.A. Selby-Bigge, 8 Sep. 1914.

72 ED 22/58 Memorandum to HMIs, 22 Dec. 1915.

73 ED 24/1869 Memorandum, 9 Jan. 1918.

74 ED 24/1980 L.A. Selby-Bigge to H.A.L. Fisher, 7 Jan. 1918, and annotation by Fisher.

75 Michael Sanderson, *The Universities and British Industry 1850– 1970* (London, 1972) p.218.

76 ED 22/58 Memorandum, 10 Sep. 1915.

77 Board of Education *Annual Report 1914–15*, p.13.

78 ED 22/58 Memorandum to HMIs, 3 Aug. 1915.

79 J.H. Badley, *Education after the War* (Oxford, 1917) pp.5–6, 73. See also Sir Graham John Bower, 'The state view: International' in Huntley Carter (ed.) *Industrial Reconstruction* (London, 1917) p.17: 'German Kultur has destroyed the mind and conscience of a people'.

80 Sarah Burstall, 'The education of the girl' in *Problems of Reconstruction: Lectures and Addresses at Hampstead Garden Suburb, August 1917* (London, 1918) p.117.

81 Spencer J. Gibb, *Boy Work, Exploitation or Training* (London, 1919) pp.10–11.

82 Sir Stanley Leathes, *What is Education*? (London, 1913) pp.56–7. Leathes, of Eton and Trinity College, Cambridge, had been a lecturer in history at Cambridge and Secretary of the Civil Service Commission.

83 Edith Waterfall, *The Day Continuation School* (London, 1923) p.164.

84 Fabian Ware, *Educational Reform* (London, 1900) p.53.

85 C.F.G. Masterman, *The Condition of England* (London, 1909) p.283.

86 Martin Weiner, *English Culture and the Decline of the Industrial Spirit 1850–1980* (Cambridge, 1981).

87 ED 24/1849 Minutes of a conference of principals of junior technical schools, 18 May, 8 Jun. 1917.

88 G. Kendall, 'The influence of vocation on school education' in *Problems of Reconstruction, Lectures and Addresses at Hampstead Garden Suburb, August 1917* (London, 1918) pp.132–3. Also Edith Waterfall, *The Day Continuation School*, p.50 on the same lines.

89 1917–18 XI Cd 8512 *Final Report of the Departmental Committee on Juvenile Education in Relation to Employment after the War*, vol. II, p.78.

90 Dearle, *Industrial Training*, pp.478–9.

91 ED 24/1849 Letter, Major Ernest Gray to Selby-Bigge, 24 Jul. 1914. Gray wanted to counter these views with which he disagreed.
92 1909 XVII Cd 4757 (A.H.D. Acland) vol. I, p.143.
93 Fisher, *Educational Reform Speeches*, p.61.
94 Fisher, *An Unfinished Autobiography*, p.111.
95 *Board of Education Annual Statistics.*
96 ED 24/1849 List of recognised junior technical schools, a memorandum prepared for the Lewis Committee, 1916.
97 1917-18 XI Cd 8577 (J.H. Lewis) vol.II, p.55.
98 1919 XXI Board of Education *Annual Report 1917–18*, p.38.

CHAPTER 3 The Problems of the Junior Technical Schools

1 ED 10/147 Boots Pure Drug Co. memorandum to the Hadow Committee, 28 May 1925.
2 ED 10/151 British Association of Commercial and Industrial Education to the Consultative Committee, 26 Oct. 1934.
3 1923 X Board of Education *Annual Report 1921–2*, p.46.
4 1918 XI Cd 9011 *Report of the Committee to Enquire into the Position of Natural Science in the Educational System of Great Britain* (Sir Joseph Thomson) p.43.
5 *Association of Teachers in Technical Institutions Report of an Inquiry into the Relationships of Technical Education . . . to Industry and Commerce* (Lord Emmott) (Bootle, 1927) p.47.
6 *Memorandum on the Place of the Junior Technical School in the Educational System*, Board of Education pamphlet no. 83 (1930) p.21.
7 *Report of the Consultative Committee on Secondary Education* (Sir Will Spens) 1938, p.270.
8 *Report of the Consultative Committee on the Education of the Adolescent* (Sir Henry Hadow) 1926, p.48.
9 *Memorandum on the Place of the Junior Technical School in the Educational System*, Board of Education pamphlet no. 83 (1930) p.17.
10 *Review of Junior Technical Schools in England*, Board of Education pamphlet no.111, 1937, p.8.
11 A. Abbott, *Education for Industry and Commerce in England* (Oxford, 1933) p.107.
12 W.A. Richardson, *The Technical College* (Oxford, 1939) pp.48–9.
13 ED 10/151 National Association of Inspectors of Schools, 23 Mar. 1934.
14 ED 12/373 Letter, R.E.S. Hart to A.F. Fennell, 30 Mar. 1925 (£90–£100); Parliamentary Reply, Duchess of Atholl to W. Baker, 19 Nov. 1925 (£100); Lord Percy to Sir Charles Oman. 25 Mar. 1926 (£100–£200); ED 10/147 F. Clay to R.F. Young, average of 23 schools built 1924–5 (£108).

15 *Suggestions in Regard to Teaching in Junior Technical Schools*, Board of Education pamphlet no.113 (1937).
16 ED 20/151 Verbal evidence, J.W. Bispham to the Consultative Committee 23 March 1934.
17 ED 98/72 Manchester Dressmaking Junior Technical Schools. Officials' comments on this and other schools, 4 and 15 May 1934, 2 Jul. 1934.
18 ED 98/223 Accrington Junior Technical School. Letter, Sir Gilbert Flemming to Accrington LEA, 24 May 1938.
19 ED 10/147 Evidence of Miss B.N. Cunnington HMI, 23 May 1924.
20 Dorothy Pannett, 'A comparison of girls' junior technical schools in London and Paris', MA thesis, University of London, (1939) p.33.
21 ED 10/151 National Association of Inspectors of Schools, 23 Mar. 1934.
22 ED 98/83 Leicester. Suggested reorganisation of the junior technical school and craft schools, 28 Sep. 1927.
23 ED 12/419 Minute, Mr Swan, 28 Sep. 1933.
24 Richardson, *The Technical College*, p.49.
25 ED 22/219 Memorandum, 5 Jan. 1939.
26 *Report of the Consultative Committee on Secondary Education* (Sir Will Spens) 1938, p.106.
27 Sir Michael Sadler, *Report on Secondary Education in Liverpool* (London, 1904) p.158.
28 Richardson, *The Technical College*, pp.48–9.
29 R.F. Cholmeley, *Secondary Education in England* (London, 1913) pp.50, 52; Sadler *Report on Secondary Education in Liverpool*, p.137; H.A.L. Fisher, *Educational Reform: an Address at the University of Manchester, 26 September 1917* (Manchester, 1917) p.13.
30 F.C.C. Egerton, *The Future of Education* (London, 1914) p.166.
31 ED 24/1849 Draft memorandum on junior technical schools, WBH to HMI Mr Owen, 23 Mar. 1916.
32 ED 108/17 Letter, Lord Burnham to H.A.L. Fisher, 9 Jun. 1921.
33 ED 108/18 e.g. Letter, Sir Robert Horne of the Treasury to H.A.L. Fisher, 15 Jul. 1921.
34 ED 108/18 Minutes of the Standing Joint Committee on Salaries of Teachers in Technical Schools, 26 Jun. 1925, 30 Sep. 1927, 6 Dec. 1929.
35 *Second Report of the Standing Joint Committee . . . on . . . Salaries of Teachers* (Lord Burnham) 30 Sep. 1927.
36 ED 108/18 Minutes of the Joint Standing Committee, 22 May 1931. Paley Yorke of the Association of Teachers in Technical Institutions.
37 Ibid., 17 Oct. 1935.
38 ED 46/223 Memorandum Mr Marris, 29 Nov. 1938.

39 ED 98/1 Chipping Wycombe Junior Technical School.
40 ED 98/53 Barrow Junior Technical School.
41 Pannett, 'A Comparison of Girls Junior Technical Schools in London and Paris', MA thesis, p.132.
42 ED 22/220 Letter, W.S.E. to H.B. Wallis, 27 Mar. 1940.
43 ED 98/119 Board of Education to E.W. Woodhead, 14 Nov. 1935.
44 Pannett, 'A comparison of girls' junior technical schools', MA thesis, p.130.
45 *Report of the Consultative Committee on Secondary Education* (Sir Will Spens) 1938, p.106.
46 ED 98/54 *Bolton Junior Technical School Prospectus*, 1931–2.
47 ED 10/152 Hull Junior Technical School, Memorandum E.P. Bates, n.d. 1935.
48 ED 10/151 Memorandum on junior technical schools, J.W. Bispham, 23 Mar. 1934.
49 ED 46/224 Training of technical teachers, by a joint committee (ATI, APTI, BACIE) n.d. 1938. Also *Education after the War* (The Green Book) July 1941, p.45, makes the same point.
50 ED 22/145 Short courses on instruction for teachers in technical and evening schools, 1924, 1925.
51 ED 22/155 The training of technical and commercial teachers, 3 Jan. 1935.
52 ED 46/224 E.G. Savage to HMIs, 11 Jul. 1936.
53 ED 22/63 Recognition of new junior technical schools, 23 Nov. 1920.
54 ED 12/419 Report of HMI on London junior technical schools for boys, 31 Jul. 1928.
55 ED 22/152 E.G. Savage, Memorandum on fees in junior full time institutions, 21 Dec. 1932.
56 ED 136/31 Minute of E.G. Savage to H.B. Wallis, 3 May 1939.
57 Pannett, 'A comparison of girls' junior technical schools', MA thesis, reprints the 1939 London levels, pp. 139–41. Kenneth Lindsay, *Social Progress and Educational Waste* (London, 1926) pp. 213–15 reprints the 1926 scales.
58 1933–4 XI Board of Education *Annual Report 1934*, p.32.
59 D.W. Thoms, 'Market forces and recruitment to technical education, the example of the junior technical schools', *History of Education*, 10 (1981) no.2.
60 ED 10/153 W.P. Wheldon and C.J. Williams to the Consultative Committee *c.*1935.
61 R. Edgar, 'The organisation of junior technical education', MA thesis, University of Manchester (1946) p.93.
62 Edgar, 'The organisation of junior technical education', p.94; Thoms 'Market forces and recruitment to technical education', p.131.

63 ED 98/83 H.C. Dent, The constitution and organisation of the Gateway School 12 Jul. 1929. Dent, well known as a historian and writer on education, was described as 'A Dreamer but not a visionary' in a note by C.J. Phillips HMI on this document.

64 ED 22/48 Age limits and duration of course and curriculum of junior technical schools, 28 Apr. 1920.

65 'Junior technical schools and their regulations', *Education*, 3 Jul. 1925; and Herbert Schofield in *Education*, 10 Jul. 1925.

66 *Review of Junior Technical Schools*, Board of Education pamphlet no.111, p.13.

67 A. Little and J. Westergaard, 'The trend of class differentials in educational opportunity in England and Wales', *British Journal of Sociology*, 15 (1964); Jean Floud, 'The educational experience of the adult population of England and Wales as at July 1949' in D.V. Glass (ed.) *Social Mobility in Britain* (London, 1954).

68 *Review of Junior Technical Schools*, Board of Education pamphlet no.111, p.14.

69 Richardson, *The Technical College*, p.43.

70 Ibid., p.475.

71 1934–5 VII Board of Education *Annual Report 1935*, p.36.

72 *Memorandum on the Place of the Junior Technical School in the Educational System*, Board of Education pamphlet no.83 (1930) p.29.

73 ED 98/59 Memorandum 'Smethwick', 6 Oct. 1932, in file on Bootle.

74 ED 99/119 Norwich Junior Technical School. Letters, R.F. Betts, 25 Oct. 1930, E.W. Woodward, 27 Jul. 1935.

75 ED 98/54 Bolton Junior Technical School. Letter, John Cox, 21 Apr. 1932.

76 ED 98/10 Sunderland, Villiers Street. Interview memorandum 14 Jul. 1931; Notes of a conference with the governing board, 15 Jun. 1933.

77 ED/419 Letter, James Strachan to A. Abbott, 29 Jul. 1930.

78 ED 98/16 Letter, James Strachan to E.G. Savage, 12 Jul. 1933.

79 ED 12/149 A. Abbott to W.R. Davies, 17 Apr. 1930.

80 ED 13/419 A. Abbott to James Strachan, 7 Aug. 1930.

81 ED 22/153 Memorandum, G.E. Savage, March 1933.

82 ED 10/152 Summary of evidence relating to the age of entry to junior technical schools.

83 ED 98/84 Gateway School, Leicester.

84 ED 98/4 Workington Junior Technical School. Letter, G.B. Brown, 18 Jul. 1920. Case for decision, 5 Aug. 1930. Minute, 15 Oct. 1935.

85 *Education*, 27 Jan. 1939.

86 Edgar, 'The organisation of junior technical education', MA thesis, pp.144–5.

87 *Report of the Consultative Committee on the Education of the Adoles-*

cent (Sir Henry Hadow) 1926.

88 *The New Prospect in Education* Board of Education pamphlet no. 60, (1928) p.7.

89 Eustace Percy, *Some Memories* (London, 1958) p.95.

90 ED 136/789 The secondary technical school. Draft (1946) p.5.

91 ED 10/152 Mr G. Thompson, Headmaster of Toxteth Technical Institute, Liverpool, Dec. 1934.

92 *Review of Junior Technical Schools*, Board of Education pamphlet no.111, pp.29, 31, 33.

93 1948–9 XIV Ministry of Education *Annual Report 1949*, p. 18; E.W. Jenkins, 'Junior technical schools 1905–1945: the case of Leeds', *History of Education*, 16 (1987) no.2, shows early hopes for a city-wide system of trade schools destroyed by the inability to provide adequate buildings required by the Board and HMIs.

94 ED 98/7 Exeter Junior Technical School. Letter, A.C. Badcoe, 28 Jan. 1921, and Memorandum, R.R.C., 3 Feb. 1921.

95 ED 98/109 Westminster School of Retail Distribution, 1932.

96 *Report on Policy in Technical Education by a Joint Committee* (ATI, APTI, ATTI, National Association of Art Masters, 1938) p.42.

97 Kenneth Lindsay, *Social Progress and Educational Waste* (London, 1926) p.69.

98 ED 10/151 Memorandum, W.C. Eaton and E.G. Savage, 25 Jan. 1934. ED/147 Evidence of F.T. Howard, 26 Jun. 1924.

99 ED 10/147 HMI A.T. Kerslake, 22 May 1924.

100 ED 10/147 Evidence to the Hadow Committee of Bolton King (Warwickshire), 23 Oct. 1924; H.W. Household (Gloucestershire), 24 Oct. 1924; Spurley Hey, 23 Oct. 1924.

101 ED 10/147 James Graham, Sir Benjamin Gott, 27 Nov. 1924.

102 Thoms, 'Market forces and recruitment to technical education'.

103 C.T. Millis, 'Junior technical schools, their status and position', *Education*, 15 Apr. 1921.

104 ED 98/16 A. Abbott to W.C. Eaton, 28 Jul. 1931, expressing disquiet and reporting Meardon's speech at St Annes.

CHAPTER 4 The Junior Technical Schools and Industry, 1918–1939

1 ED 10/147 Albert Abbott in evidence to the Hadow Committee, 27 Jun. 1924.

2 *Report of an Inquiry into Apprenticeship and Training, Ministry of Labour*, 1925–6, vol. 7, pp.34, 43–5, 59.

3 ED 10/147 A.S. Bright HMI, *c*.1924.

4 *Report of an Inquiry into Apprenticeship*, Vol 7, p.61.

5 Ibid., pp.64–5.

6 Ibid., pp.105–6.

7 *Factors in Industrial and Commercial Efficiency (Committee on Industry and Trade)* (Sir Arthur Balfour) 1927, p.19.
8 *Report of an Inquiry into Apprenticeship*, vol 7.
9 ED 98/53 Report of HMI on certain alternative courses in secondary schools in Yorkshire (West Riding) 8 Apr. 1935.
10 ED 12/479 *National Council on Commercial Education, Policy on Commercial Education*, 1942.
11 ED 10/147 Evidence of Sir Robert Blair, 27 Feb. 1925.
12 *Final Report of the Committee on Education for Salesmanship* (Sir Francis Goodenough) 1931, pp. 34, 45, 129.
13 ED 136/669 Technical education, some social factors, Feb. 1942.
14 ED 10/147 Evidence of A. Abbott, 27 Jun. 1924. Ironically Abbott became Assessor to the Goodenough Committee.
15 *Report of the Consultative Committee on Secondary Education with Special Reference to Grammar Schools and Technical High Schools* (Sir Will Spens) 1938, pp. 283–4.
16 ED 10/152 Memorandum, Miss M. Dunn, Headmistress of Blackpool Collegiate (Girls' Grammar) School, *c.*1935.
17 As did the author's mother, a pupil of Manchester High School for Girls and the Blackpool Collegiate referred to in the previous note.
18 *Trade and Domestic Training for Girls*, Board of Education pamphlet no.72 (1929).
19 ED 10/147 Evidence of Miss B.M. Cunnington HMI, 23 May 1924.
20 ED 10/152 Evidence of E.M. Rich, 26 Nov. 1935.
21 Dorothy Pannett, 'A comparison of girls' junior technical schools in London and Paris' MA thesis, University of London (1939).
22 ED 10/151 Association of Principals of Technical Institutes, 22 Nov. 1934, specimen curricula.
23 ED 10/147 Evidence of Miss B.M. Cunnington, 23 May 1924.
24 ED 24/1849 Recognition of new junior technical schools, 23 Nov. 1920.
25 ED 10/147 Miss B.M. Cunnington, 23 May 1924.
26 ED 10/151 Miss H. Johnston HMI, 26 Jan. 1934.
27 ED 10/152 Miss E.H. Horniblow CBE, HMI, 28 May 1936.
28 ED 10/152 Memorandum, Miss H. Sanders, n.d. 1934.
29 1914–16 XVIII Board of Education *Annual Report 1913–14*, p.115.
30 ED 98/118 Elmham Watts Naval Training School letters, 3 Apr. 1930, and minutes, 16 Nov. 1932, 17 May 1933. *Training Ships and Training Schools for the British Merchant Marine*, Departmental paper no.319 (1916).
31 ED 13/669 Merchant Navy Training Board, outline plan for post war training, n.d. *c.*1942.
32 ED 22/153 F. Bray HMI, Account of a voyage from Hull to the Faroe

Isles in the steam trawler *Sir John Hotham*, 11 Oct. 1933.

33 1913 L Cd 6919 *Board of Education Regulations for Junior Technical Schools in England and Wales*, clause 2(b).

34 R. Inwards, *William Ford Stanley, His Life and Work* (London, 1911) p.25.

35 A.E. Evans and J. Wilson, *The Association of Teachers in Technical Institutions, the First-Half Century 1904–1954* (London, 1955) p.18.

36 1918 IX Cd 9036 *Report of the Committee . . . Position of Modern Languages in the Educational System of Great Britain* (Sir Stanley Leathes).

37 ED 10/147 House of Commons questions, 1 and 3 Aug. 1922.

38 ED 98/75 Preston Junior Technical School, HMI report, 1932.

39 ED 10/152 Memorandum on Hull Junior Technical School by E.P. Bates.

40 ED 98/4 Workington Junior Technical School. Letter, G.B. Brown, 18 Jul. 1929.

41 ED 10/152 Memorandum by A.B. Coles, n.d. probably 1935.

42 J. Dover Wilson, *The Schools of England* (London, 1928) Ch. VIII by E. Salter Davies, p.172.

43 ED 98/4 Workington Junior Technical School. Memorandum, W.S.D., 21 Aug. 1929.

44 ED 98/20 Colchester Junior Technical School. Letter, W.H. Whyte, 29 May 1933, and Memo., J.E. to Mr Jenkins, 2 Jun. 1933.

45 ED 98/16 Sunderland Junior Technical School. Letter, Herbert Reed, 21 Mar. 1933. Notes of a conference with the governing body, 15 Jun. 1933.

46 ED 98/152 Doncaster Junior Technical School, Spring 1934.

47 Personal interview with Mr John Neal, 4 Jan. 1991.

48 Sir Michael Sadler, *Report on Secondary Education in Liverpool* (London, 1904) pp. 9, 10, 74.

49 *Kent Education Committee Special Report on Higher Education in the County of Kent* (London, 1906) p.241.

50 1909 XVII Cd 4757 *Report of the Consultative Committee on Attendance at Continuation Schools* (A.H.D. Acland) p.121.

51 *Report of the Committee on Education and Industry (England and Wales)* (Sir Dougal Malcolm) 1928, pt.II, p.42.

52 Eustace Percy, *Education at the Crossroads* (London, 1930) p.66.

53 1937–8 X Board of Education *Annual Report 1938*, p.28. This phrase was recurrent, e.g. ED 136/132 Robert Wood to E.G. Savage, 17 May 1938, and ED 136/669 Technical education, some social factors, Feb. 1942.

54 R.W. Ferguson (ed.) *Training in Industry, a Report . . . by the AEIC* (London, 1935) p.112.

55 *Report of the Committee on Education and Industry (England and Wales)* (Sir Dougal Malcolm) pt.II, p.43.
56 Ibid., p.33.
57 ED 136/132 Letter, H.B. Wallis to Gilbert Flemming, 19 Jul. 1939.
58 ED 24/1869 A. Abbott, 9 Mar. 1925.
59 ED 98/16 Sunderland Junior Technical School.
60 ED 10/152 E.P. Bates, referring to the period 1915–35.
61 ED 98/123 Particulars of Newark Junior Technical School, 29 May 1935.
62 ED 10/151 Evidence of A. Abbott to the Consultative Committee, 26 Jan. 1934.
63 ED 136/132 Memorandum, E.G. Savage, 25 Mar. 1928.
64 ED 10/147 Boots Pure Drug Co., 27 May 1925, and R.W. Ferguson of Cadbury's, 24 Apr. 1925, evidence to the Hadow Committee.
65 ED 12/479 ICI evidence to the Norwood Committee, n.d. *c.*1943.
66 A.P.M. Fleming, 'Critical review of education and training for engineers', paper to the Institute of Electrical Engineers, 1 Jan. 1942, sent by Fleming to Norwood in ED 12/479.
67 ED 10/151 Memorandum of the National Association of Inspectors of Schools, 23 Mar. 1934.
68 *Education for the Engineering Industry* (Sir Dugald Clerk) 1931, pp. 7, 25.
69 *Education for Industry and Commerce, the West Midlands Metal Working Area* Board of Education pamphlet no.74 (1930) pp.19, 38.
70 *Survey of Technical and Further Education in England and Wales*, Board of Education pamphlet no.49 (1946) p.49.
71 Ibid., p.52.
72 *Factors in Industrial and Commercial Efficiency* (Sir Arthur Balfour), p.195.
73 ED 24/1868 The Institute of Builders. Papers read before a conference, 21 Jul. 1924. A.H. Adamson and various papers in this file.
74 1909 XVII Cd 4757 (Acland) p.114.
75 F.C.C. Egerton, *The Future of Education* (London, 1914) pp.158– 9.
76 ED 136/669 H.B. Wallis, Training of young workers in the coal mining industry, Dec. 1941.
77 *Survey of Technical and Further Education in England and Wales*, Board of Education pamphlet no.49, p.56.
78 Ibid., p.52.
79 Ibid., p.52, and *Factors in Industrial and Commercial Efficiency* (Sir Arthur Balfour) p.206.
80 *Report of an Inquiry into Apprenticeship*, vol. 4, p.5.
81 Arthur W. Ashby and Phoebe G. Byles, *Rural Education* (Oxford, 1923) p.214.

82 ED 10/152 H.M. Spink, Director of Education for Northumberland, 19 Jul. 1935.
83 ED 10/153 Mr Hacking, Applied biology in rural central schools, n.d. 1935.
84 ED 10/152 See T. Owen for Wales, E.P. Le Breton for Dorset, C.Foster for Somerset, all in 1935.
85 ED 10/153 Evidence of the County Councils Association 24 May 1935.
86 *Report of the Consultative Committee on Secondary Education* (Sir Will Spens) 1938, p.325.
87 ED 12/497 National Union of Agricultural Workers, April 1942.
88 ED 136/669 H.B. Wallis, Some problems in technical education, 7 Apr. 1941.
89 Radio 4 'On Your Farm' 25 Jan. 1992.
90 ED 22/145 The encouragement of technical education by employers, 29 Jul. 1925, statistical appendix. These figures were then reprinted in the Malcolm Report, pp. 78–9.
91 ED 22/146 List of gifts, money and equipment to technical colleges and junior technical schools to 29 Jan. 1926.
92 ED 10/147 Evidence of H.E. Boothroyd HMI, 27 Jun. 1924.
93 ED 98/189 Sunderland Villiers St Junior Technical School.
94 ED 98/53 Barrow Junior Technical School.
95 ED 98/1 Chipping Wycombe. W.H. Healey, 22 Jul. 1927.
96 ED 10/153 Gateway School, Leicester. E.C. White on leavers of 1933–4.
97 ED 12/472 Enquiry into conditions of employment of ex-secondary school boys by Balham Rotary Club, 26 Aug. 1937.
98 ED 12/427 Letters between Sir Philip Dawson, MP, Sir Maurice Holmes, H.M. Emmerson (Ministry of Labour) and H.B. Wallis, 12–25 Feb. 1938.
99 ED 10/147 Dr H. Schofield, 25 Jun. 1925.
100 *Trade and Domestic Training for Girls*, Board of Education pamphlet no.72 (1929) p.16.
101 ED 10/152 Memorandum, Miss H. Sanders (LCC organizer of womens' technical classes) n.d. 1934.
102 C.F.G. Masterman, *England after the War* (London,1922) pp. 71–2.
103 Guy Routh, *Occupation and Pay in Great Britain 1906–1960* (London, 1965) pp. 104, 107.
104 ED 136/669 Data in memorandum, Technical education, some social factors, Feb. 1942.
105 ED 136/296 The education and training of the adolescent, memorandum from Sir William Jowitt to Earl de la Warr, 4 May 1942. These points were repeated in other Board memoranda.

106 *Report of an Inquiry into Apprenticeship and Training*, 1925–6 vol. 6 Engineering, 1928, p.115.
107 ED 12/419 Report of HM Inspectors on the London junior technical schools for boys, 21 Jul. 1928.
108 1934–5 VIII Board of Education *Annual Report 1935*, p.35.
109 ED 98/223 Accrington Junior Technical School. Printed letter by Sir Percy Meardon, June 1938.
110 ED 10/272 Nuffield Survey, The education services in Stoke-on-Trent 4 Aug. 1942.
111 ED 147/195 File of letters from JTSs to Antony Part, 1946.
112 ED 147/195 Letter, Antony Part to R.A.R. Tricker, 15 Jul. 1946.
113 1934–5 VIII Board of Education *Annual Report 1935*, p.31.
114 *Memorandum on the Place of the Junior Technical School in the Educational System*, Board of Education pamphlet no.83 (1930) p.18.
115 ED 24/1849 Address by Herwald Ramsbotham MP (Parliamentary Secretary to the Board of Education) at the opening of Sheffield Junior Technical School, 16 Dec. 1933.
116 A. Abbott, *Education for Industry and Commerce in England* (Oxford, 1933) p.106. Maurice Holmes told Hadow that 20,000 was the minimum catchment population: ED 10/147, 23 May 1924.
117 1934–5 VIII Board of Education *Annual Report 1935*, p.33.
118 *Co-operation in Technical Education. Report of a Conference of Representatives of the Association of Local Education Authorities and the LCC.* (HMSO, 1937).
119 W. McG. Eager and H.A. Secretan, *Unemployment among Boys* (London, 1925) pp. 31, 33.
120 J. Jewkes and A. Winterbottom, *Juvenile Unemployment* (London, 1933) p.26.
121 Ibid., p.27.
122 *Report of the Committee on Education and Industry* (1928) p.37.
123 Dorothy Pannett, 'A comparison of girls' junior technical schools', MA thesis, p.154.
124 ED 10/152 Memorandum, Miss H. Sanders, *c*.1934.
125 ED 10/273 Educational organisation for the age range 14 to 16+ in relation to conditions of employment, 10 Nov. 1937.
126 ED 12/478 H.B. Wallis, Intake into employment from full time schools, Oct. 1942.
127 R.A. Butler Archive, RAB K10/126 Address to the Union of Lancashire and Cheshire Institutes, Wigan, 2 Oct. 1942.
128 R.H. Tawney, *Secondary Education for All, a Policy for Labour* (London, 1922) pp. 107–113.
129 J. MacTavish (Secretary of the WEA) in Huntley Carter (ed.) *Industrial Reconstruction* (London, 1917) p.147.

130 William Temple cited in G. Sherington, *English Education, Social Change and War 1911–1920* (Manchester, 1981) p.102.
131 ED 10/147 TUC evidence to Hadow Committee, 26 Jun. 1925.
132 ED 10/151 TUC evidence to the Consultative Committee (Spens), 19 Jul. 1934.
133 ED 10/147 NUT evidence to Hadow Committee, 18 Dec. 1924.
134 ED 10/152 NUT evidence to the Consultative Committee (Spens), May 1935.
135 D.W. Thoms, 'Market forces and recruitment to technical education, the example of the junior technical schools', *History of Education*, 10 (1981) no.2, p.130.
136 ED 12/479 Norwood Papers. Responses to 'Question 21'.
137 ED 10/151 Incorporated Association of Headmasters, 19 May 1934, and Incorporated Association of Assistant Masters in Secondary Schools, 22 Mar. 1934.
138 ED 10/151 Headmasters Conference (Spencer Leeson and G.C. Turner) n.d. 1934.
139 ED 10/150 Evidence of Professor H.A. Harris, 24 Jan. 1935.
140 ED 10/147 Memorandum by Dr Cyril Burt presented to the Hadow and Spens Committees.
141 ED 10/151 Evidence of Professor Cyril Burt, 25 Jan. 1935.
142 ED 10/150 Evidence of Professor C.W. Valentine, 24 Jan. 1935.
143 ED 10/152 Evidence from the National Institute of Industrial Psychology and verbal evidence from Dr C. S. Myers and A. Macrae, 27 Jun. 1935.

CHAPTER 5 The Junior Technical Schools and Second World War

1 H. C. Dent, *Education in Transition, a Sociological Study of the Impact of War on English Education 1939–1943* (London, 1944) p.136.
2 Circular 1473 Schooling in an emergency, 29 Aug. 1939.
3 ED 121/257 Education in the first four months of the war, Jan. 1940. A memorandum produced for the Netherlands Government.
4 ED 135/2 The re-opening of secondary and junior technical schools in evacuation areas.
5 ED 136/669 Further education in war-time, n.d. probably Nov. 1939.
6 ED 22/221 Note on the position of junior technical and similar schools at the end of November 1940.
7 ED 10/272 A. Bentwich, A survey of wartime education in London, 30 Mar. 1942.
8 ED 10/272 Nuffield College Social Reconstruction Survey report on public education services in Devon, 1 Feb. 1943.
9 ED 22/219 Requisition of technical schools by other departments, 5 Oct. 1939.

10 ED 22/220 Memorandum to HMIs about mobilising premises and equipment of technical colleges, 23 Mar. 1940.
11 ED 10/272 Nuffield College Social Reconstruction Survey report on public education services in Devon, 1 Feb. 1943.
12 ED 22/220 Training for war industries, 7 Aug. 1940.
13 ED 121/217 The use of teachers for certain war time activities, 12 Mar. 1941.
14 ED 121/217 The employment of aliens, 14 Feb. 1941.
15 ED 12/217 Letters, A. F. Rouse to R. N. Dunkley, 1 May 1941. R. N. Dunkley to G. D. Rokeling, 1 Jul. 1941.
16 ED 98/174 Luton JTS, 19 Jun. 1942.
17 ED 136/669 R. A. Butler, Technical colleges and the war effort, Nov. 1941. A memorandum for the War Cabinet produced by H. B. Wallis.
18 ED 10/272 Nuffield College Social Reconstruction Survey report on public education services in Devon, 1 Feb. 1943.
19 ED 10/272 A. M. Lewis, The effect of the war upon London education, Nov. 1942. Interview with Mr Reynolds, Juvenile Employment Officer, King's Cross Exchange.
20 Dent, *Education in Transition*, p.219.
21 ED 77/158 Full time technical and commercial instruction for pupils under 16 years of age in the CB of Bristol, Apr. 1940.
22 ED 98/174 Luton. Letter, H. E. Baines to Board of Education, 19 Jun. 1940.
23 ED 98/210 Canterbury. Letter, R. H. Stevens to Board of Education, 29 May 1941.
24 ED 98/174 Luton. Memorandum, Mr Rokeling, 23 Apr. 1942.
25 ED 22/219 Letter to aircraft firms, 1 May 1939, following Board of Education consultation with the Education Committee of the Society of British Aircraft Construction.
26 ED 22/219 Pre-nursing courses in secondary and technical schools, 30 Jun. 1939.
27 ED 98/210 Canterbury JTS.
28 R. Edgar, 'The organisation of junior technical education', MA thesis, Manchester University, (1946) pp. 32–4.
29 G. F. Taylor, 'Selection for junior and secondary technical education' *Vocational Aspect*, 20 (1965) no.47, Autumn, pp. 157–64.
30 ED 98/210 Canterbury JTS.
31 1943 Cmd 6433 *Report of the Committee on Post War Agricultural Education* (Lord Luxmoore) pp. 37, 74, 83.
32 ED 147/207 A. G. Gooch, Secondary technical education, 28 Dec. 1954.
33 P.H.J.H. Gosden, *Education in the Second World War, a Study in Policy and Administration* (London, 1976) p.137.

34 ED 135/2 Memorandum to Inspectors. Junior technical schools and the building industry, 4 Feb. 1942.
35 ED 135/2 Notes on junior technical schools for the building industry, 10 Aug. 1942.
36 1943 Cmd 6433 *Training for the Building Industry*, p.5.
37 Taylor, 'Selection for junior and secondary technical education', pp. 148–9.
38 ED 98/201 Southampton Building JTS.
39 Taylor, 'Selection for junior and secondary technical education', p.151.
40 ED 135/4 Inspectors' memorandum. Junior technical schools for building, 4 Aug. 1944.
41 ED 46/224 Letter, W. H. Jackson to C.I. Mr Elliott, 25 Jun. 1942.
42 ED 46/224 Training of technical teachers in women's subjects, 23 Jan. 1943, and many letters about Miss Browning, 1942–3.
43 ED 46/224 Memorandum, 5 Mar. 1943.
44 ED 46/224 Letter, H.B. Wallis to H. J. Shelley, 10 Aug. 1944.
45 ED 46/224 Letter, H.B. Wallis to H. J. Shelley, 12 Aug. 1944.
46 ED 46/224 G. N. Flemming, Training for the teaching of technical subjects, 12 Aug. 1944.
47 ED 46/224 Letter, H. B. Wallis to H. J. Shelley, 6 Aug. 1944.
48 ED 46/223 Nuffield College. Analysis of replies from industrial workers who are considering entering into the teaching profession, 1 Jun. 1944. G. D. H. Cole sent a copy to R. A. Butler.
49 ED 136/427 Memorandum, Sep. 1943.

CHAPTER 6 Policy and the Technical School from Spens to Butler

1 ED 136/669 H.B. Wallis to R.A. Butler, 27 Sep. 1941.
2 ED 10/273 Memorandum, R.S. Wood, 30 Jul. 1937, and discussion on Wood's paper.
3 ED 10/273 Memorandum on a meeting of G.G. Williams and Dr Innes, 7 Dec. 1937.
4 ED 10/273 Memorandum on the organisation of post-primary education, 31 May 1938.
5 *Report of the Consultative Committee on Secondary Education with Special Reference to Grammar Schools and Technical High Schools* (Sir Will Spens) 1938.
6 ED 10/151 Association of Teachers in Technical Institutions, 28 Jun. 1934.
7 ED 10/151 Association of Principals of Technical Institutions, 22 Nov. 1934. See also ATTI and APTI, *Report on Policy in Technical Education* 1937 (copy in Cambridge University Library, 1938. 8. 790).
8 ED 10/151 BACIE, 26 Oct. 1934.

9 *Report of the Consultative Committee* (Spens) 1938, p. 270.
10 Ibid., p. 282.
11 Ibid., p. 276.
12 Ibid., p.278.
13 Ibid., p.277.
14 Ibid., p. *xxx*.
15 Ibid., p. 374.
16 Ibid., p. 322.
17 ED 136/131 Estimate of increased cost of salary proposals in the Spens Report.
18 ED 136/131 Secondary Advisory Committee, 7 Feb. 1939.
19 ED 136/131 LEA Advisory Committee, Sir Percival Sharp, 30 Jun. 1939.
20 ED 136/131 Minute of E.G. Savage and H.B. Wallis, 3 May 1939.
21 ED 136/131 Secondary Advisory Committee, 7 Feb. 1939.
22 ED 136/131 T. Boyce, LEA Advisory Committee, 30 Jun. 1939.
23 ED 136/131 G.G. Williams, Note on the Spens Report, 16 Jun. 1939.
24 ED 136/131 Minute of E.G. Savage and H.B. Wallis, 3 May 1939.
25 ED 136/131 LEA Advisory Committee, 30 Jun. 1939.
26 ED 136/131 Sir Maurice Holmes, 5 Jul. 1939. Holmes had first entered the Board in 1909 in Sir Robert Morant's day.¯
27 ED 136/132 Memorandum, E.G. Savage, 25 Mar. 1938, and Postscript to the report . . . Berlin, 25–29 July 1938.
28 ED 136/132 Letter, Lord Stanhope to Sir Thomas Inskip, n.d. 1938.
29 ED 136/132 Memorandum, R.S. Wood, 4 Nov. 1938.
30 ED 136/132 Letter, Lord de la Warr to Oliver Stanley, and Memorandum to the Chancellor of the Exchequer, 19 Dec. 1938 and 1 Mar. 1939.
31 ED 136/132 Letter, Sir John Simon, 8 Mar. and 4 May 1939.
32 ED 136/132 Letters, Sir Horace Wilson to Sir Maurice Holmes, 13–18 Jul. 1939, and Letter, Holmes to Sir Frank Tribe, 18 Jul. 1939.
33 Viscount Simon, *Retrospect* (London, 1952) pp.232–3.
34 R.G. Wallace, 'The origins and authorship of the 1944 Education Act', *History of Education*, 10 (1981) no. 4.
35 Noel Annan, *Our Age, Portrait of a Generation* (London, 1990) p. 362.
36 *Education after the War* (The Green Book) June 1941. A copy is in file ED 136/124.
37 ED 136/257 Education after the war. Discussions of the Association of Technical Institutions and APTI on the Green Book.
38 ED 136/257 H.B. Wallis, 16 Jan. 1942 and Green Book discussions, 16 Feb. 1942.
39 Anthony Howard, *RAB, the Life of R.A. Butler* (London, 1987) p. 115;

R.A. Butler, *The Art of the Possible* (London, 1971) p. 94.

40 ED 136/296 H.B. Wallis to R.A. Butler, 5 Sep. 1941.

41 ED 136/669 H.B. Wallis, Some problems in technical education, 17 Apr. 1941. This was written before RAB took office but read by him.

42 R.A. Butler Archive. RAB H70/381. R.A. Butler's annotation on a memorandum by H.B. Wallis and Maurice Holmes, 24 Sep. 1941.

43 ED 136/296 H.B. Wallis, Technical education in post war policy and organisation, 15 Oct. 1941.

44 ED 136/669 Technical education, some social factors, Feb. 1942. This important document seems to have been compiled by R.S. Wood for Butler.

45 The Diaries of James Chuter Ede. British Library Add MS 59690 vol. I, 15 Aug. 1941.

46 Ibid., vol. II, Add MS 59691, 21 Oct. 1941.

47 Ibid., vol. IV, Add MS 59693, 24 Mar. 1942.

48 Ibid., vol. II, Add MS 59691, 13 Oct. 1941.

49 Ibid., vol. V, Add MS 59694, 24 Apr. 1942.

50 Ibid., vol. VI, Add MS 59695, 28 Oct. 1942.

51 RAB H70/351 *The Statutory Educational System*, Jan. 1944, pp.10, 22–3, and the various drafts H70/244, 256, 277.

52 RAB H70 Suggestions for discussion, 30 Mar. 1944.

53 RAB H70/178 Memorandum, H.B. Wallis to R.A. Butler, 15 Jan. 1945.

54 RAB H70/173 R.A. Butler to H.B. Wallis, 18 Jan. 1945.

55 Dame Margaret Cole, *The Life of G.D.H. Cole* (London, 1971) pp. 235–252; L.P. Carpenter, *G.D.H. Cole, an Intellectual Biography* (Cambridge, 1973) pp. 197–202; G.D.N. Worswick, 'Cole and Oxford 1938–1958' in Asa Briggs and John Saville (eds) *Essays in Labour History* (London, 1967).

56 ED 10/272 Papers of the Nuffield College Social Reconstruction Survey 'Education in relation to industry and vocation', 27 Jun. 1942, E.G. Savage, J. Paley Yorke, G.D.H. Cole.

57 Nuffield College, *Industry and Education, a Statement* (Oxford, 1943). Butler's copy is in file ED 10/272.

58 ED 12/478 Letter, Cyril Norwood to R.A. Butler, 6 Mar. 1942.

59 ED 10/272 Letter, R.A. Butler to G.D.H. Cole, 26 Jan. 1943.

60 Samuel Courtauld, 'An industrialist's reflections on the future relations of government and industry', *Economic Journal*, 52 (1942) Apr. pp.10–11. The script of a speech Courtauld gave as a follow-up to his article in R.A. Butler's papers RAB K/11.

61 *From School to Work: Education, Recruitment and Training for Industry and Commerce. Report of a Conference of the British Association for Commerce and Industrial Education*, 27 Mar. 1942.

In R.A. Butler Archive RAB K/13.

62 R.A. Butler Archive. RAB K10/126 Script of address to the Union of Lancashire and Cheshire Institutes meeting, Wigan, 2 Oct. 1942.

63 RAB K10/135 Script of address to the Federation of Education Committees for Wales, 23 Oct. 1942.

64 RAB K10/145 Script of address to the AGM of the Institute of the Plastics Industry, 28 Oct. 1942.

65 RAB K11/37 *Cotton Industry and Education, Recruitment and Training of Cotton Workers. Report of a Conference Convened by the Cotton Board*, 24 Mar. 1943. RAB K11/33 Script of R.A. Butler's address to this conference.

66 RAB K11/88 Scripts of speech at Birmingham Town Hall, 8 Sep. 1943 and RAB K11/104 Lunchtime lecture at St Paul's, 13 Oct. 1943.

67 Cyril Norwood, *The English Tradition of Education* (London, 1929) pp. 90–1, 185, 257.

68 Cyril Norwood, *The Curriculum in Secondary Schools* (Association for Education in Citizenship, 1937?) in ED 10/273.

69 ED 136/131 R.A. Butler's personal notes on an interview with Sir Will Spens, 20 Mar. 1942.

70 ED 12/478 Letter, Sir Walter Citrine to R.A. Butler, 3 Mar. 1942.

71 ED 12/478 Memorandum by R.H. Barrow, 16 Oct. 1941.

72 ED 12/478 G.G. Williams to R.A. Butler, 23 Dec. 1941.

73 ED 12/478 Notes of a discussion with Sir Cyril Norwood and Technical Branch, 25 Feb. 1942.

74 ED 12/478 *Trades Union Congress Statement on the Spens Report* sent to Norwood.

75 ED 12/479 e.g. G.T.R. Potter of High Pavement School, Nottingham, J.W. Stork of Portsmouth G.S., A.L. Nichols of Exeter; also Incorporated Association of Headmasters, *The Future of Education*.

76 ED 12/479 e.g. National Association of Inspectors of Schools, Institute of Builders in Letter, 5 June 1942; Ministry of Labour and National Service.

77 ED 12/479 Memorandum by Dr W.P. Alexander, n.d.

78 L.S. Hearnshaw, *Cyril Burt, Psychologist*, (London, 1979) p. 117.

79 Sir Antony Part, *The Making of a Mandarin* (London, 1990) p. 19.

80 ED 12/478 Letter, R.S. Wood to H.B. Wallis, 13 Apr. 1942.

81 ED 12/478 Letter, R.H. Barrow to G.G. Williams, 25 Oct. 1942.

82 ED 12/478 Letter, Cyril Norwood to G.G. Williams, 6 Jun. 1942.

83 ED 12/479 Norwood Committee meeting, 5–7 Jan. 1942.

84 Ibid., 12–13 Jun. 1942.

85 Ibid., 18–19 Sep. 1942.

86 Ibid., 2–3 Oct. 1942.

87 Board of Education, *Curriculum and Examinations in Second-*

ary Schools. Report of the Committee of the Secondary Schools Examinations Council (Sir Cyril Norwood) 1943, pp. 2–4, 14, 20, 130–33.

88 C.L. Burt, 'The psychological implications of the Norwood Report', *British Journal of Educational Psychology*,13 (1943).

89 Hearnshaw, *Cyril Burt*, p. 117.

90 W.P. Alexander, *Intelligence, Concrete and Abstract* (Cambridge, 1935).

91 RAB F/103 Draft clauses and schedules, 24 Feb.-26 Nov. 1943. R.A. Butler's copies.

92 Diaries of Chuter Ede, vol. 7, BL Add MS 59696, 24 Feb. 1943.

93 Ibid., 1 Mar. 1943.

94 Ibid., 6 and 7 Apr. 1943.

95 Diaries of Chuter Ede, BL, vol. 7, 19 and 27 May 1943, for conversations between Ede, Sir Maurice Holmes and Butler about whether Morant was a 'thug', 'unscrupulous', 'unprincipled' or 'mad'.

96 1943 Cmd 6458 *Educational Reconstruction*, pp. 9–10, 32.

97 House of Commons debates 1942–3, vol. 391, Debate on education reconstruction, 29 Jul. 1943, R.A. Butler col. 1832.

98 Ibid., Mrs Cazalet-Keir col. 1922, Mr Linstead col. 1955, Mr Cove col. 1962.

99 Thelma Cazalet-Keir, *From the Wings* (London, 1967) p.142.

100 House of Lords debates 1942–3, vol. 128, Lord Selborne, Aug. 1943 col. 986.

101 House of Lords debates 1942–3, vol. 126, Lord Selborne, 17 Feb. 1943 col. 98.

102 ED 136/427 Memorandum on the White Paper proposals in so far as they affect technical education, Aug. 1943.

103 *The Times*, Letter, H. Richardson of Bradford Technical College, 30 Sep. 1943.

104 ED 136/427 Memorandum, H.B. Wallis 30 Sept. 1943 and R.S. Wood, 5 Oct. 1943.

105 ED 136/427 Letter, R.A. Butler to Sir John Anderson, 19 Oct. 1943.

106 House of Commons debates 1943–4, vol. 397, Chuter Ede, 14 Feb. 1944 col. 119, and Mr Silkin, 16 Feb. 1944 col. 245.

107 The Education Act 1944. 7 and 8 Geo. 6 Ch. 31, clauses 7 and 8.

108 Kevin Jeffereys, 'R.A. Butler, the Board of Education and the 1944 Education Act', *History*, Oct. 1984; Nigel Middleton, 'Lord Butler and the Education Act of 1944', *British Journal of Educational Studies*, 20 (1972) no.2.

CHAPTER 7 Change and Decay, 1945–1960s

1 ED 147/207 Memorandum, Sir David Eccles, 20 Dec. 1954.
2 G. L. Payne, *Britain's Scientific and Technological Manpower* (Stanford, 1960) pp. 121–2.
3 Lord Butler, *The Education Act of 1944 and After* Noel Buxton Lecture at the University of Essex, 1965 (London, 1966) pp. 7–8.
4 Lord Butler, *The Art of Memory, Friends in Perspective* (London, 1982) pp. 161–2.
5 *The Nation's Schools, their Plan and Purpose*, Ministry of Education pamphlet no.1 (1945) pp. 17–19.
6 Lord Eustace Percy, *Education at the Crossroads* (London, 1930) p.58.
7 *Higher Technological Education* (Lord Eustace Percy) (HMSO, 1945) p.20.
8 ED 136/789 The secondary technical school. Memorandum, Antony Part to Sir Robert Wood, 2 Apr. 1946.
9 ED 136/789 Antony Part's annotation on memoranda on the secondary technical school, n.d. 1946.
10 ED 136/789 Memorandum by Part, 17 Sep. 1946.
11 *The New Secondary Education*, Ministry of Education pamphlet no.9, (1947) pp. 49–57.
12 F. B. Sullivan, *Lord Butler, the 1944 Act in Retrospect* (Milton Keynes, 1960) p.25.
13 Betty D. Vernon, *Ellen Wilkinson 1891–1947* (London, 1982) pp. 204, 222, 217; D. W. Dean, 'Planning for a post war generation: Ellen Wilkinson and George Tomlinson at the Ministry of Education, 1945–51', *History of Education*, 15 (1986) no.2, p.107.
14 Fred Blackburn, *George Tomlinson* (London, 1954).
15 1948–9, XIV Cmd. 7724 Ministry of Education *Annual Report 1949*, p.10.
16 ED 147/207 Memorandum, Sir David Eccles, Secondary technical schools 20 Dec. 1954.
17 ED 147/207 The problems of secondary education. A series of questions and pencilled responses by David Eccles, n.d. Dec. 1954-Jan. 1955.
18 ED 147/207 R. N. Heaton to Sir Gilbert Flemming, 18 Jan. 1955.
19 ED 147/207 D. H. Morrell, Secondary technical schools, 3 Jan. 1955.
20 ED 147/207 Memorandum, Toby Weaver, 14 Jan. 1955.
21 ED 147/207 A. A. Part, 17 Jan. 1955. See also Obituary 'Sir Antony Part', *The Independent*, 16 Jan. 1990.
22 ED 147/207 HMI A. Bray, 17 Jan. 1955.
23 ED 147/207 Sir Gilbert Flemming to Sir David Eccles, 19 Jan. 1955.
24 ED 147/207 The Minister's meeting, 23 Feb. 1955.

25 ED 147/207 Note, Mr Humphreys to Sir David Eccles, 3 Jan. 1955.
26 ED 147/207 Memorandum, Toby Weaver to Antony Part, 29 Nov. 1955, includes the text of the Minister's speech.
27 Ibid.
28 ED 147/207 Secondary technical education, a statement of policy by the Association of Heads of Secondary Technical Schools, Mar. 1953. A. G. Gooch commented on this document that he now preferred the grammar technical school, 27 Nov. 1955.
29 ED 147/207 Interview memorandum of the meeting of the Minister and the Association of Heads of Secondary Technical Schools, 5 Dec. 1955.
30 M. Kogan (ed.) *The Politics of Education* (London, 1971) p.162. David Eccles told this to Anthony Crosland.
31 Christopher Knight, *The Making of Tory Education Policy in Post War Britain 1950–1986* (Lewes, 1990) p.17.
32 Sir Antony Part, *The Making of a Mandarin* (London, 1990) pp. 89–90.
33 ED 136/870 Technical college development plan, 12 Oct. 1955.
34 ED 136/870 Gilbert Flemming, Draft paper on proposed developments, 26 Nov. 1955.
35 ED 136/870 Mr Routh, Further education, 6 Dec. 1955.
36 1956–7 X Cmnd Ministry of Education *Annual Report 1957*, p.10.
37 *The Future Development of Higher Technological Education* (HMSO, 1950).
38 1955–6 XXXVI Cmd. 9703 *Technical Education*, p.6.
39 1958-9 XXV Cmnd 604 *Secondary Education for All, a New Drive*, (1958) p.6.
40 1960–1 XXVII Cmnd 1254 *Better Opportunities in Technical Education*; Part, *The Making of a Mandarin*, p.98.
41 Payne, *Britain's Scientific and Technological Manpower* (Stanford U.P.) pp.121–2.
42 Reese Edwards, *The Secondary Technical School* (London, 1960) pp. 44–5.
43 Typescript of Sir Edward Boyle's address to the Conference of Headmasters of Secondary Technical Schools, Liverpool, 28 Mar. 1958.
44 Eustace Percy, *Some Memories* (London, 1958) pp. 94–5.
45 1962–3 XI Cmnd 1990, Ministry of Education *Annual Report*, p.50.
46 *Early Leaving, A Report of the Central Advisory Council for Education* (1954) p.19.
47 *15 to 18 A Report of the Central Advisory Council for Education* (Sir Geoffrey Crowther) (1959) vol. I, p.204, also pp. 396–7.
48 M. P. Carter, *Home, School and Work* (Oxford, 1962) pp. 131, 210.
49 Peter Willmott, *Adolescent Boys of East London* (London, 1966).

50 *Training for Skill, Recruitment and Training of Young Workers in Industry* (Robert Carr) (HMSO, 1958) pp. 2, 11.
51 Stuart Maclure, *One Hundred Years of London Education 1870– 1970*, (London, 1970) pp. 130, 170–5.
52 W. Jacob, 'The London secondary technical schools for girls', *Journal of Education* (1954) August.
53 Rene Saran, *Policy Making in Secondary Education* (Oxford, 1973).
54 Sir Edward Boyle in Kogan (ed.) *The Politics of Education* p.115.
55 John Mander, *Leicester Schools 1944–1974* (Leicester, 1980) pp. 35, 161.
56 P.H.J.H. Gosden and P.R. Sharp, *The Development of an Education Service, the West Riding 1889–1974* (Oxford, 1978) pp. 163–75.
57 Gary McCulloch, *The Secondary Technical School: a Usable Past?* (Lewes, 1989) pp. 142–57.
58 *The Nation's Schools, their Plan and Purpose*, Ministry of Education pamphlet no.1 (1945) p.15.
59 1951–2 X Cmd 8554, Ministry of Education *Annual Report*, p.11.
60 ED 147/207 C. I. Elliott, Paper on progress in the secondary modern school, 1948.
61 R. Edgar, 'The organisation of junior technical education', MA thesis, Manchester University (1946), pp. 97–104.
62 Edwards, *The Secondary Technical School*, p.62.
63 Deborah Thom, 'The 1944 Education Act, the art of the possible' in H.L. Smith (ed.) *War and Social Change, British Society in the Second World War* (Manchester, 1986) p.119.
64 ED 147/207 J. H. Newsom, Secondary technical education, n.d. *c.*1953, and Report on secondary technical education to Hertfordshire County Education Committee, 31 Jan. 1955, cited in Edwards, *The Secondary Technical School* p.62.
65 Reese Edwards, *Entry into Secondary Technical Education* (Manchester, 1952) pp. 24–5. Typescript in British Library 08311.K.26.
66 Edwards, *The Secondary Technical School*, p.62.
67 Edwards, *Entry into Secondary Technical Education*, p.41.
68 ED 147/207 A. G. Gooch, Secondary technical education, 28 Dec. 1954.
69 G. F. Taylor, 'Selection for junior and secondary technical education', *Vocational Aspect*, 20 (1968) no.47 (Autumn).
70 ED 135/11 Secondary technical education, 31 Jan. 1951.
71 McCulloch, *The Secondary Technical School: a Usable Past?*, pp. 85–93.
72 Michael Sanderson, *The Universities and British Industry 1850– 1970* (London, 1972) pp. 355–6 for this trend.
73 McCulloch, *The Secondary Technical School*, p.90.

74 P. F. R. Venables, *Technical Education, its Aims, Organisation and Future Development* (London, 1955) p.95.

75 David Rubinstein and Brian Simon, *The Evolution of the Comprehensive School 1926–1972* (London, 1973); and I. G. K. Fenwick, *The Comprehensive School 1944–1970, the Politics of School Reorganisation* (London, 1976).

76 Maclure, *One Hundred Years of London Education*, pp. 171, 175.

77 Michael V. Wallbank, 'Secondary education in Walsall 1902– 1968', *Vocational Aspect*, 21 (1969) no.48 (May).

78 *The Organisation of Secondary Education, a Policy Statement by the Association of Teachers in Technical Institutions*, Aug. 1966.

79 Association of Heads of Secondary Technical Schools, Annual conference presidential address, A. B. Moffat, 27 Feb. 1958.

80 Ibid., E. Semper, 10 Jun. 1961.

81 Ibid., Dr H. Frazer, Mar. 1962.

82 ED 147/207 A. G. Gooch, Secondary technical education, 28 Dec. 1954, on reasons for increasing scale.

83 C. H. Dobinson, *Technical Education for Adolescents Some Thoughts on Present Problems* (London, 1951) p.71.

84 J. C. Kingsland, 'Cray Valley Technical High School for Boys' in R. E. Gross, *British Secondary Education* (Oxford, 1965) p. 340.

85 A survey by A. G. Gooch HMI, cited in Taylor, 'Selection for junior and secondary technical education', p.305.

86 Dr H. Frazer, 'Present trends in secondary technical education', n.d. *c*. 1960, in Papers of the Association of Headmasters of Secondary Technical Schools.

87 *15 to 18* (Crowther) (1959) vol. I, p.249.

88 Ibid., p.432.

89 Interview with Mr Frank Cooper, the Headmaster of Chelmsford STS, 1961–75, 1 Jul. 1991.

90 Kingsland, 'Cray Valley Technical High School for Boys', p.367.

91 J. E. Phillips, 'The Development of the Secondary Technical School', *Journal of Education*, (1954) February.

92 Edgar 'The organisation of junior technical education', MA thesis, p. 223.

93 E. Guy, 'The secondary technical school today', *Journal of Education* (1954) January.

CHAPTER 8 Why This Matters

1 B.W.E. Alford, *British Economic Performance 1945–1975* (London, 1988) p.15.

2 *Enquiry into the Flow of Candidates in Science and Technology into Higher Education* (Sir Frederick Dainton) Interim Report 1966, Cmnd

2893. Final Report 1968, Cmnd 3541.

3 G. McCulloch, E. Jenkins and D. Layton, *Technological Revolution? The Politics of School Science and Technology in England and Wales since 1945* (Lewes, 1985) p.165.

4 *Daily Telegraph*, 30 Jan. 1970. Michael Sanderson, *The Universities and British Industry 1850–1970* (London, 1972) p.375.

5 Sir Peter Venables, *Higher Education Developments: the Technological Universities* (London, 1978) p.295.

6 *The Independent*, 26 Aug. 1989, prints the UFC assessments. What is here termed 'poor' is defined by the UFC as 'research quality that equates to attainable levels of national excellence in none or virtually none of the sub-areas of activities'.

7 1963 Cmnd 2154 *Higher Education* (Lord Robbins) p.127.

8 Anthony Peaker, *Economic Growth in Modern Britain* (London, 1974) p.49.

9 Lord Eustace Percy, *Education at the Crossroads* (London, 1930) p.58.

10 Lord Eustace Percy, *Some Memories* (London, 1958) p.101.

11 S. J. Prais, 'Vocational qualifications of the labour force in Britain and Germany', *National Institute Economic Review*, 1982.

12 Roger Jowell, Sharon Witherspoon and Lindsay Brook, *British Social Attitudes, the 1987 Report* (Aldershot, 1987) p.33.

13 Derek H. Aldcroft, *Education, Training and Economic Performance 1944 to 1990* (Manchester, 1992) p.127.

14 Sir John Cassels, *Britain's Real Skill Shortage and What to Do About It* (London, Policy Studies Institute, 1990) pp. 5, 8.

15 Thelma Veness, *School Leavers* (London, 1962). Her study was in 1956.

16 Martin Wiener, *English Culture and the Decline of the Industrial Spirit 1850–1980* (Cambridge, 1981); G. C. Allen, *The British Disease*, Hobart Paper 67, Institute of Economic Affairs (London, 1979).

17 Robert Bacon and Walter Eltis, *Britain's Economic Problem, Too Few Producers* (London, 1978) p.11.

18 K. Williams, J. Williams and D. Thomas, *Why are the British Bad at Manufacturing*? (London, 1983)

19 Percy *Education at the Crossroads*, p.53.

20 C. P. Snow, *The Two Cultures and the Scientific Revolution*, The Rede Lecture 1959 (Cambridge, 1959); 'The Two Cultures', *New Statesman*, 6 Oct. 1956.

21 Michael Sanderson, 'Social equity and industrial need; a dilemma of English education since 1945' in T. R. Gourvish and Alan O'Day, *Britain since 1945* (London, 1991).

22 Sir Edward Boyle in Maurice Kogan, *The Politics of Education* (London, 1971) p.123.

23 S. J. Prais, 'What can we learn from the German system of education and vocational training?' in G. D. N. Worswick (ed.) *Education and Economic Performance* (Aldershot, 1985); F. Naylor, 'Technical schools, a tale of four countries', *Daily Telegraph*, 18 Apr. 1985; *'The Independent' Schools Charter, a Policy Study for Education in the Nineties* (June 1991) pp. 13–15 on Germany by Colin Hughes.
24 Personal information from Tim Lambillion-Jameson of the University of East Anglia who visited Japan in August 1984 to study the education system. Also *'The Independent' Schools Charter* pp. 16–18 on Japan by Tim Jackson. 'Nippon, the Learning Machine' BBC2 TV 11 Nov. 1990.
25 Gary McCulloch, Edgar Jenkins and David Layton, *Technological Revolution? The Politics of School Science and Technology in England and Wales since 1945* (Lewes, 1985).
26 Ibid., p.207.
27 Aldcroft, *Education, Training and Economic Performance 1944– 1990* is excellent on this, and this paragraph is based on it.
28 Ibid., p.72.
29 *Technical and Vocational Initiative Review* 1990 and Seminar by Mr Michael Fahey, former head of TVEI, 6 Dec. 1991, University of London Institute of Education.
30 Alan Smithers and Pamela Robinson, *Technology in the National Curriculum* (The Engineering Council, 1992).
31 *The Independent*, 8 Oct. 1986; Geoffrey Walford and Henry Miller, *City Technology College* (Milford Keynes, 1991).
32 Kenneth Baker interviewed on *Weekend World*, Radio 4, 3 Sep. 1988.
33 *The Independent*, 28 Sep. 1988.
34 Jack Straw in *The Independent*, 29 Jul. 1988.
35 'A Class Apart', *Panorama*, BBC1 TV, 26 Sep. 1988.
36 *The Independent*, 29 Jun. 1989.
37 *The Independent*. 18 Oct. 1990.
38 Walford and Miller, *City Technology College*, pp. 114–15.
39 1978–80 LXVII Cmnd 7794 *Engineering Our Future* (Sir Montague Finniston) (1980) p.24.
40 Helvia Bierhoff and S.J. Prais, *Britain's Industrial Skills and the School-Teaching of Practical Subjects*, NIESR Discussion Paper no.33, March 1993, p.2.
41 Ibid., pp.8–9 and *Passim*.
42 Andy Green and Hilary Steedman, *Educational Provision, Educational Attainment and the Needs of Industry*, NIESR Report Series no.5 (1993) p.12.
43 Bierhoff and Prais, *Britain's Industrial Skills*, pp.32–6.
44 See *Independent*, 17 June 1993 for these fears.

Selected Bibliography

UNPUBLISHED PAPERS

Public Record Office, Kew

ED 10/147, 151, 152, 153, 212a, 212b, 272, 273

ED 12/50, 211, 373, 419, 472, 478, 479, 480

ED 22/20, 39, 40, 48, 52, 54, 55, 56, 57, 58, 59, 63, 64, 87, 142, 144, 145, 146, 152, 153, 154, 155, 218, 219, 220, 221

ED 24/1412, 1849, 1860, 1868, 1870, 1871, 1872, 1873, 1875, 1876, 1877, 1878, 1879

ED 35/233, 1786, 1814, 2085, 2299

ED 36/6

ED 46/223, 224

ED 98/1, 4, 7, 16, 20, 27, 29, 53, 54, 59, 72, 75, 76, 83, 84, 109, 118, 119, 123, 129, 140, 147, 152, 174, 189, 201, 210, 223

ED 108/17, 18, 19

ED 121/54, 63, 69, 217, 247, 257

ED 135/2, 3, 4, 6, 9, 11

ED 136/131, 132, 214, 257, 296, 427, 669, 789, 870

ED 147/195, 207

British Library

Additional MSS 59690-5 The Diaries of James Chuter Ede, 1940–5.

Trinity College, Cambridge

R.A. Butler Archive

RAB F/103

G 15/25; 16/163, 173; 151/1

H 70/6, 224, 256, 277, 351

K 9/33; 10/31, 126, 135, 145; 11/33, 37, 88, 104

Mr Frank Cooper

Miscellaneous papers of the Association of Heads of Secondary Technical Schools.

THESES

Pannett, D.A., 'A comparison of girls junior technical schools in London and Paris', University of London, MA (1939).

Edgar, R., 'The organisation of junior technical education', Manchester University, MA (1946).

Taylor, G.F., 'Developments in secondary technical education 1944–1960', Sheffield University, MA (1965).

GOVERNMENT PUBLICATIONS

Parliamentary papers

1897 XXV C 8447 *The French System of Higher Primary Schools* (R.L. Morant).

1898 XXCV C 8943 *The London Polytechnic Institutions* (Sidney Webb).

1904 LXXV Cd 2172 *Regulations for Evening Schools.* 1905 LIX Cd 2574 *Regulations for Evening Schools, Technical Institutions and Schools of Art and Art Classes*, 1 Aug. 1904–31 Jul. 1905.

1909 XVII Cd 4757 *Report of the Consultative Committee on Attendance at Continuation Schools* (A.H.D. Acland).

1909 XXXVII Cd 4499 *Report of the Royal Commission on the Poor Law*, pp.407–11, 630.

Annual Reports of the Board and Ministry of Education 1912/13 to 1963

1913 L Cd 6919 *Board of Education Regulations for Junior Technical Schools in England and Wales.*

1917–18 XI Cd 8512 *Final Report of the Departmental Committee on Juvenile Education in Relation to Employment* (J.J. Lewis).

1917–18 XI Cd 8577 *Evidence and Appendices to the Report on . . . Juvenile Education in Relation to Employment.*

1918 IX Cd 9011 *Report of the Committee to Enquire into the Position of Natural Science in the Educational System of Great Britain* (Sir Joseph Thomson).

1918 IX Cd 9036 *Report of the Committee . . . Position of Modern Languages in the Educational System of Great Britain (Sir Stanley Leathes).*

Report of the Standing Joint Committee . . . on Scales of Salaries for Teachers . . . Junior Technical Schools (Lord Burnham) 1921, 1927.

Report of an Inquiry into Apprenticeship and Training, Ministry of Labour, 1925–6, vols 1–7.

Report of the Consultative Committee on the Education of the Adolescent (Sir Henry Hadow) 1926.

Factors in Industrial and Commercial Efficiency, (Committee on Industry and Trade) (Sir Arthur Balfour) 1927.

Report of the Committee on Education and Industry (England and Wales) (Sir Dougal Malcolm) 2 parts 1928.

Education for the Engineering Industry (Sir Dugald Clerk) 1931.

Final Report of the Committee on Education for Salesmanship (Sir Francis Goodenough) 1931.

Co-operation in Technical Education, Report of a Conference of Representatives of the Associations of Local Education Authorities and the LCC 1937.

Report of the Consultative Committee on Secondary Education With Special Reference to Grammar Schools and Technical High Schools (Sir Will Spens) 1938.

Education After the War (The Green Book) 1941.

Curriculum and Examinations in Secondary Schools. Report of the Committee of the Secondary Schools Examinations Council (Sir Cyril Norwood) 1943.

1943 Cmd 6428 *Training for the Building Industry.*

1943 Cmd 6433 *Report of the Committee on Post War Agricultural Education* (Lord Luxmoore).

1943 Cmd 6458 *Educational Reconstruction.*

Higher Technological Education (Lord Eustace Percy) 1945.

The Future Development of Higher Technological Education 1950.

Early Leaving, A Report of the Central Advisory Council for Education 1954.

1955–6 XXXVI Cmd 9703 *Technical Education.*

Training for Skill, Recruitment and Training of Young Workers in Industry (Robert Carr) 1958.

1958–9 XXV Cmnd 604 *Secondary Education for All, a New Drive.*

15 to 18 A Report of the Central Advisory Council for Education (Sir Geoffrey Crowther) 1959.

1960–1 XXVII Cmnd 1254 *Better Opportunities in Technical Education.*

1979–80 LXVII Cmnd 7794 *Engineering Our Future* (Sir Montague

Finniston).

Board of Education (Ministry of Education) Pamphlets

Survey of Technical and Further Education in England and Wales, Board of Education pamphlet no. 49 (1926).

The New Prospect in Education, pamphlet no.60 (1928).

Junior Technical Schools, pamphlet no.63 (1928).

Education for Commerce, pamphlet no.64 (1928).

Trade and Domestic Training for Girls, pamphlet no.72 (1929).

Education for Industry and Commerce, the West Midlands Metal Working Area, pamphlet no.74 (1930).

Memorandum on the Place of the Junior Technical School in the Educational System, pamphlet no.83 (1930).

Trade Schools on the Continent, pamphlet no.91 (1932).

Review of Junior Technical Schools in England, pamphlet no.111 (1937).

Suggestions in Regard to Teaching in Junior Technical Schools, pamphlet no.113 (1937).

The Nations Schools, their Plan and Purpose, Ministry of Education pamphlet no.1 (1945).

The New Secondary Education, Ministry of Education pamphlet no.9 (1947).

Education 1900–1950, Report of the Ministry of Education (1950).

Acts of Parliament

2 Edward VII Chapter 42 *An Act to Make Further Provision with Respect to Education in England and Wales*, 18 Dec. 1902.

8 & 9 Geo 5 Chapter 39 *An Act to Make Further Provision With Respect to Education in England and Wales and for Purposes Connected Therewith*, 8 Aug. 1918.

7 & 8 Geo 6 Chapter 31 *The Education Act*, 1944

PUBLICATIONS OF OTHER BODIES

Report of the Mosely Educational Commission to the United States of America 1903, London, 1904.

Kent Education Committee Special Report on Higher Education in the County of Kent, London, 1906.

Education and Training for the Electrical and Allied Engineering Industries, Report of the Education Committee of the British Electrical and Allied Manufacturers' Association, London, 1920.

Association of Teachers in Technical Institutions, Report of an Inquiry into the Relationships of Technical Education to Other Forms of Education and to Industry and Commerce (Lord Emmott) Bootle, 1927.

Technical College Buildings, their Planning and Equipment, Association of Technical Institutions and Association of Principals of Technical Institutions, London, 1935.

County Council of Middlesex Education Committee, Report of a Delegation on their Visit to Continental Technical Institutions, May 1936. Greater London Record Office and Library 22.14.MID.

ATTI and APTI Report on Policy in Technical Education, 1937.

Report on Policy in Technical Education by a Joint Committee, ATI, APTI, ATTI, National Association of Art Masters, 1938.

From School to Work, Report of a Conference of the British Association for Commerce and Industrial Education, 27 Mar. 1942.

Nuffield College, *Industry and Education, a Statement*, Oxford, 1943.

Cotton Industry and Education, Report of a Conference Convened by the Cotton Board, 24 Mar. 1943.

The Organisation of Secondary Education, a Policy Statement by the Association of Teachers in Technical Institutions, Aug. 1966.

Policies for Higher Education in the 1980s, OECD, 1983.

BOOKS

Abbott, A., *Education for Industry and Commerce in England*, Oxford, 1933.

Aldcroft, Derek H., *Education, Training and Economic Performance 1944 to 1990*, Manchester, 1992.

Alexander, W.P., *Intelligence, Concrete and Abstract*, Cambridge, 1935.

Alexander, W.P., *The Educational Needs of Democracy*, London, 1940.

Alexander, W.P., *Education in England*, London, 1954.

Alford, B.W.E., *British Economic Performance 1945–1975*, London, 1988.

Allen, Bernard M., *Sir Robert Morant*, London, 1934.

Allen, G.C., *The British Disease*, Hobart Paper 67. Institute of Economic Affairs, London, 1979.

Anderson, Gregory, *The White Blouse Revolution, Female Office Workers since 1870*, Manchester, 1988.

Anderson, L.F., *History of Manual and Industrial School Education*, New York, 1926.

Annan, (Lord) Noel, *Our Age, Portrait of a Generation*, London, 1990.

Apprenticeship and Skilled Employment Association, *Trades for Boys and How to Enter Them*, London, 1912.

Ashby, Arthur W. and Byles, Phoebe G., *Rural Education*, Oxford, 1923.

Bacon, Robert and Eltis, Walter, *Britain's Economic Problem, Too Few Producers*, London, 1978.

Badley, J.H., *Education after the War*, Oxford, 1917.

Banks, Olive, *Parity and Prestige in English Secondary Education*, London, 1955, 1963.

Barker, Rodney, *Education and Politics 1900–1951, A Study of the Labour Party*, Oxford, 1972.

Barnett, Corelli, *The Audit of War* London, 1986.

Bell, Lady Florence, *At The Works, A Study of a Manufacturing Town*, London, 1907.

Bernbaum, Gerald, *Social Change and the Schools 1918–1944*, London, 1967.

Best, R.H. and Ogden, C.K., *The Problem of the Continuation School and its Successful Solution in Germany*, London, 1914.

Bierhoff, Helvia and Prais, S.J., *Britain's Industrial Skills and the School-Teaching of Practical Subjects*, NIESR Discussion Paper no.33, March 1993.

Blackburn, Fred, *George Tomlinson*, London, 1954.

Bray, Reginald A., *Boy Labour and Apprenticeship*, London, 1911.

Butler, C.V., *Social Conditions in Oxford*, London, 1912.

Butler, R.A. (Lord) *The Education Act of 1944 and After*, Noel Buxton Lecture at the University of Essex, 1965, London, 1966.

Butler, R.A. (Lord) *The Art of the Possible*, London, 1971.

Butler, R.A. (Lord) *The Art of Memory, Friends in Perspective*, London, 1982.

Cardwell, D.S.L., *The Organisation of Science in England*, London, 1957.

Carpenter, L.P., *G.D.H. Cole an Intellectual Biography*, Cambridge, 1973.

Carr-Saunders, A.M. and Caradog-Jones, D., *A Survey of the Social Structure of England and Wales*, Oxford, 1937.

Carter, Huntley, *Industrial Reconstruction*, London, 1917.

Carter M.P., *Home, School and Work*, Oxford, 1962.

Cassels, Sir John, *Britain's Real Skill Shortage and What to Do About It*, Policy Studies Institute, London, 1990.

Cazalet-Keir, Thelma, *From the Wings*, London, 1967.

Cholmeley, R.F., *Secondary Education in England*, London, 1913.

Cole, Dame Margaret, *The Life of G.D.H. Cole*, London, 1971.

Cooley, Edwin G., *Vocational Education in Europe, a Report to the Commercial Club of Chicago*, 2 vols, Chicago, 1912, 1915.

Creasey, Clarence H., *Technical Education in Evening Schools*, London, 1905.

Dearle, N.B., *Industrial Training*, London, 1914.

Dent, H.C., *Education in Transition, a Sociological Study of the Impact of War on English Education 1939–1943*, London, 1944.

Dent, H.C., *Secondary Education for All, Origins and Development in England*, London, 1949.

Dent, H.C., *Secondary Modern Schools*, London, 1958.

Dobinson, C.H., *Technical Education for Adolescents, Some Thoughts on Present Problems*, London, 1951.

Dunlop, J.O., *English Apprenticeship and Child Labour*, London, 1912.

Eager, W. McG. and Secretan, H.A., *Unemployment Among Boys*, London, 1925.

Eaglesham, E., *From School Board to Local Authority*, London, 1956.

Edwards, Reese, *Entry into Secondary Technical Education*, Manchester 1952.

Edwards, Reese, *The Secondary Technical School*, London, 1960.

Egerton, F.C.C., *The Future of Education*, London, 1914.

Evans, A.E. and Wilson, J., *The Association of Teachers in Technical Institutions, the First Half Century 1904–1954*, London, 1955.

Fenwick, I.G.K., *The Comprehensive School 1944–1970, the Politics of School Reorganisation*, London, 1976.

Ferguson, R.W. (ed.) *Training in Industry, a Report . . . by the AEIC*, London, 1935.

Findlay, J.J. (ed.) *The Young Wage Earner, and the Problem of his Education*, London, 1918.

Fisher, H.A.L., *Educational Reform, an Address at the University of Manchester, 26 September 1917*, Manchester, 1917.

Fisher, H.A.L., *Educational Reform Speeches*, Oxford, 1918.

Fisher, H.A.L., *An Unfinished Autobiography*, London, 1940.

Freeman, Arnold, *Boy Life and Labour*, London, 1914.

Friedberg, Aaron L., *The Weary Titan, Britain and the Experience of Relative Decline 1895–1905*, Princeton, 1988.

Gibb, Spencer J., *The Problem of Boy Work*, London, 1906.

Gibb, Spencer, J., *The Boy and His Work*, London, 1911.

Gibb, Spencer, J., *Boy Work, Exploitation or Training*, London, 1919.

Glover, A.H.T., *New Teaching for a New Age*, London, 1946.

Gollan, John, *Youth in British Industry, a Survey of Labour Conditions Today*, London, 1937.

Gosden, P.H.J.H., *Education in the Second World War, a Study in Policy and Administration*, London, 1976.

Gosden, P.H.J.H. and Sharp, P.R., *The Development of an Education Service, the West Riding 1889–1974*, Oxford, 1978.

Gospel, Howard (ed.) *Industrial Training and Technological Innovation*, London 1991.

Graves, John, *Policy and Progress in Secondary Education 1902-1942*, London, 1943, 1949.

Green, Andy and Steedman, Hilary, *Education Provision, Educational Attainment and the Needs of Industry*, NIESR Report Series no.5, 1993.

Grier, Lynda, *Achievement in Education, the Work of Michael Ernest Sadler 1885–1935*, London, 1952.

Gross, R.E., *British Secondary Education*, Oxford, 1965.

Halsey, A.H., *Trends in British Society since 1900*, London, 1972.

Hawkins, C.B., *Norwich, A Social Study*, London, 1912.

Hearnshaw, L.S., *Cyril Burt, Psychologist*, London, 1979.

Hendrick, Harry, *Images of Youth, Age, Class and the Male Youth Problem 1880–1920*, Oxford, 1990.

Hogg, Ethel M., *The Polytechnic and its Founder Quintin Hogg*, London, 1904, reprinted 1932.

Howard, Anthony, *RAB, the Life of R.A. Butler*, London, 1987.

Humphries, Stephen, *Hooligans or Rebels? An Oral History of Working Class Childhood and Youth 1889–1939*, Oxford, 1981.

Hurt, J.S., *Outside the Mainstream*, London, 1988.

'The Independent' Schools Charter, 1991.

Inwards, Richard, *William Ford Stanley, His Life and Work*, London, 1911.

Jebb, Eglantyne, *Cambridge, a Brief Study in Social Questions*, Cambridge, 1906.

Jewkes, John and Sylvia, *The Juvenile Labour Market*, London, 1938.

Jewkes, John and Winterbottom, Allan, *Juvenile Unemployment*, London, 1933.

Jowell, Roger, Witherspoon, Sharon, and Brook, Lindsay (eds) *British Social Attitudes, the 1987 Report*, Aldershot, 1987.

Jowell, Roger, Witherspoon, Sharon, and Brook, Lindsay, *British Social Attitudes, Special International Report*, Aldershot, 1989.

Kazamias, A.M., *Politics, Society and Secondary Education in England*, Pennsylvania, 1966.

Kirby, M.W., *The Decline of British Economic Power Since 1870*, London, 1981.

Klemm, L.R., *Public Education in Germany and the United States*, New York, 1914.

Knight, Christopher, *The Making of Tory Education Policy in Post War Britain 1950–1986*, Lewes, 1990.

Kogan, Maurice (ed.) *The Politics of Education*, London, 1971.

Lawson, W.R., *John Bull and his Schools, a Book for Parents, Ratepayers and Men of Business*, London, 1908.

Leathes, Stanley, *What is Education?*, London, 1913.

Leybourne, G.G., and White, K., *Education and the Birth Rate*, London, 1940.

Lindsay, Kenneth, *Social Progress and Educational Waste*, London, 1926.

Lowe, Roy, *Education in the Post War Years, a Social History*, London, 1988.

Lowndes, G.A.N., *The Silent Social Revolution 1895–1965*, Oxford, 1969.

Maclure, Stuart, *One Hundred Years of London Education 1870–1970*, London, 1970.

McCulloch, Gary, *The Secondary Technical School, a Usable Past?*, Lewes, 1989.

McCulloch, Gary, Jenkins, Edgar, and Layton, David, *Technological Revolution? The Politics of School Science and Technology in England and Wales since 1945*, Lewes, 1985.

Mander, John, *Leicester Schools 1944–1974*, Leicester, 1980.

Masterman, C.F.G., *The Condition of England*, London, 1909.

Masterman, C.F.G., *England after the War*, London, 1922.

Mess, Henry A., *Industrial Tyneside, a Social Survey*, London, 1928.

Middleton, Nigel, *A Place for Everyone*, London, 1976.

Millis, C.T., *Technical Education, its Development and Aims*, London, 1925.

More, C.V., *Skill and the English Working Class 1870–1914*, London, 1980.

Newton, A.P., *The English Elementary School*, London, 1919.

Norwood, Sir Cyril, *The Curriculum in Secondary Schools*, Association for Education in Citizenship, 1937?.

Norwood, Sir Cyril, *The English Tradition of Education*, London, 1929.

Parkinson, Michael, *The Labour Party and the Organisation of Secondary Education 1918–65*, London, 1970.

Part, Sir Antony, *The Making of a Mandarin*, London, 1990.

Paterson, Alexander, *Across the Bridges, or Life by the South London River-side*, London, 1911.

Payne, P.L., *Britain's Scientific and Technological Manpower*, Stanford, 1960.

Peaker, Antony, *Economic Growth in Modern Britain*, London, 1974.

Pearson, Geoffrey, *Hooligan, a History of Respectable Fears*, London, 1983.

Pelham, Rev. H.S., *The Training of the Working Boy*, London, 1914.

Percy, Lord Eustace, *Education at the Crossroads*, London, 1930.

Percy, Lord Eustace, *Some Memories*, London, 1958.

Problems of Reconstruction, Lectures and Addresses at Hampstead Garden Suburb August 1917, London, 1918.

Rackham, C., *Education in Norwich, an Independent Survey 1920–1940*, Norwich, n.d.

Richardson, W.A., *The Technical College*, Oxford, 1939.

Roderick, Gordon and Stephens, Michael, *The British Malaise*, Falmer, 1982.

Roman, F.W., *The Industrial and Commercial Schools of the United States and Germany*, New York, 1915.

Routh, Guy, *Occupation and Pay in Great Britain 1906–60*, London, 1965.

Rubinstein, David and Simon, Brian, *The Evolution of the Comprehensive School 1926–1972*, London, 1973.

Sadler, Sir Michael, *Report on Secondary Education in Liverpool*, London, 1904.

Sadler, Sir Michael, *Continuation Schools in England and Elsewhere*, Manchester, 1908.

Sanderson, Michael, *Educational Opportunity and Social Change in England*, London, 1987.

Saran, Rene, *Policy Making in Secondary Education*, Oxford, 1973.

Searle, Geoffrey, *The Quest for National Efficiency*, Oxford, 1971.

Selby-Bigge, L.A., *The Board of Education*, London, 1927, 1934.

Sheldrake, J. and Vickerstaff, S., *The History of Industrial Training in Britain*, Aldershot, 1987.

Sherington, Geoffrey, *English Education, Social Change and War 1911–1920*, Manchester, 1981.

Simon, Brian, *Education and the Labour Movement 1870–1920*, London, 1965.

Simon, Brian, *The Politics of Educational Reform 1920–1940*, London, 1974.

Simon, Brian, *Education and the Social Order 1940–1990*, London 1991.

Simon, Viscount, *Retrospect*, London, 1952.

Smithers, Alan and Robinson, Pamela, *Technology in the National Curriculum*, The Engineering Council, 1992.

Snow, C.P., *The Two Cultures and the Scientific Revolution*, (The Rede Lecture, 1959) Cambridge, 1959.

Spalding, T.A., *The Work of the London School Board*, London, 1900.

Springhall, John, *Coming of Age: Adolescence in Britain 1860–1960*, Dublin, 1986.

Sullivan, F.B., *Lord Butler, the 1944 Act in Retrospect*, Milton Keynes, 1960.

Summerfield, Penny and Evans, Eric, (eds) *Technical Education and the State since 1850*, Manchester, 1990.

Sutherland, Gillian, *Ability, Merit and Measurement, Mental Testing and English Education 1880–1940*, Oxford, 1984.

Tawney, R.H., *Secondary Education for All, a Policy for Labour*, London, 1922.

Tawney, R.H., *Juvenile Employment and Education*, Barnett House Paper no.17, Oxford, 1934.

Taylor, William, *The Secondary Modern School*, London, 1963.

Technical and Vocational Initiative Review, 1990.

Thomas, Leslie, *In My Wildest Dreams*, London, 1984.

Thompson, Joan, *Secondary Education for All*, London, 1947.

Thompson, Joan, *Next Steps in Education*, Fabian Tract no. 274, London, 1949.

Thompson, Joan, *Secondary Education Survey*, London, 1952.

Thoms, D.W., *Policy Making in Education, Robert Blair and the London County Council*, Education Administration and History Monograph no.10, Leeds, 1980.

Urwick, E.J. (ed.) *Studies of Boy Life in Our Cities*, London, 1904.

Venables, P.F.R., *Technical Education, its Aims, Organisation and Future Development*, London, 1955.

Veness, Thelma, *School Leavers*, London, 1962.

Vernon, Betty D., *Ellen Wilkinson 1891–1947*, London 1982.

Walford, Geoffrey and Miller, Henry, *City Technology College*, Milton Keynes, 1991.

Ware, Fabian, *Educational Reform*, London, 1900.

Waterfall, Edith, *The Day Continuation School*, London, 1923.

Welpton, W.P., *Primary Artisan Education*, London, 1913.

Wiener, Martin, *English Culture and the Decline of the Industrial Spirit 1850–1980*, Cambridge, 1981.

Williams, K., Williams, J. and Thomas, D., *Why are the British Bad at Manufacturing?*, London, 1983.

Willimott, Peter, *Adolescent Boys of East London*, London, 1966.

Wilson, J. Dover, *The Schools of England*, London 1928.

ARTICLES

Aldcroft, D.H., 'Investment in and utilisation of manpower: Great Britain and her rivals 1870–1914' in B.M. Ratcliffe, *Great Britain and her World*, Manchester, 1975.

Barnett, C., 'Long term industrial performance in the UK: the role of education and research 1850–1939' in Morris D.J., *The Economic System in the UK*, Oxford, 1985.

Bray, R.A., 'The Apprenticeship Question' *Economic Journal*, 19 (1909).

Burt, Sir Cyril, 'The Psychological implications of the Norwood Report' *British Journal of Educational Psychology*, 13 (1943).

Courtauld, Samuel, 'An industrialist's reflections on the future relations of government and industry', *Economic Journal*, 52 (1942) Apr.

Day, C.R., 'Education for the industrial world, Technical and modern instruction in France under the Third Republic 1870–1914' in R. Fox and G. Weisz (eds) *The Organisation of Science and Technology in France 1808–1914*, Cambridge, 1980.

Dean, D.W., 'H.A.L. Fisher, Reconstruction and the Development of the 1918 Education Act', *British Journal of Educational Studies* (1970) Oct.

Dean, D.W., 'Conservatism and the national education system 1922–40', *Journal of Contemporary History*, 6 (1971) no.2.

Dean, D.W., 'Planning for a post war generation: Ellen Wilkinson and George Tomlinson at the Ministry of Education 1945–51', *History of Education* 15 (1986) no.2.

Firmager, Jennifer, 'The Consultative Committee under the chairmanship of Sir Henry Hadow', *History of Education*, 10 (1981) no.4.

Floud, Jean, 'The educational experience of the adult population of England and Wales as at July 1949' in D.V. Glass (ed.) *Social Mobility in Britain*, London, 1954.

Gillis, John R., 'The evolution of juvenile delinquency in England 1890–1914', *Past and Present*, (1975) May.

Gomulka, Stanislaw, 'Britain's slow industrial growth - increasing inefficiency versus low rate of technical change' in Wilfred Beckerman, *Slow Growth in Britain*, Oxford, 1979.

Guy, E., 'The secondary technical school today', *Journal of Education*, (1954) Jan.

Harley, C.K., 'Skilled labour and the choice of technique in Edwardian industry', *Explorations in Economic History* 11 (1974).

Harney, Klaus, 'The emergence of the technical school system in Prussia' in Ian Inkster, *The Steam Intellect Societies*, Nottingham, 1985.

Jacob, W. 'The London secondary technical schools for girls', *Journal of Education*, (1954) Aug.

Jeffreys, Kevin, 'R.A.Butler, the Board of Education and 1944 Education Act', *History*, (1984) Oct.

Jenkins, E.W., 'Junior technical schools 1905–1945: the case of Leeds', *History of Education*, 16 (1987) no.2.

Jenkinson, A.J., 'The technical education of Members of Parliament', *Vocational Aspect*, 17 (1965) no.37 (Summer) and 18 (1966) no.40 (Summer).

Kendal, G., 'The influence of vocation on school education' in *Problems of Reconstruction, Lectures and Addresses at Hampstead Garden Suburb, August 1917*, London, 1918.

Kingsland, J.C., 'Cray Valley Technical High School for Boys' in R.E. Gross, *British Secondary Education*, Oxford, 1965.

Knox, William, 'Apprenticeship and deskilling in Britain 1850–1914', *International Review of Social History*, 31 (1986) pt 2.

Landymore, P.J.A., 'Education and industry since the war' in D.J. Morris, *The Economic System in the UK*, Oxford, 1985.

Little, A. and Westergaard, J., 'The trend of class differentials in educational opportunity in England and Wales', *British Journal of Sociology*, 15 (1964).

Lyon, J., 'Engineering apprenticeship and education in Bolton 1900–1914' *Vocational Aspect*, 15 (1963) no.32, Autumn.

Martin, F.M., 'An inquiry into parents' preferences in secondary education' in Glass, D.V., *Social Mobility in Britain*, London 1954, reprint 1966.

Middleton, Nigel, 'Lord Butler and the Education Act of 1944', *British Journal of Educational Studies*, 20 (1972) no.2.

Millis, C.T., 'Junior technical schools, their status and position', *Education*, 15 Apr. 1921.

Peck, Merton J., 'Science and technology' in Richard E. Caves, *Britain's Economic Prospects*, Washington and London, 1968.

Phillips, J.E., 'The development of the secondary technical school', *Journal of Education*, (1954) Feb.

Prais, S.J., 'What can we learn from the German system of education and vocational training?' in G.D.N. Worswick (ed.) *Education and Economic Performance*, Aldershot, 1985.

Richardson, Malcolm, 'Education and politics: the London Labour Party and schooling between the wars' in Andrew Saint, *Politics and the People of London*, London, 1989.

Saint, Andrew, 'Technical education and the early LCC' in Andrew Saint, *Politics and the People of London*, London, 1989.

Sanderson, Michael, 'The missing stratum, the problem of secondary technical education in England 1900–1960s' in Gabriel Tortella (ed.) *Education and Economic Development since the Industrial Revolution*, Valencia, 1990.

Sanderson, Michael, 'Social equity and industrial need: a dilemma of English education since 1945' in Terry Gourvish and Alan 0'Day (eds) *Britain since 1945*, London, 1991.

Sanderson, Michael, 'French influences on technical and managerial education in England 1870–1940' in T.R. Gourvish and Y. Cassis (eds) *Management in the Age of the Corporate Economy* (forthcoming).

Savage, Gail L., 'Social class and social policy: the Civil Service and secondary education in England during the interwar period', *Journal of Contemporary History*, 18 (1983).

Simon, Brian, 'The Tory Government and education 1951–60: background to breakout', *History of Education*, 14 (1985) no.4.

Tawney, R.H., 'The economics of boy labour', *Economic Journal*, 19 (1909).

Taylor, F., 'Technical schools, a tale of four countries', *Daily Telegraph*, 18 Apr. 1985.

Taylor, G.F., 'Selection for junior and secondary technical education', *Vocational Aspect*, 20 (1965) no.47, Autumn.

Thom, Deborah, 'The 1944 Education Act, the art of the possible' in Harold L. Smith (ed.) *War and Social Change, British Society in the Second World War*, Manchester, 1986.

Thoms, D.W., 'Market forces and recruitment to technical education, the example of the junior technical schools', *History of Education*, 10 (1981) no.2.

Vaizey, John, 'Education, training and growth' in P.D. Henderson (ed.) *Economic Growth in Britain*, London, 1968.

Wallace, R.G., 'The origins and authorship of the 1944 Education Act', *History of Education*, 10 (1981) no.4.

Wallbank, Michael V., 'Secondary education in Walsall 1902–1968', *Vocational Aspect*, 21 (1969) no.48 (May).

Worswick, G.D.N., 'Cole and Oxford 1938–1958' in Asa Briggs and John Saville (eds) *Essays in Labour History*, London, 1967.

Wrigley, Julia, 'Technical education and industry in the nineteenth century' in B. Elbaum and W. Lazonick, *The Decline of the British Economy*, Oxford, 1986.

Index